Black Culture, White Youth:

The Reggae Tradition from JA to UK

Simon Jones

Published by Bassline Books, 2016
ISBN: 9781521919033

First published in 1988

Contents

Acknowledgements

This book was first published in 1988 in Macmillan's *Culture and Communications* series. It stemmed from a doctoral thesis undertaken at Birmingham University's Centre for Contemporary Cultural Studies between 1982 and 1986. But this book always had other, non-academic origins. Forged out of the experience of living and studying in Birmingham for most of the 1980s, it was the result of a very personal involvement with its subject matter, and the product of a life-long love of Jamaican popular music.

The second half of the book is best read as a snapshot of urban multiculture in a specific historical and regional context. While this study has gained documentary value with the passing of time, the book is also republished here to answer the continuing interest in many of its central themes.

Despite minor editorial revisions, the book's structure and content are unchanged from the first edition. The original cover has been retained in order to showcase Pogus Caesar's photo once again. The main changes to this edition are a revised introduction and a new epilogue. Republishing the book digitally has also provided the opportunity to include some photos taken at the time, and originally intended to illustrate the first edition. They are included here partly as a tribute to the person who took them, Jonathan Girling, (1964-2012) who was a major contributor to this book, but is tragically no longer here to witness its second coming. Jon, this is for you.

I am deeply indebted to all the other participants and interviewees for sharing their insights. They remain the book's hidden co-authors. Special request to Johnny Aitken, Michelle Dawes, David Rodigan, and the Scientist posse (especially Robbo, Roy, Nicky, Desmond and Flux) to whom I shall always be the other "Rodigan". Various academic colleagues and friends were crucial in inspiring and helping to realise the book, first and second time around, particularly Richard Johnson, Stuart Hall, Paul Gilroy, Dick Hebdige, John Solomos and Les Back. Respect to one and all of you. Finally, love and gratitude to the Joneses; Bernard, the two Joans, Jade and Jacqueline.

Simon Jones, 2016

"What sort of country will Britain be when its capital, other cities and areas of England consist of a population of which at least one-third is of African and Asian descent? My answer...is that it will be a Britain unimaginably wracked by dissension and violent disorder, not recognisable as the same nation as it has been, or perhaps as a nation at all." (J. Enoch Powell, Birkenhead, 1985)

"It's like we've all turned out the same in Balsall Heath. There's no racial fuckries round this way! It's like, I know there's no such thing as "England" any more...Welcome to India brothers! This is the Caribbean! Nigeria!...There is no "England" man! When will they wake up? This is the new world, man, this is what is coming!" (Jo-Jo, Balsall Heath, Birmingham, 1983)

Introduction: Rewind Selecta

Balsall Heath, Birmingham, 1986

It's mid December and the local community centre is holding a pre-Christmas disco for both its junior and senior youth clubs. I'm on my way to the centre, accompanied by Jon who is armed with his camera to take some photos. Walking past the inner-city council houses that have replaced the terraced rows of "old" Balsall Heath, we can hear reggae music echoing from a side-street up ahead. As we approach, the music grows louder and becomes identifiable as Smiley Culture's "Police officer". And then, as if to deliberately confound our expectations, around the corner come jaunting two Asian boys, one carrying a boombox, accompanied by a white girl who can distinctly be heard reciting the song's lyrics perfectly, word-for-word.

Outside the community centre, a group of boys—white, mixed-race, Afro-Caribbean and Asian—are milling around, decked out in the ubiquitous styles of mid-80s youth: ski jumpers, baggy trousers, buttoned-up shirts, trainers and moccasin shoes. Inside the club, a sound system run by two older dreads provides the musical backdrop to the evening's proceedings with a mix of reggae, soul and pop. While the younger children from the junior club dance energetically in the middle of the room, a group of senior youth clubbers stand on the perimeter, coolly surveying the scene. As the posse from outside bursts into the club, the place comes alive with a youthful exuberance (photo 1). Shortly, another boy enters with a selection of 12" records under his arm. The posse descend on him, relieve him of the records and begin scrutinising the titles one by one with endorsements and nods of approval (photo 2). Cameo's electro-funk hit "Word Up" starts to play on the sound system. A white boy with a curly perm hair-style, sporting baggy check trousers and a knitted sweater deftly snatches a pair of white-rimmed Polaroid's off the face of his black friend. He perches them provocatively on the end of his nose and begins to move, body-popping style, to the music. As his friend attempts to recover them, a friendly wrestling match ensues. There is much horseplay in the club tonight, plenty of energy and high-spiritedness, but no fights, and no "racial fuckries."

1

Photo 1: Mount Pleasant Community Centre, Highgate, Birmingham, 19th December 1986 [Jon Girling]

Photo 2: Mount Pleasant Community Centre, Highgate, Birmingham, 19th December 1986 [Jon Girling]

Balsall Heath, Jo-Jo tells me, is a special place; "It's like ebony and ivory", he eulogises, "you know...perfect harmony." Jo-Jo is very much a product of the area, a "black boy/white boy" as he describes himself, raised within the interlocking social networks and shared living spaces that have evolved between its black and white communities over the course of three decades. The fruits of those networks are evident amongst a whole generation of young black and white people who have grown up alongside one another and shared the same streets, classrooms and youth clubs. They are visible everywhere in cross-cultural affiliations and shared leisure spaces, on the streets, around the games machine in the local chip shop, in the playgrounds and parks, through to the mixed rock and reggae groups for which the area has become renowned.

As a result of these proximities, nothing is quite as "black and white" as it first appears in Balsall Heath. For some young whites like Jo-Jo the exact point at which one ends and the other begins has become somewhat blurred. "I don't look at it like borders, man" he tells me. Sitting here, talking to Jo-Jo, trying to pin down the slippery contours of "race", I make a clumsy attempt to remind of his whiteness, but he isn't having any of it:

> Yeah, but just because I'm *white*, I don't go around saying "I'm a white man", or any crap like that, you know...Man is man, you know, what's the big fucking difference? I mean, it's like, I never met many English people, you know what I mean? Cos when I used to sit down with my mates when I was younger, you know, my mates used to turn round and say like "Oh my daddy comes from Trenchtown!" and all this kind of stuff you know, sort of, Montego Bay! Spanish Town! All them kinda places man, that's all I ever used to hear about. And you'd think to yourself, well where's Portsmouth?! [laughs]....You know what I mean? When one of the teachers mentioned Portsmouth, like, you thought you was off to Jamaica man!

Photo 3: Jo-Jo, New Street, Birmingham city-centre, 1987 [Jon Girling]

How was it that sentiments like these could come to be expressed with such conviction by a young white person in Britain in the early 1980s? What kinds of histories and cultural processes did they presume? These cameos of inner-city multiculture offered a microcosmic glimpse of embryonic identities and cultural formations that were already emerging in some areas of urban Britain. They spoke of profound cultural changes in the fabric of post-war British society, changes, in turn, kindled by social and historical movements which spanned the course of several centuries. *Black Culture, White Youth* attempted to capture some of these changes by looking at just one aspect of their history, the impact of Jamaican popular cultural forms on the lives of young white people in one specific historical and regional context. It was concerned with white youth's collective and individual encounters with these cultural traditions, how these encounters came about, the forms they assumed and their political effects.

In a speech made in the wake of the 1985 riots in Birmingham and Tottenham, Enoch Powell reiterated his earlier warnings and prophecies from 1968 about the dire consequences of black settlement in Britain (see above). The language and themes of Powell's prognosis were taken up by a number of right-wing politicians and echoed in some sections of the popular press. Amidst fears of Britain's inner-city areas being turned into "no-go" zones where the only law was that of the "jungle", a number of newspapers dwelt on the theme that somehow this was not "England" anymore. Through the imagery of disorder, violence and racial conflict, the inner-city was perceived as a different, "alien" country, one whose inhabitants did not share the cultural values of "ordinary" English people.

The riots were represented explicitly in terms of racial conflict in some sections of the popular press. Tales of whites abused and terrorised by their black neighbours, and living in perpetual fear of being mugged and harassed, were corroborated in a number of papers and lent a bogus objectivity. The salient images were of whites put upon and "under siege" in their own country (*Daily Mail*, 9 October 1985, p. 7). The inner-city was defined as a site of negative interracial encounters, one where black and white people lived side by side, yet estranged from one another. These were areas which lacked a community spirit, where neighbourliness was "spat on" (*Daily Mail*, 8 October 1985, p. 3).

In the dominant political and media responses to the 1985 riots, the use of "race" as a metaphor for urban crisis went further than ever before (Solomos, 1986). These responses also marked the beginnings of a new onslaught on "multiracialism". Peregrine Worsthorne of the Sunday Telegraph suggested that "separate development may be the only sensible answer...mixed schooling in Bradford does not work. Nor truth to tell, do mixed housing estates work. Nothing mixed really works" (*Sunday Telegraph*, 29 September 1985, p. 18). These images of fundamental incompatibility between different ethnic and racial groups were recurrent themes in the discourse of contemporary racism, in which "race" was defined in terms of the interchangeable discourses of patriotism, xenophobia and Britishness (Barkcr, 1981; Lawrence, 1982a, Gilroy, 1987). Cultures were seen as fixed, neo-biological properties, and as mutually exclusive expressions of racial and national identity.

5

These were ubiquitous themes in the dominant political ideologies of the time. Far from being the exclusive property of the Right, such themes operated across the spectrum of formal political opinion (Gilroy, 1987). These same categories also found an echo in mainstream academic research on "race relations" with its compartmentalised study of the relatively fixed cultural characteristics of different ethnic and racial minorities (Lawrence, 1982b).

This view of cultures as solid, impermeable categories, however, suggested a false discontinuity between the experiences and identities of black and white young people. The interactive dimensions of these relations had attracted little serious academic attention. Much of the discussion of white youth culture on the Left had focused on the more reactive and overtly racist elements in white responses. The dominant imagery that held sway was that of the shaven-head, swastika-bedecked skinhead, an image which had become something of an archetypal portrait of English racism by the early 80s.

Black Culture, White Youth was intended as a counterweight to some of these prevailing assumptions and images. It was written partly to challenge such discourses, by representing what were, at the time, relatively hidden and unacknowledged social phenomena. These phenomena were concealed under the sheer weight of public media and political discourse that viewed "race relations" as a "problem" of cultural incompatibility and "natural" antagonism between different racial groups. The youth clubs and sound system dances of south Birmingham, however, were playing host to cross-cultural interactions that were completely off the radar of such discourses. Most striking was the widespread adoption of elements of black youth culture by young people in general, and young whites in particular, and the significant numbers of white participants in parts of the local reggae scene.

Powell's forebodings were oddly archaic and completely out of tune with these social realities. For in a sense, Powell and others were already too late. By the time of his 1985 speech, the cultural and musical traditions of Britain's black communities, far from being "alien" or "external" to the British way of life, were well on their way to becoming permanent, organic features of the political and cultural landscape.

6

By the early 1980s, there were signs that the scale and intensity of these cross-cultural movements was increasing amongst the young in some areas of urban Britain. *Black Culture, White Youth* attempted to explore the more dynamic and enabling aspects of these movements. By doing so, it attempted to open up the question of "race" in a different way, offering some fresh insights into the complexities with which young black and white people related to one another in contemporary Britain.

Popular music has, of course, long been acknowledged as a key channel of communication across racial and ethnic boundaries. In the US context, it has been the site of repeated, and well-documented, cross-cultural exchanges. The interaction between European and African-derived musical traditions has long been identified as one of the central dynamos of American popular music history. These traditions have co-shaped one another in a complex process of cross-fertilization that has taken place over the course of three centuries.

These interactions, however, have never been neutral processes of "free" musical exchange. They have always been politically charged, complicated by economic and cultural power relations, and rendered problematic by racism. This has produced a number of tensions that run through the course of popular music history, and has lead to recurring patterns in the entertainment industry's handling of black music; white economic control and colonization of the black music business, patterns of racial segregation in musicianship, and the marketing of black music in specific, racialised forms. Styles pioneered by black performers have consistently been bowdlerized and popularized by white performers. Detached from the cultural institutions that nourished them, black musical forms have been repeatedly appropriated as unacknowledged sources for myriad imitations.

Historically, white fears and fantasies have long been projected onto black music, refracted through discourses that tap into centuries-old racial mythologies in which African music and culture came to symbolize the "exotic" and "primitive" Other of European culture (Walton, 1972). Within the mind/body dualities of European racist discourse, black music connoted the "corporeal", defined against a European musical tradition that represented the "cerebral" (Middleton, 1972). Black music was seen to possess certain innate

7

qualities that white bourgeois society lacked; qualities of passion, spontaneity, emotion and sexuality. These discourses have framed the way black musical cultures have been packaged and sold to white audiences, whether as signs of exoticism, or pure "authentic" forms to be protected and preserved (Gilroy, 1991).

These have resulted in the fundamental paradox whereby musical traditions forged out of experiences of racial oppression, and a crucial means through which black people affirmed their identities and expressed their collective aspirations, became, for white listeners, objects of pleasure and spectacles of entertainment (Frith, 1983). From black-faced minstrelsy in the nineteenth century, through the bohemian romanticism of jazz, to the various subcultural appropriations of blues and r'n'b, successive generations of whites have lived their own particular imaginary relation to black music and black performers (Hobsbawn, 1959; Hoare, 1975; Hebdige, 1979; Frith, 1988; Ross, 1989, Jones, 1993).

These discourses and power relations continue to render problematic the ways in which black musics are commodified, consumed and appropriated by white musicians and audiences. But this narrative of black creativity and white cultural expropriation is only part of the story, and one that conceals many layers of complexity in these processes. It glosses over the contributions of white and non-black musicians to genres such as jazz, r'n'b, soul and funk, and the integrated cultures of recording and musicianship that have been a key part of these traditions (Back, 2002). It also obscures the complex ways in which black musical forms have acted as a catalyst for successive generations of young white musicians seeking to create their own forms of musical expression in pop and rock cultures. Black musical traditions have continually been adopted and rearticulated by white youth to register their independence, signify generational difference, and reject mainstream and dominant cultures.

In this process, the technologies of music production and dissemination have played a central role in enabling the mass public circulation of black musical performances. From the phonogram and the microphone, to radio and the recording studio, these technologies provided a bridge across which black music crossed over into mainstream American culture. Sounds and airwaves became crossing-places that undermined and broke down patterns of racial segregation elsewhere in society.

8

These same technologies also became the means by which the music, style and culture of black America was circulated globally. These bridges became conduits for latent social and political forces, along which oppositional sensibilities and liberating pleasures were carried. In Britain, black American music became central to the development of white youth culture and popular music. From skiffle and rockabilly in the 1950s to the beat groups and blues-based rock bands of the 1960s, black American forms were appropriated and adapted by a succession of young white musicians. Blues, r'n'b and soul provided the musical conventions, the vocal and instrumental techniques, and the modes of performance through which to articulate the collective experience and rebellion of youth, and the community of rock. Black musics were championed by white youth to signify their non-conformity with the cultural mainstream, and declare their opposition both to the dominance of bourgeois high culture and to older working-class musical traditions.

Within post-war British popular culture, however, black American musics were consumed at a relative distance from Britain's own indigenous black population, and its internal dynamics around "race". This contrasted, in important ways, with the impact of Jamaican music, which from the outset was more heavily mediated by the *presence* of black settlers in Britain. White engagement with Jamaican music was consequently bound up with a closer relation to that presence, and the forms and conditions of that engagement shaped by accompanying encounters with the contradictions of race and class identity.

It was only with the emergence of a "second-generation" Afro-Caribbean population in Britain that the possibilities of widespread contact between black and white youth had existed. Even in the early 80s, the cultural and political implications of this contact had yet to be fully examined. One of the few existing studies was Dick Hebdige's exploration of the stylistic connections between black and white youth subcultures (Hebdige, 1979). Hebdige looked at how successive white subcultures had grown up around the Afro-Caribbean community. He found a "phantom history of race relations" played out on the stylistic surfaces of post-war British youth culture, and proceeded to "decode" their meanings. However, in focusing on the submerged, symbolic links between black and white youth, his approach tended to overlook the more self-conscious forms of attachment to black culture in conditions of

9

sustained contact between young black and white people. For these connections had a substantive and not just a stylistic history, one that was rooted in shared, lived experience.

In the mid 80s, the ramifications of these social encounters had only just started to be explored. Roger Hewitt's ethnographic study of Jamaican creole usage amongst young white Londoners was the only substantial piece of research that existed (Hewitt, 1986). In its approach and subject matter, Hewitt's formative work on interracial communication and friendship patterns was an important precedent for my own ethnographic study. I wanted to similarly give primacy to young people's own lived experiences and knowledges, but focusing on *music*, rather than language, as the primary medium through which these relations were enacted. The Birmingham study explored the subjectivities and life histories of one particular group of young white people. It undertook a close-up investigation of the responses generated by their engagement with black youth culture. I wanted to know what it meant to young whites themselves to have grown up alongside their young black peers, and shared the same classrooms, neighbourhoods and leisure spaces. How did they identify with, and adopt the language, style and music of their black peers? How were the contradictory effects of racism lived out in their everyday social experience?

Since most of the participants were in their late teens and early twenties when interviewed, what emerged was a series of autobiographical narratives and personal histories. Current attitudes were interspersed with reflections on past experiences from earlier adolescence and teenage years.

The slender sample of respondents meant that the ethnography was never going to be a representative cross-section of white youth in Birmingham or in Britain generally. Instead, the aim was to examine the qualitative, inner dimensions of those responses, to capture their narrative detail and richness, and the subtle patterns of thinking and feeling that lay behind them.

From the outset, the focus was on *white* responses, partly because it was these responses that were under-researched, but also as a conscious attempt to use my own identity as a white researcher as a resource in the interview process. This approach was vindicated time and again by the wealth of insights that came out of those interviews, and by the richness of the responses that were frequently moving in their candour. For me, this was a powerful affirmation of the value of

10

ethnographic research, and of the importance of talking to people, letting them speak, and listening to them with empathy and an open mind.

Part I History

1 400 Years

1.1 Roots and Culture

To understand how particular forms of Jamaican popular culture acquired a resonance in the British context means understanding the long-term historical origins of those forms. For the cultural and political traditions which became significant within Britain's black communities and beyond have their roots in non-European forms. These traditions are indelibly marked with, and shaped by, the experience of slavery and colonialism. The historical range of this chapter is therefore far-reaching in scope, extending back into these deep roots of Jamaican popular culture and music.

Up until quite recently, it was still widely assumed in mainstream sociological approaches to Caribbean cultures that the African cultural heritage of black Caribbeans was largely destroyed by slavery and replaced by appropriated imitations of European culture. The view that African-derived forms were eliminated or abandoned in the Caribbean context, however, is contradicted by the historical evidence. Afro-Caribbean people, far from losing their African cultural heritage, retained many important elements of it in their language, religion, political philosophies and music. Premised on an increasingly detailed knowledge of traditional West African cultures, historians and anthropologists have shed light on the mechanisms of retention under slavery by which key aspects of those cultures were preserved, blended with European forms and maintained in a whole array of practices and beliefs in the New World. While the number of convincing cases of survivals traceable to *specific* West African origins has been reduced, researchers have focussed on retentions in fundamental values, cognitive orientations and basic assumptions about social relations (Price and Mintz, 1976; Kopytoff, 1976; Crahan and Knight, 1979; Robinson, 1983). Enormous amounts of knowledge were carried over into the New World in the form of spiritual belief systems, frames of reference, moral codes, medical and healing crafts, and concepts of kinship and land tenure (Robinson, 1983). The oral character of linguistic and musical forms increased the likelihood of their successful retention in the New

World (Barrett, 1976; Brathwaite, 1981). For the slave owners, these apparently non-material aspects of African culture proved almost impossible to eradicate. While plantation slave cultures developed within the parameters of the slave system, they did so at a relative distance from white institutions. Because of the impossibility of constant surveillance, the slaves were able to construct their own autonomous spheres of social and cultural life that lay beyond the control of the slave owners (Henry et al., 1982; Robinson, 1983). It was in these spaces that the slaves organised themselves and created their own characteristic cultures.

It is the uniquely syncretic *creole* quality of these forms which marks the distinctiveness of Afro-Caribbean cultures. These cultures were not simply derivative or imitative of European forms, anymore than they were straightforwardly "African". They were the product of intermixture between different African traditions, a process in which many survivals lost their ethnic specificity and become "African" in a more general sense (Bilby, 1985). These cultures were dynamic syntheses of European and African elements in which European cultural forms were creatively appropriated by the slaves, welded with retained African forms and remoulded into indigenous Afro-Caribbean cultures in a complex process of transculturation that evolved over the course of four centuries.

In Jamaican plantation society the African element of this creole culture was stronger and more prominent than in many other New World slave systems. The specific social and cultural configurations of that society combined to create something of a cultural vacuum in which Africanisms could survive and develop. From the outset, the Jamaican slave system faced a number of internal problems and contradictions, including widespread corruption, inefficiency and absenteeism amongst the planter class. The large-scale sugar plantations of the Jamaican system resulted in particularly large concentrations of African labour in which the proportion of African slaves to Europeans was amongst the highest in the Western Hemisphere (Patterson, 1967). The particular harshness and brutality of the Jamaican slave system also produced a relatively high turnover of labour, and a steady transfusion of African slaves from markedly similar regional and tribal origins (Patterson, 1967). The rugged and mountainous interior of the island, moreover, enhanced the possibilities for revolt and successful escape, enabling groups of slaves to establish large, enduring *maroon* communities from as

14

early as the seventeenth century (Price, 1973). These maroon settlements were perhaps the most visible sign that black Jamaicans never fully consented to European domination. Within their confines were nurtured music and dance forms in which the African heritage was stronger than anywhere else on the island (Bilby, 1985). The very existence of the maroon communities was a continual thorn in the side of the British, while for those enslaved on the plantations they remained a source of cultural and political inspiration, providing a symbol of rebellion as much as a real avenue of escape.

Together, these factors go far in explaining the greater incidence of rebellion in Jamaican slave society and the countless examples of slave insurrection that run through the course of its history (Craton, 1982; Patterson, 1967; Price, 1973). Besides marronage and open revolt, resistance also manifested itself in a myriad of preserved African religious and cultural forms. From the very inception of slavery, these forms emerged in contradiction to those of the dominant European culture, consistently undermining the colonialists' attempts at cultural hegemony over the slaves. Their preservation under slavery thus became a key site of political struggle.

Cabral has noted how the cultural sphere often acquires an overriding significance in channelling and mobilising resistance amongst colonised peoples (Cabral, 1973). Since slavery could only be maintained by the organised repression and denial of the slaves' cultural life, it was accordingly within that culture that the seeds of opposition were to be found. The domination of slavery was experienced collectively by blacks in the form of cultural and racial oppression. It followed, then, that their specifically *cultural* responses to that oppression often became the raw material out of which resistance was manufactured. This is not to suggest that *all* the cultural expressions of the slaves and their descendants were invested with political meaning or reducible to conditions of political and economic struggle. Rather, it is to acknowledge the specificity of ideological struggles over the signification of culture, struggles at the heart of which lay a complex negation of European cultural dominance.

The rebellious implications and unifying potential of African-derived cultures were recognised by the slave owners who attempted to brutally suppress their every expression. In the British West Indies the legitimacy of colonial authority and the existence of social order

15

were seen to depend on the eradication of African religious and cultural practices, and the outlawing of traditions that celebrated blackness. For the slaves, conversely, the preservation of an autonomous, collective black identity was a basic impulse of resistance and a necessity of survival under conditions of enslavement (Hoetink, 1979; Robinson, 1983). Language provides a clear example of how creole cultural forms were forged out of this fundamental political dialectic.

Under the plantation system, the use of African languages was forbidden by the slave owners and subject to harsh punishment. African linguistic elements nevertheless survived through a complex process of language recomposition out of which distinctive creole tongues emerged (Dalphinis, 1978). The various West African languages spoken by the slaves were reworked and blended with European forms in the need for a common means of communication, not only between the slaves and the planters, but also between the slaves themselves. These processes would have been facilitated by relatively similar speech patterns and common tribal origins amongst the slaves (Patterson, 1967; Barrett, 1976). The pidgins spoken by the earliest slaves were progressively expanded over the course of two or three generations into a comprehensive creole vernacular with its own characteristic, African-inflected vocabulary, syntax and grammatical structures (Dalby, 197 l, 1972; Dalphinis, 1985).

From their very inception, these creole languages fulfilled a semi-clandestine function, enabling slaves to communicate with one another in the presence of whites with some measure of safety. In the American context, a catalogue of research on black speech patterns sheds light on some of the cultural mechanisms involved in these processes. It shows how the dominant white values and racist caste definitions that were built into the slave system were challenged, broken down and reconstituted through the use of various linguistic strategies. Such strategies included the use of ridicule, subterfuge, inversion and allusion in speech, and a reliance on intonation, rhythm, contextual definitions of words and various non-verbal and paralinguistic features to convey meaning (Kochman, 1972; Sims Holt, 1972; Smithermann, 1977; Genovese, 1976).

Initially forged as a language of resistance under conditions of racial domination, Jamaican creole emerged as the inherited speech of the black peasantry and working class in the post-slavery period. Its importance in the lives of black Jamaicans reflected the strong

16

oral traditions in Jamaican popular culture as a whole. These traditions functioned as key repositories of the Afro-Jamaican cultural heritage. Aphorisms, practical knowledge, communal values and folk history were faithfully preserved and transmitted in rhymes, proverbs, anecdotes and metaphors, many of which were African in origin (Barrett, 1976).

Of all the cultural elements retained by black slaves in the New World, musical forms were amongst the most apparent legacies of their African past. Studies of both traditional West African and Afro-Caribbean music have shown how various musical features and principles were retained in the New World in the form of musical styles, rhythmic constructions, vocal and instrumental techniques, and in basic aesthetic traditions, modes of communication and idioms of expression (Nketia, 1975, 1978, 1979, 1982; Chernoff, 1979; Bebey, 1975; Storm Roberts, 1973). These features amounted to a whole reference system of musical practices which was carried over from traditional West African societies and recreated within New World slave cultures. Of all these features, the principles and aesthetics of polyrhythm were amongst the most audible legacies of the slaves' West African musical heritage. The strict adherence to metre and tempo remained a basic building block of musical expression in Afro-Caribbean music. As an organising principle, and an aesthetic of musical evaluation, rhythmic sensibilities became one of the fundamental matrices underlying all black musical expression in the New World.

In Jamaican slave society these musical sensibilities and principles were retained at all levels of the island's musical culture. Opportunities for music-making amongst the slaves, however, were heavily determined by the social relations of the plantation system and by the responses of individual slave owners. Such responses varied from outright hostility, to indifference and active encouragement. Those forms that were considered too "African" and threatening by the colonialists were officially banned and suppressed (Johnson, 1983; Clarke, 1980). Dancing and music-making were permitted to flourish only when not interfering with work, for example during seasonal holidays and festivals, or when actively assisting the labour process through work-songs (Patterson, 1967; White, G., 1983a).

Work-songs were amongst the earliest forms of music to be practised by the slaves in the New World context where music

17

retained its traditionally intimate connection to the labour process. These invariably synthesised European sea-shanties and melodies, with call-and-response vocal patterns drawn from West African work-songs. The content of work-songs, however, took on an added political significance under plantation conditions where they were used to scandalise and ridicule the slave owners and overseers, and protest against the slaves' status (Patterson, 1967; Brathwaite, 1981; Johnson, 1983).

From the very earliest days of slavery, the influence of European music forms was indelibly stamped on the slaves' musical culture. In Jamaica, the diversity of those influences was considerable, ranging from French and Spanish music, to various regional forms of British folk and religious music. Such influences were invariably mediated to the plantation slaves through "freed" and house slaves, by mulattos, or by various European staff and indentured labourers. Appropriated by black musicians, these European forms were infused with African creative models, motifs and rhythmic structures. The results were indigenous, uniquely creole music forms which became central in the music and dance culture of the slaves. This "creolisation" process was precipitated by slave musicians being required to play in two distinct settings; as "entertainers" for the slave-owners, and as performers in the autonomous spaces of the slaves' social and cultural life. It was in this latter context that the most audibly "African" modes of musical expression were practised during slavery. Many of these practices were related to secret cultural and religious observances such as myalism, obeah and kumina. Initially developed within the confines of maroon culture, such practices were later transmitted to the plantation slaves by myal and obeah leaders. These leaders were invariably themselves musicians and, in keeping with West African political and religious traditions, often combined the roles of healer, historian and military organiser (Brathwaite, 1981).

In many West African societies musicians were traditionally the guardians of historical knowledge and spiritual wisdom, responsible for preserving the cultural heritage of a community and transmitting it through song. The music-making process served to strengthen communal bonds by encouraging collective behaviour and referring people to shared traditions and sensibilities (Chernoff, 1979; Nketia, 1975; Bebey, 1975). This traditional status of music as a vehicle through which communal values and collective sentiments were

18

expressed took on an added significance in the slavery context where music came to be one of the most effective ways of articulating a *collective* response to racial domination. Its ability to preserve a sense of racial identity was especially important in slave cultures, where music-making became a site in which self-dignity could be restored, as much as a relief from oppression (Patterson, 1967; Storm Roberts, 1973).

Under conditions of enslavement, musical activity became a crucial autonomous space of cultural and political freedom, a site of unsupervised "freetime" onto which non-musical activities were displaced. Funerals, frequent events because of high slave mortality, likewise became important spaces in which to plot revolts and cement loyalties, since they were often the only opportunities for slaves to associate with any degree of privacy (White, G., 1983a; Patterson, 1967). Out of these funeral rites emerged various African-derived wakes and forms of ancestor worship such as kumina, a practice introduced to Jamaica in the post-emancipation period by indentured labourers from central Africa (Johnson, 1983; Bilby, 1985). Forms like myalism and obeah played a crucial role in unifying different tribal groups amongst the slaves, serving as powerful ideologies of resistance through the administering of oaths and fetishes to protect insurgents (Patterson, 1967; Schuler, 1979). Burru was another musical practice in which African traditions were retained virtually intact throughout the slavery period. From its origins as a work-song, burru developed into a topical musical form addressed to current events and to individuals in the community who were guilty of misdeeds. Its use by black musicians as a form of moral control and social criticism in slave communities was strongly reminiscent of the *griots*, the professional musicians of traditional West African society. Like the griots, burru musicians served both as popular historians and commentators on topical issues, using humour and satire to circumscribe anti-social behaviour or moral infringements (Bebey, 1975; Chernoff, 1979).

The musical forms that were associated with these various practices were strongly African in character. Of all their constituent elements, perhaps the most audibly "African" was the drum. The drum stood as a vivid reminder to the European colonialists that the slaves had not fully lost their African cultural heritage. Universally feared for its ability to convey messages, rally crowds and instil courage into the slaves, the drum came to be identified with sedition

19

and revolt in the minds of the slave owners. To the slaves themselves it was a powerful signifier of blackness and racial solidarity (Martins, 1983). The semantic importance attached to drumming traditions was a reflection of the strongly vocal and language-like qualities of instrumental music and non-verbal sounds generally in many traditional forms of West African musical expression. The practice of using instruments as speech surrogates was a common one in African music and was partly a product of the analogous features of speech patterns and musical forms in African oral cultures, whereby music "spoke" as much as speech was musical. The renowned "talking drums", for example, were able to duplicate speech patterns by producing tones that were linguistically comprehensible.

It is in this relationship between language and music that the African heritage retains one of its most profound and enduring legacies in the folk culture of black Jamaicans. For the same rhythmic sensibilities that permeate Jamaican creole speech patterns are also to be found throughout the island's musical culture. These sensibilities are rooted in traditional West African musical practices where the semantic inflexions and communicative power of music can be modified by different playing techniques, and by the manipulation of melodic movement, tonality, musical texture and rhythmic organisation. As Nketia has pointed out, in much African music the verbal meanings imparted in songs are complemented and enhanced by those which lie within the structure of the music itself:-

> While the song texts provide the significant changes in thought, mood or feeling, it may be the music that defines or expresses the general character of the occasion or the spirit of the performance. Hence, the musical function of a category of songs and consequently its form of expression would be maintained even where the texts contain nonsense syllables, archaic words or difficult allusions, or where the style of delivery makes comprehension difficult. We must thus recognize that the basis for the appreciation of a song may be linguistic, musical or both. (Nketia, 1975, p. 205)

These aesthetics of musical performance and communication became central features of black musical expression in the New World. In Jamaican slave culture, African rhythms of great complexity were preserved in forms such as kumina, while burru duplicated the exact pitch, size and number of drums of its West African parent form (Clarke, 1980). In the New World context, however, drums were often restricted to the beating of dance rhythms, losing their explicitly communicative function. The harsh punishment meted out by the slave owners to practitioners of drumming also meant that drums had to be substituted by improvised percussive devices such as shakers, graters, rattlers and stamping tubes. Drums were also supplanted by other instruments which took on highly rhythmic, drum-like functions and qualities. This practice of substituting instruments for one another, and shifting rhythmic functions from percussive to melodic instruments, was an established practice in African music, and one that was accelerated in the New World context by the adoption of Western instruments and sound sources (Nketia, 1979). Although forced underground during slavery, African drumming, dancing and singing traditions were never completely eradicated. Resurfacing periodically during rebellions, they were maintained throughout the post-emancipation era into the contemporary period, providing an unbroken link with Jamaican folk culture's African heritage.

1.2 From Revival to Rastafari

The abolition of slavery in Jamaica in 1838 marked the beginnings of a spiritual and cultural renaissance amongst black Jamaicans, the most dramatic expression of which was the growth of various mass religious movements amongst the former slaves. Sparked by the introduction of Baptist forms into Jamaica in the late seventeenth century by black American preachers, these "native" forms of Christianity drew an enthusiastic response from black Jamaicans. The mass support they engendered climaxed in the Jamaican Revival movement in the early 1860s.

Revival became the dominant Afro-Christian tradition in post-emancipation Jamaica. Like many forms of black Christianity, Revival fused rites and ceremonies drawn from the European church, such as prayers, hymns and Bible-reading, with African-based forms of worship and practices absorbed from myalism and kumina, including drum music, spirit possession and dance (Johnson, 1983). A rich variety of African musical features was retained in the music of Revival, not only in drumming and percussion, but also in

21

African-derived vocal idioms such as parallel harmony, antiphony (the repetition and answering of musical phrases), glissando (the slurring and sliding of notes) and melisma (pushing a single syllable through several separate notes) (Clarke, 1980). The participatory qualities of traditional African music, through its emphasis on *group* musical activities and dialogue between audience and musicians, were particularly evident in black church music. Here, the retention of these qualities was clearly audible in audience response and participation (through handclapping, dancing, percussion and other forms of rhythmic embellishment) and in call-and-response singing patterns and verbal exchanges between preacher and congregation (White, G., 1983a; Johnson, 1983).

The political importance of these movements in the historical experience and consciousness of the Jamaican masses is often overlooked in Eurocentric accounts of Jamaican popular culture. A close examination of Jamaican religious traditions reveals a complex fusion of spiritual and secular themes, and a strong present-world orientation, one which goes a long way in explaining why, throughout Jamaican history, resistance and political protest have consistently manifested themselves in religious terms (Schuler, 1979; Post, 1970). The colonialists, for their part, knew only too well that upsurges in religious activity amongst the black masses were often the prelude to rebellion and armed revolt.

From its inception black Christianity sought to rework European Christian doctrines. Black church leaders inverted accepted Christian themes in a complex semantic and ideological struggle over the theology of the Christian Gospel. The Bible became a major source of alternative values, ideas and images in the collective popular consciousness of the black masses (Post, 1970). As the only reading matter permitted to them by the colonialists, it had provided the means through which to make sense of their subordination and expose the hypocrisy of slavery. Black Jamaicans drew analogies between their own historical experience and that of the Old Testament Jews. Of particular interest to them were those biblical passages which either concerned themselves with the liberation of oppressed people (the Israelites), those which referred to people as "black" (Psalm 68) or which mentioned Ethiopia. God was seen as the liberator of the weak and downtrodden from the power of the oppressor. The symbols of redemption, judgement and the Promised Land provided black Jamaicans with metaphors of liberation in

22

which they saw their own reflection, and through which they channelled their hopes and aspirations for earthly freedom (Post, 1970; Cone, 1972).

The development of the Revival tradition and the growing connections between black church movements in the Caribbean, America and Africa bore fruit in the rudiments of an emergent black nationalism amongst the Jamaican masses in the late nineteenth and early twentieth centuries. It was within these movements that the seeds of a pan-African racial consciousness were first sown, thereby laying the foundations for the emergence of Garveyism and Ethiopianism in the 1920s and 30s and, eventually, Rastafarianism (Post, 1978). That consciousness was spearheaded by black churchmen who travelled freely between Africa and the New World, and communicated a knowledge and awareness of Africa to those in the Caribbean in a real and dramatic way (Clarke, 1980). The struggles of African nations and peoples against European colonial domination became stamped on the collective consciousness of the black masses (Campbell, 1980). The independence of Ethiopia, in particular, from white colonial rule stood as a symbol of African resistance. The sparse but significant biblical references made to Ethiopia cultivated a renewed awareness of Africa amongst the Jamaican masses and a sense of having participated in history (Post, 1970).

It was from these various traditions that Rastafarianism emerged in the mid-1930s out of a unique coincidence of historical events in Jamaica and against a backdrop of severe economic deprivation on the island. These events included Haile Selassie's coronation in Ethiopia and that country's subsequent invasion by Italy. Combined with the pronouncements of the Bible, the prophecies of Garvey and the knowledge of African people's anti-colonial struggles, this confluence of events provided the framework for a new deification amongst a small section of Jamaican peasants and workers, that of Rastafari (a name taken from the pre-coronation title of Haile Selassie). For these early forerunners of the Rastafari movement, Selassie took on the role of messiah and liberator, a black king of the only African nation free from colonisation by Europe (Post, 1978; Campbell, 1985). From its inception, the Rastafari movement sought to rejuvenate a sense of pride in blackness amongst the Jamaican working class and peasantry. It inverted the doctrines of white Christianity by placing God in Africa and the exiled "sufferers" in

23

Jamaica. Rastafari built on the long traditions of black radicalism in Jamaican popular culture by fusing the pan-Africanist themes of Garveyism and Ethiopianism with various folk elements drawn from burru, kumina, Revival and maroon culture (Campbell, 1980, 1985).

The creolisation of Jamaican folk music, meanwhile, continued over the post-emancipation period, accelerated in the latter half of the nineteenth century by the input of European dance forms into the island's musical culture. Polkas, reels, waltzes and the quadrille in particular, were learned by black musicians who were required to play at the "grand balls" of planter society. Once learnt, they were fed back into the black population. There, unsupervised and unhindered by Europeans, the traditional fiddles and fifes of forms like the quadrille were combined with creole musical elements such as drums, banjos and the rumba box (Johnson, 1983; White, G., 1983a). More importantly, perhaps, these ballroom styles introduced a common harmonic system, based on the European, 8-note diatonic scale, one that was quickly grasped and adapted by slave musicians (Bilby, 1985). The musical results of this process were a more syncopated, Africanised form of the quadrille, whose tonalities were similar, but whose rhythmic orientations were decidedly non-European. These distinctly creole forms provided the basis for Jamaica's first national popular music genre, *mento*.

Mento incorporated a whole range of folk elements, such as work-songs, wakes, and ring-songs. The similarity of its syncopations and rhythmic patterns to those of its close Trinidadian relative, *calypso* reflected the increasing inter-island migration in the Caribbean area during the late nineteenth and early twentieth centuries. Like calypso, mento was a topical song genre of protest, ridicule and gossip, one which continued firmly in the African musical tradition of satire and social criticism (White, G., 1983a). Forms like mento and calypso functioned as important channels of news and dissent through which the colonial authorities could be mocked and criticised. Here, the retention of African-derived musical principles was again audible in the use of music as an effective vehicle of political protest.

The 1930s and 1940s saw a number of fundamental changes in Jamaican popular culture and music, changes precipitated by the growing industrialisation and urbanisation of Jamaican society. Shifting patterns of migration throughout the Caribbean and Americas in this period, together with the break-up of rural

24

communities through forced expropriation and lopsided economic growth, caused a massive displacement of the Jamaican peasantry and a rapid rate of rural-urban migration (Beckford and Witter, 1980). The result was a dramatic expansion of surplus labour in the urban slum areas of Kingston. Drawn from the rural areas of Jamaica, this floating surplus population brought with it cultural and musical elements from the whole range of Jamaica's creole folk culture, including kumina, myalism, Revival, mento and burru.

The traditional functions of many of these forms were maintained and adapted to the urban context. The burru tradition, for example, was upheld by the large numbers of migrants who settled in the ghettoes of Kingston in the 1940s. Its singing, drumming and dancing traditions became absorbed into the culture of the urban black poor, being used specifically to welcome home ex-prisoners into the community (White, G., 1983a). With its close proximity to the newly-born movement of Rastafari, burru was seized upon by the early Rasta brethren as a "pure" African form untainted by Western influences. Lacking any musical forms of their own, the drumming traditions of burru were adopted and progressively taken over by the Rastafari as their traditional mode of musical expression.

The evolution of burru illustrates one of the enduring features of Jamaican popular music; the continuous infiltration of African-based reference points and cultural principles into contemporary, urban, popular forms. It is this feature which lies behind much of the indigenous, "roots" character of contemporary Jamaican music. Those roots are audible in the music's concrete links with the whole spectrum of traditional, neo-African and creole folk music forms. They can be heard in the many remnants and echoes of those forms which are detectable throughout modern Jamaican popular music (Johnson, 1983).

This unique juxtaposition of traditional and modern forms is one of the defining characteristics of contemporary Jamaican popular music in the post-war period. For while the changes wrought in Jamaican society by rapid industrialisation and urbanisation brought about a unique merging and fusion of these long-standing musical and cultural traditions, they also had the effect of exposing Jamaicans to a wider variety of external popular music forms. It is at the juncture of these various traditional and external, modern influences, that contemporary forms of Jamaican popular music begin to emerge.

25

1.3 These Sounds Lead the Way

By the 1940s the popularity of mento amongst black Jamaicans was beginning to be eclipsed by a growing fondness for contemporary black American music such as swing, jazz and especially r'n'b. While still popular in urban areas, younger Jamaicans began to disassociate themselves from mento as a rural music, reminiscent of the deprivations of peasant life and less capable of reflecting the sensibilities of urban, working-class experience (White, G., 1983a). The harder, electronic rhythms of urban jump blues and the loping, shuffle tempo of southern r'n'b artists like Amos Milburn, Fats Domino and Louis Jordan proved more appealing to working-class Jamaicans. Born out of a similar rural-urban transition in the American context, the preoccupations and subject matter of r'n'b proved more relevant to the conditions and pressures of urban life. The emergence of a state broadcasting corporation, the growth in radio ownership and the importing of recorded music by returning migrant workers and US servicemen stationed on the island, all contributed to the growing availability of black American music. However, it was the sound system which was perhaps most responsible for the popularisation of r'n'b amongst urban, working-class Jamaicans.

Sound systems first began to appear in the late 1940s as mobile entertainment institutions playing recorded music at dances held in local halls, nightclubs and backyards. By tapping the growing demand for r'n'b, the early sound systems attracted a large, predominantly working-class following, particularly in the poorer areas of Kingston. The early sound operators attempted to keep abreast of their rivals with the most exclusive and popular tunes of the day, thereby attracting the largest crowd and custom. The keen sense of inter-sound rivalry, in which survival and keeping ahead of one's opponents depended on wits, originality and improvisation, provided a certain stimulus to musical and technological innovation. As the sound systems expanded in economic scale and size, they developed into important community resources, providing a genuinely popular source of collective entertainment for working-class Jamaicans, many of whom, especially in the 1940s and 50s, were unable to afford record-players. In terms of cultural importance and popularity, they rivalled and often superseded "live", stage-based musical performances. From their inception, the sound systems were tightly bound to the communities which they served and which, in turn, sustained them. Jamaican popular music was forged out of this close cultural dialectic between the sound system and its audience. Perhaps more than any other form, this uniquely Jamaican cultural institution has exerted the greatest influence on contemporary Jamaican music, so much so that many of its key musical and technological innovations have originated from the sound system.

By the late 1950s and early 1960s, r'n'b had begun to lose much of its original impetus. The less robust, more diluted rhythms of rock 'n' roll failed to capture a mass appeal amongst black Jamaican audiences (Clarke, 1980). It was the sound-system operators who responded to the diminishing supply of danceable r'n'b by stimulating the production of an indigenous Jamaican version for local consumption (Johnson, 1983). This Jamaican r'n'b, which became known as "blues" or "boogie", evolved through the late 1950s and early 1960s into a uniquely Jamaican popular music genre in the form of *ska*.

Ska emerged out of a melting-pot of modern and traditional influences, including folk music forms that existed in the ghettoes and slums of Kingston in the late 1950s. Since many early ska musicians hailed from these self-same ghettoes, it was not surprising that many of these influences were reflected in the music, in its rhythmic echoes of kumina, burru and mento, and its call-and-response vocal and instrumental passages drawn from Revival music (Reckford, 1982). While ska drew heavily on all these indigenous folk forms, its immediate origins were in American r'n'b. Working-class musicians, with formal training in jazz and military music, appropriated the 12-bar blues, stabbing piano rhythms and walking bass patterns of r'n'b and blended them with the polyrhythms and strumming off-beat guitar of mento (White, G., 1983b; Clarke, 1980).

The influence of r'n'b on Jamaican music was a sign of the growing cultural and political dialogue between black people in the Caribbean and America, and the increasing homogenisation of black music in the western hemisphere as a whole (White, G., 1983b). The use of parallel developments in black American music by Jamaican

27

musicians was to become an ongoing feature of the reggae tradition, reflected in various appropriations of gospel, soul, jazz and funk.

Ska, however, was always more than a Jamaican approximation of black American music. It was a conscious reworking and *Jamaicanising* of r'n'b, its most noticeable difference being its accentuated off-beat rhythm. Ska also placed an even greater emphasis on the bass, originally one of the most attractive features of r'n'b and one that was crucial to the music's danceability. Both these features, bass and off-beat rhythm, were to become recurring characteristics and anchor principles of nearly all subsequent Jamaican popular music.

The production of Jamaican r'n'b and early ska revolved around a small caucus of recording studios and artists who were tied almost exclusively into the sound system business. The manufacture of records for public consumption was initially limited and secondary to the requirements of the sound systems. It was not until the turn of the decade that other, non-sound system entrepreneurs began to explore the commercial possibilities of manufacturing locally recorded music for more widespread consumption. The sound system businessmen, however, were better equipped to respond to the needs of their audiences, and soon followed into mass production of records, establishing an embryonic infrastructure of studios and recording labels (Johnson, 1983). As consumption of recorded music increased, the industry gathered momentum throughout the 1960s. It was in this period that most of the present-day economic structures and cultural practices of the Jamaican recording industry were forged.

A unique method of production and distribution was evolved in this period to suit the peculiar nature of the Jamaican market. It involved the production of one-off custom-made acetates, or *dubplates*, for exclusive play on individual sounds, alongside variants of those recordings intended for general consumption. Such recordings would be released in limited editions as a way of testing their popularity before making them generally available through retail networks. This method of consumer enticement was an effective way of guaranteeing sales and lessening investment risks in a fragile and relatively small record-buying market. In addition, the exclusivity of much sound-system music was a means of ensuring high attendance at dances.

The production of Jamaican music, from its very inception, became a focal point of struggle over its economic and cultural

28

control, a struggle waged largely between a small group of entrepreneurs who supplied the financial backing for recordings and who hired vocalists on a song-by-song basis, and the abundance of predominantly working-class musicians and singers. The non-existence of copyright and publishing contracts opened the way to exploitative practices by the handful of owners who monopolised recording and production facilities (Clark, 1980). Many of these early "producers" were businessmen and sound-system operators who exercised minimal control over the actual composition of songs. Musical arrangement was left largely in the hands of the musicians themselves. Thus while the producers had an ear for the most popular and profitable sounds, it was these session-players who controlled the music's formal possibilities. This established a recurring pattern in the Jamaican recording industry where music was crafted primarily for consumption in the dancehall context, and encoded with formal qualities that were aligned to that context. From this point on, the identifying characteristics of Jamaican music, and its unique cultural conventions, were heavily mediated by the requirements and social relations of the dancehall.

Through these mechanisms, disseminated via the sound system, ska rapidly became a vibrant, popular cultural force and a key vehicle of expression amongst working class Jamaicans. Held in contempt by middle and upper-class Jamaicans, and initially excluded from the state-controlled broadcasting media, ska undermined the domination of white American popular music in the island's official musical culture (Hylton, 1975). Early attempts by government representatives to incorporate the music, and control the direction of its development by diluting its musical and political content, were largely unsuccessful, and the music's creative base remained firmly rooted in the working-class ghettoes of Kingston.

The gaining of independence in Jamaica in 1962 signalled a growing disparity in the distribution of wealth on the island. Distorted economic growth served to widen the gap between the dispossessed masses and the ruling elite (Beckford and Witter, 1980). The legacies of slavery and colonialism were inherited in the apprenticeship system, in the neo-colonial power structure and in the unchanged colour-class basis of Jamaica's social structure (White, 1967). These economic and social realities resulted in a dramatic intensification of the class struggle in the mid-1960s, with social

29

unrest reaching a peak in the political violence that surrounded the nation's first general election in 1966.

The changing social and economic climate of Jamaican society in this period was mirrored in corresponding shifts the in style, form and lyrical content of Jamaican popular music. The optimism of the immediate post-independence period, reflected in the vibrant, up-tempo quality of much early ska, soon began to fade into disillusionment under the impact of growing unemployment, ghettoisation and the social disequilibrium generated by underdevelopment. Jamaican music consequently began to express new moods and tensions, becoming simultaneously more sombre and introspective. By 1966, these changes were being registered in the emergence of a new musical style, *rocksteady*.

The transition from ska to rocksteady was initially dictated by the slowing-down of dance paces from the frantic "legs-work" of the former to the more sensuous "hip-work" of the latter (Johnson, 1983). These shifts soon became detectable in the changing drum and bass patterns of the music itself. Rocksteady's most noticeable difference from ska was its enhanced use of the electronic bass which by then had replaced the acoustic bass used in many ska recordings. The bass player's greater use of rests and gaps in the bass line enabled the drummer to improvise with syncopations and fills on the tom-toms and hi-hat cymbals (Griffith, 1977). Greater prominence was also given to percussion and Rasta drumming. The off-beat quality of Jamaican music was further accentuated by the drummer playing together on both snare and bass drums on the third beat of the bar in a style known as the *one drop*.

1.4 Word, Sound and Power

The emergence of rocksteady marked the beginning of a period of heightened political awareness within Jamaican music, one that reflected the growing sense of solidarity and militancy amongst black people throughout the African diaspora. By the late 1960s this incipient race and class consciousness was beginning to acquire a greater spiritual depth under the impact of Rastafari which had expanded beyond its lower working-class origins into a mass social movement and a symbol of protest for thousands of Jamaicans (Beckford and Witter, 1980). By the early 1970s Rastafari had become the dominant influence in Jamaican popular music,

30

providing a source of inspiration for many musicians and supplying the frame of reference for a whole new generation of ghetto artists typified by groups like the Wailers. Under the movement's influence, the protest element that had become such a characteristic feature of Jamaican music became more articulate and thoughtful. Political and historical themes became more prevalent, conveying an acute awareness of slavery and colonialism and the links between past and present forms of oppression.

The late 1960s also saw the beginnings of a movement towards artistic and financial autonomy amongst younger musicians dissatisfied with the exploitative practices of the old producer-artist set-up. These developments enhanced the opportunities for musicians and producers alike to record more creative and explicitly political material. The late 1960s and early 1970s was consequently a period of considerable experimentation and technological advance within Jamaican music. This period coincided with the emergence of *reggae* in late 1968.

In reggae, the rhythmic interplay of instruments reached a new level of sophistication and complexity. The rhythm guitar added an extra half-beat to the classic Jamaican offbeat that was further accentuated by keyboard phrasing. The music as a whole became a more integrated and total ensemble of complementary rhythms, highlighted by an even greater use of percussion (Reckford, 1982; Griffith, 1977). The bass took on an increasingly rhythmic, almost drum-like function and acquired a distinctly vocal quality, "saying" phrases, then pausing for effect. The bassline provided a crucial foundation for the melody and harmonic structure of songs. The pre-eminence of the bass continued to be a central aesthetic in the vernacular code of reggae. The use of pauses and rests in the bassline, together with the omission of whole bars by the bass player, served to highlight the underlying percussion and polyrhythmic instrumentation in the music. This process of rhythmic evolution entered a new phase in the mid-1970s with the emergence of styles like "rockers". Exponents of rockers drumming like Sly Dunbar and Leroy Wallace self-consciously extended the Africanisation of Jamaican popular music through the use of Nyabinghi drums and experimentation with complex cross-rhythms and syncopations (May, 1978).

The introduction of multi-track recording in the late 1960s opened up new artistic possibilities in sound engineering and recording that were most audible in dub. Dub originated through sound engineers experimenting with the separation of different tracks and instruments in the studio. Through the use of echo, reverb and phasing, and by means of skilful tape-editing, the dub engineer was able to transform the music in endlessly different ways. Originally recorded exclusively for sound-system play, by the early 1970s these "versions" had begun to appear on the B-side of every record release as a dubbed variant of the A-side.

With the advent of 16 and 24-track studios, dub evolved into a complex process of musical enrichment and an art form in its own right, with the engineer attempting to clarify or enhance the implicit meaning of a song by the selective dubbing in and reprocessing of key words and phrases from the original lyrics.

While the effectiveness of dub was dependent partly on retaining vocal and lyrical fragments of the original song, by the mid-1970s such fragments had begun to disappear altogether from the sound mix. The expressive and semantic power of dub was carried by sounds, melodies and drum and bass patterns which had the capacity to convey emotions and echo sensibilities without being linguistically comprehensible. Many commentaries on Jamaican popular music tend to overlook these non-verbal dimensions of reggae in favour of a more limited analysis of its song lyrics. Reggae's unique power, however, lies in the dynamic interplay *between* these verbal and non-verbal modes of communication and their distinctive fusion into an organic musical whole.

Dub has been seen as an extension of the subversion inherent in the musical structure of *all* reggae, by protecting itself from simplistic and fixed interpretations (Hebdige, 1974). It emerged, in part, as a response to some of the contradictions posed to reggae artists by the increasing commodification of their products by the international recording industry in the late 1960s. Dub was just one aspect of the ongoing struggle of musicians to resist the reification and packaging of reggae in specific commodity forms tailored to the international market. Gilroy sees dub as an implicit attempt to circumvent some of the obstacles posed by these processes to the dissemination of political messages. Dub, like much reggae music, relies on inferred, immanent meanings which are designed to be activated primarily in the context of performance and consumption. Dub acts as a bridge between "overtly committed and apparently unpolitical records alike", providing a consistent matrix which unites all reggae at the level of form (Gilroy, 1982, p.301).

Equally important in reggae aesthetics were the drum and bass melodies, or "riddims", which run through the course of the music's history, constantly assuming new musical forms and rhythmic patterns. The cultural sanctioning or "versioning" of these cherished standards and familiar tunes is a long-standing practice in the reggae tradition, whereby musicians continually treasure their own heritage and musical past. In this way, reggae is produced within the parameters of its own unique aesthetics and conventions which, taken together, amount to a musical language of forms and idioms which are recreated in endlessly different styles and combinations.

While reggae's meanings were is not reducible to its lyrical content, song lyrics, nevertheless, occupied a central place in Jamaican popular music as a unique chronicle of the collective historical experience of the working-class in the recorded form. Jamaican popular song has faithfully reflected that experience in its lyricism, graphically representing the complexities and contradictions of everyday working-class existence, from its problems of survival and poverty, through its many ironies and paradoxes, to its love and humour.

The lyrics of recorded songs offer topical commentary on social, economic and political issues, keeping pace with current events on an almost weekly basis. Drawn from the same backgrounds as their audiences, most reggae artists have an understanding of their problems and predicaments that is based on personal experience. The reggae lyricist attempts to translate that experience into a common language of collective symbols in which the wider audience is able to recognise itself most readily. To this end, the themes of protest, captivity, prophecy and moral exhortation which feature prominently in many reggae lyrics are often couched in biblical metaphors and imagery. The polarity of class interests in Jamaican society is also reproduced in a series of dichotomies, between "haves" and "have-nots", "righteous" and "wicked", "natty dread" and "baldhead", or "us" and "them" (Johnson, 1975, 1976). To add spiritual and philosophical weight to a particular song, the reggae lyricist also draws on a rich reservoir of rhymes, riddles, folk-stories and proverbs in Jamaican oral culture (Johnson, 1983). In this way, reggae lyricists attempt both to articulate the collective consciousness of their audience, as well as to organise and politicise it, by working on the practical ideologies that already exist in Jamaican popular culture.

Rastafari plays a critical role in this process. With the mass conversion of reggae musicians to the movement in the late 1960s and early 1970s, Jamaican music became saturated with its political discourses and symbols. Through the political vision of Rasta, the reggae lyricist attempted to jettison the Eurocentric value system of the neo-colonial bourgeoisie, by expounding Afrocentric values and fostering a sense of collective racial identity. The lyrical preoccupations of reggae, however, extended well beyond statements of solidarity and anti-racism. Gilroy identified three other principal sets of discourses that recur in reggae's subject matter; first, a critique of waged labour in the forms in which it was made available to, or withheld from, blacks, accomplished through a countervailing celebration of leisure as free time and a glorification of sexuality as symbolic of the freedom from the oppression of work; second, a questioning of the legitimacy of capitalist law and state authority, expressed in common concerns with the theme of "freedom", with the nature of "crime" and with demands for "equal rights and justice"; and, lastly, a belief in the importance of historical knowledge in the realisation of that freedom, conveyed in the emphasis on "roots", tradition, continuity and historical responsibility (Gilroy, 1987). By addressing these recurring themes, reggae continues within African traditions of music-making where performance practices are means of education as much as sources of entertainment (Small, 1987).

The oral poetry of the Jamaican DJ or "toaster" occupies a central position in these practices, and in reggae culture as a whole. Rooted, like so many features of the reggae tradition, in sound-system culture, the DJ phenomenon originated in the r'n'b/ska era, initially as a way of humanising the experience of dancing to recorded music by providing rhythmic oral embellishment and vocal interjections (Johnson, 1983). The slowing down of ska gave DJs more time to express themselves in the form of spoken introductions or *talkovers*. It was the innovations in rocksteady and dub, however, which enabled the toasting tradition to reach its full potential. The slower rhythms of rocksteady provided a suitable backing for the more fluent and poetic lyrical statements of DJ exponents like U-Roy. U-Roy's innovative style of toasting was tagged "musical talking" for its ability to correspond to the chord changes in the music. Taking

34

his cue from the lyrical fragments of the dubbed "version" of a recording, U-Roy improvised his own lyrics, modifying and expanding the song's original meaning (Clarke, 1980). From the late 1960s, toasting commentaries became increasingly articulate, addressing political and cultural themes with a high degree of stylistic originality and innovation. The early 1970s saw the emergence of Rasta-influenced DJs like Big Youth toasting over dubbed rhythms often unencumbered by vocals. Lacing his lyrics with biblical references and imagery, Big Youth delivered comments and insights into the workings of mental and material oppression, voicing a political consciousness as sharp as that of the reggae lyricist. Through the use of unrestrained patois and vocal sounds, his toasting synchronised linguistic and musical patterns at a level which transcended specific verbal meanings, conveying an overall mood of dread. Toasting, in this sense, was an attempt to extend communication beyond words, and represented a commentary on the inadequacy of language as a means of expressing certain truths and meanings.

The DJ's art, similarly to that of the reggae lyricist, grew out of the rich oral traditions of Jamaican popular culture, drawing on its wealth of proverbs, nursery rhymes, ring-songs, word games and work-songs (Johnson, 1983). The DJ phenomenon was rooted historically in those African oral traditions in which musical expression and speech forms were intimately related. The genre was steeped in the gossiping, mocking and social commentary forms of burru and mento, similarly functioning as a channel through which news and topical information could be communicated. Equally, the forms of joking, boasting and trading of ritual insults characteristic of toasting were deeply rooted in African traditions of the story-teller, broad talker and people's musician (Abrahams, 1972; Toop,1984). The similarity of toasting to its close Afro-American relatives, *scatting* in jazz and *rapping* in hip-hop, pointed to shared roots in a common African-derived musical and oral heritage.

The sound system remained the principal context of musical activity for working class Jamaicans, and one of the main institutions through which reggae's audience was able to exert some control over the music, by demanding danceable and relevant music. It was through the sound system that the DJ's art was brought to life, and through which DJs were organically connected to the audience from whom they drew their inspiration and whose collective moods and

35

concerns they sought to reflect. The close relationship between DJ and audience signified the communalism of the sound-system experience. That experience served as a key test of a DJ's popularity and relevance, one which they needed to continually pass in order to remain successful and respected.

The DJ's art was dependent on spontaneity, quick wittedness, rhyming ability, and the weaving together of poetic statements in a distinct rhythmic flow in time to the music. Delivering improvised lyrics over the dub portion of a particular track, the DJ engaged with the discourses of recorded songs, using their lyrical content as a source of inspiration, commenting on, amending and expanding their meanings. By mixing social commentary with news and stories of a topical nature, the DJ drew on time-honoured oral strategies found throughout the musical cultures of the black diaspora, including the use of parody, ridicule, impersonation, mockery, self-inflation and boasting, ritual trading of insults, and the glorification and celebration of sexuality. The space of the sound system dance represented an alternative public arena in which issues and grievances could be openly aired, uncensored, in ways impossible through dominant media channels. As such, the practice of DJing remained a democratic form of individual and collective expression throughout the 1980s and 90s.

The central role of the DJ in the live context of the dance-hall, points to one of the most important facets of the reggae tradition, the social relations of its performance. Smalls notion of *musicking* is particularly appropriate here, by encompassing all the practices of taking part in a musical performance, whether through performing, listening, rehearsing or practising, providing material for performance, or dancing (Small, 1998, p. 9). Central in sound system musicking is the activity of publicly reproducing and transforming recorded music by means of various socializing rituals and practices. Recorded music becomes the principal source of raw material in a complex process of creative improvisation in which new texts and meanings are continually reproduced. Transmitted through the sound system and consumed at a distance from their initial context of production, recorded music undergoes a series of symbolic and material transformations. Through such practices, stored musical performances in recordings are divested of their status as artistic statements with fixed meanings, and effectively re-performed.

While performance idioms centre on the orality of DJing, recorded music is also embellished through live singing by vocal performers and DJs who superimpose their own melodies over the instrumental rhythm tracks and dub versions of songs. The DJ engages the audience through various exhortations and exchanges, giving name checks, "shout outs," salutations and special dedications to particular individuals and groups in the crowd. Naming is a key signifying practice that permeates the performance, and one that serves to confer status, grace and public recognition ("respect") on key audience members and groupings. Naming also operates through the adopted aliases and personae of DJs themselves which signify their status as public performers. The DJ has a ritual function as peace keeper and mediator of tensions within the dance audience, fostering togetherness. In these ways, DJs serve as public voices for their audiences in the dance context, speaking to and for them.

Crowd response and participation through dance and vocal encouragement also play a crucial role in shaping the sound-system experience. The active, participatory character of the audience in these spaces makes them an integral part of the performance and the theatricality of the event as a whole. Audiences respond and express feedback through bodily responses in dance, and through various forms of vocal appreciation.

The practice of interrupting a popular song during its opening bars, pulling up the needle and cutting the record back to the beginning serves to increase the sense of drama and anticipation within the event. The art of selection is a central aesthetic of sound system practice. The choice of which records to play and in what order is crucial in creating a particular dramaturgy and narrative structure for an event. Through selection practices, the DJ attempts to engage with the crowd, leading it through mood shifts and building climaxes and crescendos over the course of a session.

By juxtaposing records with particular musical and lyrical content, the DJ can also set up intertextual meanings between and across selections. The meanings of songs can be underlined or expanded through the selection, ordering and counter position, or *counteraction*, of particular songs and melodies. Songs can thereby be made to comment on, critique or "answer" one another. The live "versioning" of rhythms similarly involves juxtaposing different stylistic and musical variants of timeless originals and standards. The reviving of original versions is also a way of paying homage to respected forerunners and predecessors. The intercutting of past into present music serves to articulate collective sensibilities and continuities within the reggae tradition by working around popular memory and a shared musical heritage. Here, the DJ, or *selector*, functions as a musical curator and sound archivist with an extensive knowledge of the music's history.

In the live dancehall context, recorded music is also processed at the point of transmission through a battery of technological hardware which enables the music to be transformed in an infinite number of ways through the deployment of echo, reverb, phasing, equalisation, and additional sound effects. These technologies enable the dub process to be recreated live. Sound effects can be dubbed over recorded music, while individual components of the musical mix, such as drums, vocals, guitars, and bass, can be processed or retracted, then reintroduced into the mix.

In this process, the technological means of musical reproduction, in the form of turntables, mixers, amplifiers and speakers, are humanised, made tactile, and used as musical instruments in their own right. Treble, mid-range, and bass frequencies are separated and channelled into separate speaker systems for each frequency range, in a vastly expanded version of the domestic hi-fi system. The reproduction of bass frequencies is a central aesthetic in this process, and a foundational principle in Jamaican popular music's "bass culture." Speaker boxes are custom-designed and purpose built to house large 18" bass in wardrobe-sized cabinets.

In the dancehall context, reggae's bass is a key source of pleasure for its audience, its transmission crucial to the impact and affective power of the music. Through its sheer physical weight and power of amplification, the bass is materialised in and through the body, designed to be felt as much as heard. Its periodic retraction and reintroduction into the sound mix, along with other elements of the rhythmic ensemble, serve to enhance the drama of a sound system session.

Taken together, these practices help to socialise the live event, turning it into a creative performance. The semiotic and expressive power of reggae is enhanced in the dancehall context, where the music is heard as a complex fusion of words, sounds and melodies. Through the sound system, music is experienced as an expressive totality of signifying practices, of sound, speech, singing and dance.

The characteristic forms and aesthetics of the reggae tradition, its key conventions and practices, continued to be shaped by the historical experience of the Jamaican working class in the 1980s and beyond. Reggae continued to be produced out of a particular kind of dialectic between artist and audience, sound system and crowd. Its creative base retained a firm foothold in this Jamaican point of reference. The growth of an indigenous recording industry in Jamaica in the 1960s, however, and the subsequent commodification of reggae by the global entertainment industry served to disseminate the music to disparate Caribbean communities in North America and Europe. These transnational and diasporic flows enabled reggae to acquire a mass popularity and relevance far beyond the boundaries of its original context of production, embracing not only Britain's black communities but other social groups in the population at large.

2 UK Version

2.1 Down Here in Babylon

From the very earliest days of post-war migration, Caribbean settlers began to remake and adapt their cultural and musical institutions to life in urban Britain. The need for such institutions was enhanced by the stark realities of racism in the leisure sphere. For the same racism that operated in the job and housing markets also barred black settlers from many white working-class leisure spaces, such as pubs, clubs, dance palais and bingo halls. Faced with such exclusion, black workers were forced to rely more heavily on their own entertainment institutions. Growing out of the embryonic network of jazz clubs that had existed in London since the 1930s and 1940s, a thriving music and dance culture emerged in the small number of black-owned or managed night-spots that sprang up in the metropolis. Such clubs catered for the diverse groupings that comprised London's black population in the immediate post-war period with an appropriately eclectic musical soundtrack of highlife, calypso, and latin music, as well as jazz and r'n'b.

In addition to these public leisure venues, the cultural life of Afro-Caribbean people in this early period was also expressed in various private leisure settings within the black community, in the form of church gatherings, cricket socials, wedding receptions, weekend and bank-holiday outings and house parties. Afro-Caribbean people used music in particular as a way of filling the gap in their consciousness between the lives that they had left behind and the circumstances in which they found themselves in Britain. Many Afro-Caribbean settlers, having arrived in Britain, made large radiograms one of their first purchases. These became a standard piece of furniture in black households, and provided music at social events (Phillips, 1982; Hinds, 1980). Social gatherings revolved around regular Saturday night parties which became a universal form of entertainment amongst Afro-Caribbean workers and a major focus of weekend leisure.

It was through these embryonic leisure institutions that specifically Jamaican musical traditions first became established in Britain's black communities. The growing influence of those

41

traditions, and the subsequent hegemony that they acquired in the Afro-Caribbean community, was in part a reflection of the numerical superiority of Jamaicans in the black population. While the black community embraced a diversity of Caribbean nationalities, Jamaican settlers constituted approximately 60 per cent of Britain's Afro-Caribbean population (Henry et al., 1982). While the first wave of Jamaican migrants was drawn predominantly from rural areas of the island, the second wave in the mid-1950s included a larger proportion of urban, working-class Jamaicans (Smith, 1977). Howe contends that it was representatives from this latter group who were largely responsible for importing and maintaining cultural institutions such as the gambling house and sound system (Howe, 1973).

The sound system was adapted to the specific conditions of urban British society in the form of *shebeens* or *blues parties* held in private houses or basements. The dwellings of working-class blacks were amongst the few resources available for independent entertainment and leisure activities. Growing out of its traditional function in the Caribbean, the shebeen served as much as a means of entertainment as a source of revenue; revenue acquired largely through sales of food and beverages to pay for exorbitant rents, make domestic purchases, or send money home to dependants in the Caribbean (Clarke, 1976). The recreational function of the sound system was of particular importance in the British context as a refuge from a hostile and alienating white society. In this early period of black settlement, recorded music also provided an important medium of political and cultural communication with the Caribbean, relaying news of the home society to its expatriates in the metropolis.

Howe notes that by 1955 these institutions were well established in the larger black communities such as London's Notting Hill (Howe, 1973). The blues party and gambling house, however, were largely independent of the state's laws which regulated the activities of equivalent white working-class institutions. As Howe points out, their hours of activity stood in contradiction to the rhythm of the working day. For black workers, the all-night entertainment of the blues party represented a suspension of the ordered time and place associated with waged labour and the dominant culture. In the British context, this earnest pursuit of leisure in the non-work period was all the more poignant and subversive. The practices of the shebeen indirectly impinged on the labour process by disrupting this leisure-

42

work equilibrium. As such, they quickly came to be regarded as a threat to public order and to the discipline of urban life by state agencies such as the police. This period consequently saw the beginnings of a tradition of black cultural resistance spilling over into the public domain that was to become a key feature of black struggle in the decades to come.

As early as 1957, shebeens and gambling houses began to enter into popular white consciousness in the form of various public calls for tighter supervision of these spaces (Howe, 1980). The small group of unemployed people whom such institutions had freed from waged labour increasingly began to attract attention from the police and the media. Police reports on this emerging "social problem" helped to create the climate for a clamp down on shebeens as a source of "crime" and "vice" (Howe, 1980). This was the first of many post-war moral panics around the themes of criminality and "race". Together with the support granted by prosecuting magistrates, it gave the police *carte blanche* to mobilise against the black community. The late 1950s consequently marked the beginnings of a massive police penetration of the community and its leisure spaces (Hall et al., 1978). All aspects of black cultural life, from wedding receptions to private parties, became liable to interruption and suppression. Police raids and prosecutions became commonplace in black residential areas. The pretexts for such actions were invariably contraventions of licensing laws in the form of illegal alcohol sales (Hilliard, 1981). Police intrusions into black leisure spaces were to continue throughout the 1960s in the form of systematic harassment of black cultural events.

The late 1950s marked something of a turning-point in the post-war history of the black community. The confrontations between blacks and racist white youth on the streets of Notting Hill and Nottingham in 1958, together with the murder of a Kelso Cochrane in the following year, highlighted the need for greater self-reliance and militancy (Sivanandan, 1982). The events of 1958 demonstrated the willingness and capacity of black communities to organise themselves collectively against racial attacks. During the Notting Hill disturbances, the black community's cultural and leisure institutions had been at the centre of these struggles, with shebeens and gambling houses acting as rallying points and bases from which the defence of the local community was organised (Howe, 1973).

As a consequence of these events, the early 1960s saw the emergence of a culturally more self-sufficient and cohesive Afro-Caribbean community in Britain. The 1960s as a whole witnessed the construction of a "colony society" in the larger areas of black settlement, as a defensive collective response to the more pronounced forms of public racism in British society (Hall et al., 1978). This winning of cultural space was most noticeable in the expansion of a network of autonomous cultural, economic and leisure institutions within Britain's black communities. Taken together these institutions amounted to an alternative black public sphere which provided a territorial base for the maintenance of a distinctive way of life. Black restaurants, cafes, churches, food shops and a network of night-clubs and record-shops emerged to cater for the cultural and recreational needs of Afro-Caribbean people.

One of the earliest and most important of those needs was a burgeoning demand for recorded music. The settlement of black workers in Britain created a substantial export market for Jamaican and Caribbean music in the form of thousands of potential record-buyers. In Britain, Jamaican music found an even larger and more avid audience than in its country of origin, with sales of records frequently exceeding those in Jamaica during the 1960s. Britain rapidly became one of the Jamaican recording industry's largest and most lucrative markets, its fortunes intimately bound up with the tastes and demands of Britain's black population.

In the early period of post-war black settlement it was the sound system operators and a handful of individual entrepreneurs were largely responsible for importing and disseminating Jamaican music in Britain. Much of this business was conducted on a one-to-one basis and usually involved special arrangements with personal contacts in Jamaica. However, in answer to the increasing demand for Caribbean music in the late 1950s and early 1960s, there emerged alongside this network an infrastructure of independent enterprises specialising in the wholesale import and retail of calypso, Jamaican r'n'b and early ska. One of the most significant of these labels was Island Records.

Island had been established by Chris Blackwell, a native white Jamaican, who had already been involved in record production in Jamaica. Having seen the greater marketing potential of Jamaican music in Britain, Blackwell had signed licensing deals with all of

Jamaica's top producers and set up operations there in 1962. Rapidly overtaking its main rivals, Island, with its co-label Trojan, subsequently became the principal sales and distribution outlet for Jamaican music in the 1960s, releasing over 400 singles between 1962 and 1968 alone (Dalke, 1979). In the late 1960s and early 1970s, Trojan took over the company's mantle to become the largest producer and distributor of reggae in Britain, controlling over 75% of the reggae market until its collapse in the mid-1970s (Randall, 1972).

The Island-Trojan network helped to establish an infrastructure for an indigenous reggae industry by building a mass market for Jamaican music in Britain's black communities. Around this market a largely self-sufficient, autonomous network of mostly black-owned import, distribution and retail enterprises was constructed in the early-to-mid-1970s, forming the core of a thriving British reggae industry (Gayle, 1974). Such enterprises were sustained, for the most part, by purchasing power within the black community. For the smaller record labels, working on low overheads, sales of as little as 3000 records could be sufficient to make a profit, while larger companies were routinely able to sell over 50,000 to a pre-established market, purely through exposure in clubs, record shops and sound systems. Many of these businesses operated in close conjunction with each other, forming a tight, interlocking circuit of distribution, promotion, retail and consumption that was almost wholly autonomous from the mainstream music industry.

The lifeblood of this "roots" market was the network of import record shops that existed in every major black community in Britain, and accounted for an estimated 95 per cent of reggae record sales (May, 1977). Given reggae's lack of radio exposure and the refusal of many white-owned, mainstream record shops to stock it, these shops functioned as important broadcasting and promotional channels. More than just retail outlets, they signified cultural space for the black community with their own characteristic practices and modes of consumption. Regular customers would expect to be played the whole range of latest releases by the shop-owner, and while a handful of albums might be on display, attention would be focused on the discovery, critical appreciation and celebration of the music.

Of all these institutions, however, it was the sound system that remained the principal medium through which reggae was transmitted, heard and collectively experienced. From the small nucleus of sounds in the late 1950s and early 1960s, the British-based sound-system tradition evolved into a distinct genre of its Jamaican parent form. By the late 1960s and early 1970s, sounds had become established in all of Britain's major black communities, many adopting similar titles to their Jamaican forebears such as Duke Reid and Coxsone (Gayle, 1976a). The sound system became a key site of leisure activity within black communities, and the regular accompaniment to a wide range of Afro-Caribbean social functions and family occasions, from birthday parties to wedding receptions and christenings. Sound systems could be found playing regularly in church halls, pubs and private parties in black neighbourhoods, while many kept residencies in a small circuit of commercial discos and nightclubs.

In the early 1970s, Britain's sound-system culture began to undergo something of a transition, one partly dictated by the changes in Jamaican music itself. Oppositional songs began to predominate, with Rasta and African themes increasingly prevalent in the music. The increasing preponderance of "roots" reggae, with its tougher rhythms and more conscious lyrics, served to politicise dances and blues parties in a new way. The atmosphere at such events, Gayle observes, became tangibly more tense and "dread", the attitude of dance-goers more serious and reflective (Gayle, 1976a).

These shifts were signs of a much wider process of politicisation occurring in the black community in this period. Such changes were determined by developments not only *within* Britain's black communities, but also by wider political shifts in the black diaspora as a whole. Together, these shifts laid the basis for a profound political transformation during the 1970s, a transformation that was most apparent in the mass engagement of young black people with the movement of Rastafari.

2.2 Step Forward Youth

The predicament of younger Afro-Caribbeans born or raised in Britain had been steadily worsening since the late 1960s, particularly in the areas of education, employment and relations with the police. Far from guaranteeing assimilation, black youth's experience of the British education system only served to depress their opportunities for employment and advancement by positioning them at the lowest end of the labour market (Hall et al., 1978). Those young blacks who had passed through the school system felt the closure of the job market on racial grounds all the more acutely. Confronted by racism from employers, and disproportionately affected by Britain's gathering economic crisis, Afro-Caribbean school-leavers faced an unemployment situation far worse than that of their white peers (Hiro, 1973). This predicament was further compounded by the growing polarisation between the police and the black community generally, as a result of increasingly repressive policing tactics in black neighbourhoods (John, 1970; Humphry, 1972). Such tactics bore down particularly heavily on the young, who were singled out for especially brutal treatment. The extent of such tactics was such that by the early-to-mid-1970s police malpractice had become a regular experience for young blacks.

The experience of institutional racism and economic deprivation amongst gave stimulus to already emerging forms of cultural and political consciousness in the black community. Island affiliations within the Afro-Caribbean community had already been gradually receding since the earliest days of black settlement under the immediate pressures and shared experiences of racism. Accelerated by the impact of black liberation movements in Africa and America, the 1960s witnessed the growth of a mass political consciousness based on a common "black" identity which owed no allegiance to any one particular Caribbean nationality. By the early 1970s, this process was becoming increasingly noticeable amongst the young. One of its earliest manifestations was the widespread adoption by young blacks, regardless of their ethnic origins, of speech patterns that drew on Jamaican-based creole or *patois* (Hall et al., 1978). This process was particularly evident in the education system where patois was taken up by young blacks, reinvested with political meaning and used as a weapon of cultural resistance. Its denigration by white teachers as "inferior" English or "monkey talk" only served to underline its importance amongst young blacks as a refusal of standard English and an assertion of an alternative black subjectivity. Patois became one of the principal vehicles through which the school's attempts to gain cultural hegemony over young blacks was contested. Used by black pupils to subvert and challenge the authority of the teacher, it functioned as a means of opposing the white middle-class forms in which education was experienced and received (Donald, 1982). For many young blacks, patois became *the* language and symbol of opposition, used self-consciously, and in preference to standard English, as an expression of cultural strength and a code of solidarity both inside and outside the school context.

The mass adoption of patois by Afro-Caribbean youth was just one example of the rising tempo of black cultural and political struggle in this period. It was one aspect of a more general process of radicalisation that included school strikes, refusal to register with social security agencies, resistance to police harassment and a widespread rejection of low-paid work. While the structural position of young Afro-Caribbeans in the early 1970s provided the fertile soil in which these new forms of politicisation could grow, it was developments in the reggae tradition which sparked them into motion, fostering black youth's mass engagement with the political culture and philosophy of Rastafari.

That political developments in Jamaican reggae should have had such a resounding significance for the Britain's black communities was perhaps unsurprising given the British reggae market's close cultural and economic ties to the Jamaican recording industry. With the increasing commodification of reggae internationally, this umbilical cord between Britain and Jamaica became a unique conduit of latent political forces.

This process began with Island Records' attempt to build a market for reggae amongst both black and white audiences through the release of the film *The Harder They Come* and through Chris Blackwell's careful promotion of the Wailers. While initially falling far short of its intended impact on white listeners, the Wailers' music, Gilroy observes, had a cataclysmic effect on the black community (Gilroy, 1982). The defiance and rebellion expressed in their first two Island albums, *Catch a Fire* and *Burnin'*, presented a "compulsive unity of populist, anti-imperialist and Rasta themes, which set the black community aflame" (Gilroy, 1982, p. 299). The race and class consciousness expounded in songs such as "Get Up, Stand Up" and "Burnin' and Lootin'", and the pan-Africanist historical themes of "Slave Driver" and "400 Years", fell on the receptive ears of young blacks, whose experience they were seen to directly address (Gayle, 1976a). Together with the Wailers' tour of Britain in the early 1970s, this unprecedented exposure of Rastafari aroused intense interest in the movement within the black community.

The Wailers, however, were far from the only reggae musicians to contribute to the popularisation of Rastafari. Transmitted largely through the sound systems, artists such as Big Youth, I-Roy, U-Roy, Dillinger, Junior Byles and Max Romeo also made a considerable impact on in the early 1970s. The political messages disseminated by these artists proved to be of equal relevance to conditions in Britain and in Jamaica. By the latter half of the 1970s, a whole new generation of international roots artists had emerged, following in the footsteps of The Wailers. The music of Burning Spear, Gregory Isaacs, Dennis Brown and Black Uhuru provided young blacks with a continuing source of cultural nourishment and political education, and contributed to the further popularisation of Rastafari as an international social movement.

The 1970s as a whole were characterised by an extraordinary degree of synchronisation between the political ideologies expounded in Jamaican popular music and the conditions of race and class oppression experienced by black people in Britain. From "Message to a Black Man" and "Step Forward Youth'" to "Police and Thieves" and "War Inna Babylon", Jamaican music was able to articulate a politics that was resonant to the predicament of black British youth. British sound systems played a key role in diffusing and consolidating the growth of this Rasta-informed, political consciousness. The 1970s saw a dramatic increase in the number of more powerful, militant "youth sounds" committed to the politics of Rastafari. The names of these sounds, such as *Jah Shaka, Sufferer Hi-fi,* and *Frontline International,* reflected the upsurge in Rasta consciousness and militancy amongst black youth. By the late 1970s a vibrant, youth-orientated sound system culture had developed in every major urban area of Britain with a significant Afro-Caribbean community.

Sound systems represented an important sphere of autonomous cultural production and self-activity for black youth, one which involved the co-ordination of various knowledges and skills, including carpentry, electronics and acoustic engineering. These were deployed in various primary production processes, including the manufacture of speaker boxes, and the creation, maintenance and repair of amplifiers, mixers and other sound technologies. Sounds also had their own internal forms of organisation and division of labour with roles and responsibilities delegated to various members. Core members would typically include a head *soundman* or manager, an *engineer* responsible for making and maintaining the technical equipment, an *operator* responsible for manipulating and playing

49

that equipment, a *selector* who would choose which records to play, when and in what order, and a cadre of *DJs* attached to the sound.

Larger sounds would also have a team of equipment lifters, or *box-boys*, along with various other helpers, providing security and transport to venues. Sounds were the focal point of broader networks of followers that radiated outwards from these core members. They encompassed wider formations of supporters or *posses*, invariably based on existing peer-group, friendship and neighbourhood affiliations rooted in specific localities. With its own promotional and publicity channels, and sources of revenue, sound system culture amounted to an entire cultural micro economy, one which relied on the organizational and entrepreneurial activities of its participants.

In the face of continuing and widespread discrimination from white leisure institutions, sound systems provided young blacks with a valuable cultural resource and an alternative public sphere of entertainment. Many of the new city-centre discos that flourished in the early 1970s under the management of large entertainment corporations operated racist entry quotas or dress restrictions aimed specifically at barring young blacks (Mungham, 1976). Such discriminatory door policies, together with the inability of most clubs to cater for their musical tastes, forced black youth to build their own autonomous leisure spaces out of a circuit of municipal town-halls, youth clubs, community centres and black-owned or black-frequented night-clubs (Caesar, 1976a, 1976b; Gayle, 1974, p. 14). Many sounds established residencies at these venues and with their immense drawing power would regularly attract large crowds of young blacks. As centres of cultural and leisure activity, such venues represented space won through struggle and invested with political significance. Sound system dances provided physical and spiritual shelter from the pressures of a hostile white society. They represented an autonomous sphere and a defensive enclave in which self-dignity could be restored, and a sense of collective awareness and solidarity temporarily constituted. As one of the few sites in which blackness could be openly expressed and celebrated, and political statements freely aired, the space of the sound system dance signified the ritual boundaries of the community. Transgressions of that space were therefore seen as symbolic violations of this territory.

With the increasing criminalisation of black youth culture in the early 1970s, blues parties, dances and a whole range of other cultural venues became explicitly identified as sources of disorder by state agencies. Such venues began to receive unprecedented attention from the police, for whom they represented an unacceptable level of black cultural autonomy that lay outside their jurisdiction. The police response was to systematically suppress a whole range of black cultural and political activities in a number of large-scale operations during the 1970s. The targets for such operations were invariably those which held symbolic significance for the black community, such as restaurants, night-clubs, blues parties, local fairs, reggae concerts and youth clubs (Institute of Race Relations, 1979). Mass police intrusions and persistent police harassment of these spaces provoked a series of large-scale confrontations between 1971 and 1976. This period accordingly witnessed a dramatic escalation of the struggle over cultural space, as the community's leisure institutions became the focus of particularly intense conflicts with the police. Against a backdrop of growing concern over the "problem" of black youth, the police considered any mass gathering of young black people to be a threat to public order.

This was graphically demonstrated by the events which surrounded the 1976 Notting Hill carnival. From its inception in the mid-1960s, the carnival had steadily grown from its traditional Eastern Caribbean base to become the most important public cultural celebration for Britain's black population, and for London's black community in particular. The introduction of reggae and sound systems in 1976 into a traditionally calypso-based local event dramatically increased its political content and cultural appeal (Gutzmore, 1978). Attempts by the local authorities to ban carnival and remove it from the streets were unsuccessful, and the police were consequently drafted in as the primary agents of control. The number of officers deployed was consequently increased from the 60 local constables at the 1975 carnival to approximately 15,000 at the 1976 event (*Black Music*, August 1979, p.26). The transformed carnival went ahead, attracting blacks from all over Britain and swelling the numbers attending from 100,000 in 1974 to 500,000 in 1976 (*Race Today*, September 1976). However, the harsh enforcement of the ban on alcohol and marijuana, together with the indiscriminate use of brutal policing measures, precipitated fierce resistance amongst the carnival's young black participants.

The 1976 Notting Hill Carnival signalled a new stage in the black community's mass confrontation with the state in the post-war period. The comprehensive defeat of the police's attempts at carnival's mass cultural suppression secured its place as a central symbol of defiance and survival within the black community, and marked a second turning-point in the history of black struggle in Britain, following the events of 1958.

It was little coincidence that the period in the run-up to Notting Hill had seen the symbols and rhetoric of Rastafari acquire a popular character in the black community. The confidence and militancy demonstrated by black youth was a clear indication of the central position that the movement had come to occupy at the heart of black struggle in Britain. The scope of its political influence suggested that Rastafari was much more than a separatist subculture, but part of a broader, mass social movement. Its central themes and discourses acquired a political resonance that cut across age and gender divisions within the black community.

While thousands of young black men and women embraced the stylistic trappings of Rastafari, in the form of colours, locks and headgear, the movement's political scope extended far beyond its more flamboyant adherents. Rasta symbols stood at one end of a broad continuum of belief which spanned both age and gender differences. Attempts to define Rasta affiliates by empirical membership criteria or by their adherence to a fixed set of core tenets of belief such as repatriation or the divinity of Haile Selassie, signalled a fundamental misunderstanding of the movement's populist character. For Rastafari grew out of broader religious, cultural and political traditions in the Caribbean. It attempted to bring order to the practical ideologies, political traditions and communalist sensibilities that already existed amongst Afro-Caribbean peoples (Gilroy, 1982, 1987).

These continuities were perhaps most visible in common oral traditions and political-philosophical concepts. Rasta speech patterns, for example, were an outgrowth and reworking of Jamaican patois, in which standard English words and phrases were reconstructed and given new meanings in accordance with Rasta's world-view (Pollard, 1980, 1982). It was through such speech patterns that the political culture and philosophy of Rastafari brought its greatest influence to bear on the black community. For more than any other cultural form, it was the operation of this shared language which signalled the extent of the movement's appeal. The reggae tradition, through DJing in particular, played a key role in popularising Rasta speech patterns amongst young blacks, serving as a rich source of terms and catchphrases in their everyday speech. The use of patois, generally, remained one of the single most important symbols of black identity, and the principal means by which the disparate strands of black youth culture were bound together and the boundaries of the black community signified.

By the mid-1970s, the common currency of Rasta political concepts amongst young blacks was being signalled by the ubiquitous use of Rasta terminology and expressions (Small, 1983; Hewitt, 1986). Concepts such as "Babylon system" with its incisive critique of the systematic nature of capitalist oppression prove especially relevant to young black Britons, given the nature of their encounters with the state. The notion of "Babylon" provided black youth with a critical tool with which to grasp the mechanisms and tools of oppression, while the discourses of "truths and rights" and "equal rights and justice" supplied a complementary ideology of liberation which insisted on progressive and revolutionary change. The dynamics and conditions of racial oppression in the British context gave the politics of Rasta an added poignancy, placing the movement's positive evaluation of blackness to the forefront of its appeal. Rasta's discourses of exile, estrangement and dispossession proved especially apt to the circumstances of blacks in Britain, while its notions of "tribulation" and "sufferation", founded on the specificity of black experience, provided a cultural bulwark against the racism of the dominant society. With its materialist critique of the power structures of capitalism, and its negation of the ideologies which supported them, Rasta amounted to a method of political thinking and "overstanding" social reality. The importance attached in the movement to the practice of "reasoning", the active questing after knowledge through what Gilroy called "collective processes of dialectical enquiry", pointed to Rasta's democratic and open-ended political philosophy (Gilroy, 1982). This philosophy enabled different interpretations and levels of identification to be made, but within a broad structure of central themes. As a result, the key tenets of Rasta philosophy remained a continual source of debate and reassessment.

The intervention of women into the movement was perhaps the clearest indication of how Rasta discourses remained open to specific modes of interpretation according to the different needs and experiences of its adherents. The Afro-centric aesthetics expounded by Rastafari proved particularly relevant to young black women for whom they offered an antidote to the commodified images of femininity and sexuality in white, European culture. Black women used the space they had won for themselves in the movement as a platform from which to wage their own distinctive form of feminist struggle. By questioning some of the more theological doctrines and taboos which placed restrictions on women, and by appealing to the distinction between "God" and "Man", black women were able to redefine the image of black Rasta-womanhood. The forms of communalism, kinship and supportive child-care developed by Rasta women provided a crucial foundation to the movement as a whole, providing a base from which black women organised themselves into welfare and educational collectives, and autonomous women's groups (Caribbean Times, 1981) .

The selective appropriation of Rasta concepts by those not fully engaged in the movement was an indication of Rastafari's mass character as a social movement. As an historical and political overview of racial oppression, Rasta was available as an analytic resource to all black people. Its language, symbols and ideals were used to bring philosophical and political meaning to individual and collective action in black struggles. The widespread use of kinship terms like "dread" and "rasta" as generalised forms of address amongst those with no outward signs of affiliation was perhaps the clearest indication that these forms were more deep-rooted within the black community than was commonly assumed. In the movement's insistence that all black people were Rastas lay a confirmation of its ability to create an interpretive, spiritual community. In Rastafari's attempt to establish an alternative set of ideals and a Utopian elsewhere in the form of "Zion", the movement revealed its origins within black Christianity and its overlapping connections with other, contemporary, black social movements.

2.3 UK Bubbling

One of the most significant developments in the evolution of black British culture since the mid-1970s was the emergence of an indigenous reggae tradition forged by second and third-generation black Britons out of specifically British experiences and circumstances. While expatriate Caribbean musicians had long been living and performing in Britain, the emergence of a characteristically British genre of reggae music was accelerated in the mid-1970s by the appearance of a new generation of reggae musicians inspired by Rastafari in general and the Wailers in particular. A string of British reggae groups, such as Misty, Aswad, Steel Pulse, Matumbi and Black Slate emerged in this period, reflecting the growing political awareness and confidence of black youth. Songs like Delroy Washington's "Streets of Ladbroke Grove", Steel Pulse's "Handsworth Revolution", and Tubby Cat Kelly's "Don't call us no Immigrants" sought to articulate experiences and conditions of oppression that were specific to black life in urban Britain. As Keith Drummond, lead singer of Black Slate, explained:

> You don't know what they're going through in Jamaica. You can only read about it second-hand. So sing about the sufferation you're going through here…They say you can't make reggae unless you're a sufferer. Well, it's not just the Jamaicans who suffer. We suffer too, and now we're singing about our own condition. (*Black Music*, July 1977)

This gradual weakening of artistic and creative dependency on Jamaican forms of expression was a key trend in the development of British reggae. While, musically, many of the first wave of indigenous reggae groups were derivative of the Wailers, the emergence of the Lovers Rock movement in 1975-76 was the first sign of a specifically British genre of the reggae tradition (Futrell, 1980). Lovers Rock showcased the talents of a new generation of black British female reggae vocalists. The movement partly reflected the increased financial strength and autonomy of young black women in Britain and owed a great deal, in terms of performance and consumption, to their support and independent activity.

Lovers Rock emerged initially as something of a reaction against the macho rivalry and posturing of some elements of sound system culture. The harder rhythms of Jamaican roots reggae did not always cater for the specific tastes of young women who demanded that the music represent their experiences and meet their needs (Futrell, 1980). Young black women began to make their presence felt in the reggae tradition as vocalists in their own right. A plethora of artists and female reggae groups emerged over the latter half of the 1970s, commencing with Louisa Marks and followed by Brown Sugar, 15,16,17, Black Harmony, Alpha, Sister Love, Cassandra, Jean

55

Adebambo, Carroll Thompson and Janet Kay. Musically, Lovers Rock reconciled the popularity of soft soul and reggae amongst many black women by merging the two into a specifically British reggae genre (Garratt, 1985). The sophisticated style projected by many of the music's female performers also offered an alternative model of black womanhood to the roots image of Rastafari (Steward and Garratt, 1984).

Lovers Rock acquired a universal appeal in the black community that traversed age and gender divisions. Its mass popularity was signalled by the huge sales achieved by artists like Carroll Thompson, whose album, *Hopelessly in Love*, sold over 35000, and by the domination of the reggae charts by female Lovers' artists in the latter half of the 1970s and the early 1980s (Garratt, 1985). In dance-halls, blues and parties, Lovers provided something of a relief from the heavier, roots-orientated Jamaican music which had dominated the sound-system scene since the early 1970s. The majority of Lovers Rock records were built around slow, sensuous, one-drop rhythms purposefully crafted for dancing. The social relations of the music's consumption were central to its popularity and enjoyment. The close couples dancing that accompanied the music served to foster solidarity between black men and women at a deeper level than mere courtship.

Such was the impact of Lovers Rock on the sound-system scene that, in response to the growing demand for the music, a number of identifiably Lovers sounds began to emerge, attracting large numbers of female followers. Sound systems in general began to cater for a wider cross-section of tastes within the black community. Smaller hi-fi sets and "big people" sounds, playing specifically for an older clientele, were increasingly to be found entertaining black patrons in pubs and private parties with a diverse selection of calypso, soul, Lovers, "revives" and soca. This sphere of black entertainment was only the tip of a much larger, but mostly "invisible" market that catered more for older and female record-buyers and existed outside the networks of mainstream pop.

The Lovers Rock boom precipitated a number of changes in some of the hitherto male-dominated spheres of reggae culture in Britain. Fresh from their success in the Lovers Rock market, many young black women went on to make their presence felt in all areas of the reggae industry not only as musicians and vocalists, but also as DJs, producers, label-owners and sound-system operators. Women DJs such as Ranking Ann, Bionic Rhona, Lorna Gee and Sister Audrey brought their own distinctly female styles, humour and militancy to bear on the toasting tradition. The early 1980s saw the emergence of a new style of black feminist Lovers Rock artist whose songs combined emotional and romantic themes with cultural and political issues. Ranking Ann's "Liberated Woman" and Sister Audrey's "English Girl", for example, related gender-specific issues to everyday social relationships, addressing both anti-racist and anti-sexist themes with equal assertiveness.

The success of Lovers Rock gave a financial shot in the arm to the British reggae industry. The successful recording and manufacture of reggae for local, domestic and sound-system consumption by pioneering artists like Dennis Bovell finally put paid to the notion that "authentic" versions of reggae could only come from Jamaica. In the early 1980s this process was accelerated by developments in a Jamaican music industry increasingly beset by major problems of economic recession and creative inertia associated with the Seaga period of government. In response to the dearth of creative, oppositional music emanating from Jamaica, this period saw something of a revival in music from the earlier, more vibrant era of rocksteady associated with Jamaica's formative *Studio One* label. This period also saw a shift in the locus of creativity in reggae production from Jamaica to Britain. The early 1980s consequently saw new UK-based studios, musicians, artists and labels flourishing, together with an increasing number of reggae hits being recorded in Britain.

The technical basis for this explosion of musical activity amongst young black Britons was provided by developments in digital recording technologies which revolutionized music-making in the 1980s. The falling relative costs of equipment such as drum machines, keyboard synthesisers, sequencers and cheap home computers, meant that backing tracks of relatively high quality could be produced in the confines of a spare room. These technologies put music production within the reach of anyone with rudimentary computer skills and musical knowledge. The result was an outpouring of locally-recorded music from a growing network of custom-made, DIY, home studios, and the emergence of a new kind of artist/producer recording local singers over custom-made rhythm tracks.

The wider political events of 1980/81, such as the New Cross Fire, in which thirteen young black people died in mysterious circumstances, and the wave of insurrection which subsequently swept Britain's inner-city areas, had the effect not only of galvanising black political feeling, but also of helping to unleash a burst of musical creativity within the indigenous reggae tradition. In the wake of these events, a number of records were released commenting on the riots, the fire and their political aftermath. It was in the DJ tradition that this thematic and stylistic break was perhaps most dramatically registered.

While DJs addressing local events and experiences in their lyrics was nothing new in sound-system culture, by the early 1980s new, characteristically British, linguistic forms and terms of address were beginning to emerge. These trends precipitated the emergence of original, characteristically black British styles of reggae DJing with their own unique inflexions and subject-matter. The style was best exemplified by the "fast-style chat" of *MCing* created by a group of DJs associated with south-east London's *Saxon* sound system (Back, 1987). The style has its origins in 1980 when *Ray Symbolic* became the first Jamaican sound system to tour the UK. The ultra-fast chatting style of their top deejay Ranking Joe left a deep impression on the DJs of the Lewisham-based sound system.

The stylings of Jamaican DJs were also absorbed from "yard tapes" (cassettes tapes of live Jamaican sound system sessions that were widely circulated in this period). The lyrics of Jamaican DJs were studied carefully by aspiring British DJs for coded references and social-political observations. They provided a rich source of vernacular terminology that was incorporated into their repertoire and fused with narratives about the specificities of everyday life in Britain.

The "fast style" aesthetic revolved around the ability to improvise and deliver a non-stop stream of lyrics, in rhyme, and at speed. Many such lyrics narrated incidents and anecdotes and relayed images of urban life often entirely specific to Britain. Through these articulate forms of social and political commentary, and the employment of complex narratives and characterisations, the exponents of the new style captured the specificity of the black British experience. This departure was also signalled in the structure of the music itself. While still relying on standard rhythms from the rocksteady era, the reprocessing of these rhythms in up-tempo, digitalised forms, represented a clear break from the musical and stylistic patterns of earlier British reggae.

"Cockney Translation" by Smiley Culture, one of the *Saxon* DJs, was a prime example of the new style with its fast, 4/4 drum and bass rhythm. The song typified the fast-style genre with its distinctive combination of patois terminology and cockney rhyming slang, and its literal phrase by phrase "translation" from one into the other. "Cockney Translation" represented one of the first genuinely popular forms of black British musical culture to incorporate the fundamental contradictions of black Britishness by attempting to redefine the concept of Britishness itself. By reflecting the fluid linguistic cultures that existed amongst black youth, "Cockney Translation" captured something of the changes that had occurred in black British culture over the preceding decades. The song itself was premised on the existence of a rich, indigenous black verbal culture which encompassed a diversity of linguistic practices and speech patterns. It was a culture in which young blacks did indeed move freely between "standard" English grammar and vocabulary, regional working-class accents, and Jamaican-derived forms of black British creole, often combining all three influences in their everyday speech.

The rearticulation of Jamaican popular music and culture according to the changing expressive needs of black youth was symptomatic of how black British culture was being mediated by urban British experiences, and how the meaning of blackness itself was constantly being remade and redefined in accordance with those experiences. In the 1980s, the content and character of that culture continued to be shaped by cultural and political influences from right across the black diaspora.

Black British culture had always been comprised of a whole range of distinct, but interrelated elements which drew on the culture and politics of blacks both in the Caribbean and in America. While Rasta and reggae culture were certainly the dominant political and cultural forms in the black community over the 1970s, they were by no means the only ones. Black American culture and music, and various forms of black Christianity, were highly influential in the black community as complementary and parallel vehicles of expression. By the early 80s a rich expressive black British musical culture was emerging out of a rearticulation of these various Caribbean and African-American elements. It was clearly audible in emergent forms of black British musicking, in gospel, jazz, soul and hip-hop as well as reggae.

Most notable in these developments was the shift in the centre of gravity of black musical and cultural identification towards black America. This was partly in response to the relative stagnation of Jamaican dancehall reggae in the early 1980s where slackness and gun culture were in the ascendancy. But it was also due to the political rejuvenation of American soul music and the internationalisation of the New York counter-culture of hip-hop. These developments renewed the relevance of black American music amongst many young black Britons. Hip-hop's themes of urban survival, and its body culture of dance and movement, proved more applicable to conditions of mass structural unemployment, and to the experience of police harassment and drug abuse, than much of the music emanating from Jamaica at this time. In the oral style of the South Bronx, Gilroy has observed, black British youth:

> Found a language which allowed them to speak directly about the social and political contradictions generated in the urban crises of the overdeveloped world. "The Message" had hit home. Its imagery of urban entropy, its resolute modernity and targets of its criticism all contrasted sharply with the language and style of Rastafari which were grounded in antiquity (Gilroy, 1987, p. 190).

The eclipse of Rasta's cultural hegemony opened the way to a more pluralist balance between the diverse influences and traditions which comprised black British culture. While the more dogmatic tenets of Rasta, together with its implicit distancing from Babylon society were discarded, many of its spiritual and political concepts, including its stress on black unity, its pan-Africanism and its analysis of racial domination, were maintained or articulated in different forms within the revitalised black church or from within soul and hip-hop cultures. The boundaries between these various cultural and political elements, as a result, became increasingly blurred. Premised on the continuities between "rapping" and "toasting", and "breakbeats" and dub, the previously separate cultures of soul and reggae began to coexist and overlap at several points. These continuities were evident in the mixed programming of soul and reggae on pirate radio stations, in the playing of reggae at soul venues, the opening-up of sound systems to soul culture and the mass appeal of the new styles of DJing amongst funk and hip-hop devotees.

The forms of consciousness articulated in Smiley Culture's "Cockney Translation" signalled a new phase in the political development of black British culture. As the expressive culture of young blacks continued to evolve into new, organic and uniquely British forms, the impact of the black presence on mainstream British popular culture and music became more widespread and profound. The populist appeal of black British music made it a central reference point for the struggles of young people generally, opening up new spaces for cross-racial dialogue. Through its ambiguous terms of racial and ethnic identification, and its bridging of the cultural identities of black and white working-class youth, "Cockney Translation" suggested something fundamental about the changing relationship between different groups of young people in urban Britain.

3 Reggae Gone Outernational

3.1 From *Bluebeat* to *Trojan*

In the previous chapter we saw how an embryonic network for the import, distribution and retail of Caribbean music was established in post-war Britain. While many of these enterprises were initially set up to cater for the growing demand in Britain's black communities, it soon became evident that a significant minority of white Britons were also showing interest in the music. While larger companies like EMI attempted to break into this nascent market by manufacturing their own forms of Caribbean music, it was the smaller independent companies who had the greatest success. One of these was Melodisc, which began importing Jamaican music in the late 1950s, launching its *Bluebeat* label as an outlet for ska. The label grew to be of such importance to the marketing of Jamaican music in Britain in the early 1960s that the genre of ska as a whole came to be known as "bluebeat". Melodisc acquired the release rights to music from many of Jamaica's leading producers and artists, particularly Prince Buster, whose British releases appeared almost exclusively on the Bluebeat label. Despite having no independent distribution of its own, Melodisc was nevertheless able to sell large quantities of Jamaican music to white consumers throughout the 1960s.

Of all the record labels involved in the marketing of Jamaican music, however, it was Island Records that played perhaps the most important role in connecting the music to a mass white market. Established in Britain by Chris Blackwell in 1962, Island attempted to manufacture a more marketable and widely acceptable form of Jamaican music. Island's first successful venture in this regard was in 1963 with Millie's "My Boy Lollipop". "My Boy Lollipop" was a popularised form of ska recorded by predominantly British session musicians and employing a full orchestral backing. It was a highly polished production, its clean treble-oriented sound far removed from the vigorous, bass-dominated recordings emanating from Jamaica during the same period. It was perhaps for this reason that "My Boy Lollipop" reached number two in the British pop charts in 1964 and went on to become an international hit, selling 6 million copies worldwide (Rice el al.,1977).

The success of "My Boy Lollipop" suggested the commercial potential of marketing a popularised form of Jamaican music to a mass white audience. As far as the 1960s were concerned, however, the record remained something of an anomaly. It owed much of its success to being licensed to Philips, the smallest of the four major recording companies, along with Decca, EMI and Pye, who between them controlled over 90% of the British record market in the mid-1960s (Frith, 1983). The monopoly exercised by these major recording labels over access to mainstream retail outlets, and national distribution and broadcasting networks, formed an impenetrable matrix against smaller, independent labels like Island. Apart from "My Boy Lollipop", only two other Jamaican singles made the top twenty between 1962 and 1969; Desmond Dekker's "007" and Prince Buster's "Al Capone", both only after months of exposure in the clubs. Despite this lack of pop chart success, Island continued to sell large quantities of Jamaican records to white audiences throughout the 1960s. An example of the selling power of some of Island's early releases was provided by the success of Derrick and Patsy's "Housewives Choice", which reputedly sold 18,000 copies in the first five days of its release in 1962 (Williams, 1972a).

Seeing the resistance to Jamaican music in the established pop industry, Island began to expand into the more lucrative rock market. With the money earned from the licensing and distribution of Jamaican music, Blackwell proceeded to build a profitable rock empire between 1968 and 1972, based largely on album sales in Europe and America. Reggae releases were phased out from the Island label which became reserved almost exclusively for the company's roster of rock artists, including groups such as Free, Jethro Tull, Fairport Convention, Traffic and King Crimson. As Gillett points out, this was a calculated move by Blackwell to disassociate the label from the image it had acquired in the music industry:

> After all those years as a specialist minority music label, Island had to be seen to shake off its associations in order to be taken seriously as a 'pop' and 'rock' label by the British media . . . Prejudices die hard and the simplest way was for Island to drop all West Indian names from its roster (Gillett, 1983, p. 390).

Most Jamaican music was subsequently released on Trojan, Island's partner label formed in 1968 and previously a distribution organisation called the Beat and Commercial Company. While continuing to supply the roots market, Trojan followed in Island's footsteps to seek a marketable formula for Jamaican music, and undertook the task of breaking down some of the prejudices of the entertainment industry towards reggae (Clarke, 1980). Trojan released a whole series of pop reggae productions, aimed specifically at a mass white audience. Although some of these were manufactured in Britain, many were recorded by Jamaican producers like Harry J and Lesley Kong who were aware of the commercial demands of the wider, international market. Kong in particular explored the possibilities of a popularised version of reggae that could overcome radio resistance, arguing that the music should be remixed to be "pleasing to the BBC airwaves" (Mulligan, 1969, p. 11). Trojan flooded the British pop market with a whole spate of ballads, gimmicky instrumentals and cover versions of pop and soul hits, most of which employed softer melodies, weaker bass-lines and string accompaniments.

The BBC's newly created national pop station, Radio One, succumbed to the Trojan approach, and the company achieved major success with a total of seventeen Top Twenty hits between 1969 and 1972 (Rice et at., 1977). The most successful of these was Desmond Dekker's "Israelites" which reached number one in 1969 and was the first in a whole string of Top Ten hits that included Bob and Marcia's "Young, Gifted and Black", The Upsetters' "Return of the Django" and Jimmy Cliff's "Wonderful World". The following year also saw the Pioneers and Desmond Dekker reach the top five, while in 1971 Dave and Ansell Collins had a number one hit with "Double Barrel". In this same period, budget-priced compilation LPs in Trojan's *Reggae Chartbusters* and *Tighten Up* series also proved highly popular within the mainstream record-buying market regularly selling an average of 60,000 copies each (Melody Maker, 21 July 1972).

The pop reggae boom of the late 1960s and early 1970s was the first significant intervention of Jamaican music into mainstream pop culture. Trojan's success alerted the music industry to the mass market potential of reggae. One music business commentator regarded the pop breakthrough of reggae as being one of the most important developments in the industry during 1969. "Against all odds" he observed "reggae has become a consistently saleable commodity." However, the same writer conceded that the "essential monotonous simplicity of the sound makes it an unlikely contender for mass appreciation" (Mulligan, 1969, p. 11).

Such doubts suggested the deep prejudices that existed against Jamaican music in many sections of the music industry. Some of the strongest prejudices lay within the rock market, where Jamaican music had become the object of considerable hostility. Here reggae met with trenchant criticism from fans who complained about its lowering of musical standards and its associations with skinheads (Melody Maker, 29 November 1969). For middle-class rock fans, reggae was simply "yobbo" music, its skinhead connotations "odious to any half-educated mind", while musically it was judged to be "boring", "repetitive", "joke music" and a form of "rhythmic rot" (Melody Maker, 29 November 1969).

The widespread hostility towards reggae within the rock market constituted a major marketing problem for those recording companies seeking to break Jamaican music to a wider audience. For companies like Island, who had a secure foothold in the rock market, such problems were particularly apparent. Island's answer was to evolve a specific set of marketing strategies to circumvent the racism which narrowed reggae's appeal.

The company's apparent "withdrawal" from reggae in the late 1960s was not quite as complete as it originally appeared. Island maintained their involvement in Jamaican music through artists like Jimmy Cliff, the label's prototype reggae star, and through the film project, *The Harder They Come*. The use of film to render Jamaican music more accessible to white consumers was to become a familiar marketing strategy of Island's. *The Harder They Come* was intended to whet the appetites of white record-buyers by presenting them with a caricatured and romanticised vision of the music's place of origin (Gilroy, 1982). However, while the film generated modest sales for its accompanying soundtrack album, it failed to generate the level of mass white interest which Island had hoped for. Blackwell turned his attention to the company's newly signed Jamaican group, the Wailers. Island's campaign with the Wailers, and Bob Marley specifically, established several important precedents in the mass marketing of reggae which were to have a major bearing on the way the music was subsequently handled by the international entertainment industry.

3.2 *Natty Dread*

In an attempt to anticipate trends in the rock market, Island had signed the Wailers in 1971 with a view to building a new and larger audience for reggae. Island evolved a specific promotional campaign to market the group as an alternative to the company's rock artists who by the early 1970s had already begun to fade in popularity. The thinking behind this move was later confirmed by Blackwell who admitted that rock music had become "stale" and that Marley's music had an "energy and fresh feel to it" (Gayle, 1975b, p. 13). When Blackwell paid an £8000 advance to the Wailers to record their first album, a previously unheard-of sum for a reggae group, he initiated a marketing campaign which went against all established principles of handling reggae. The decision was made to promote the band as a fixed, self-contained group, within the rock tradition. The Wailers' music was depicted in terms of a "new", "progressive" innovation in Jamaican music which represented a break from the reggae of the late 1960s that was so despised by rock fans. As Blackwell later explained:

> Reggae up until the Wailers' first album was perceived as rather quirky music in general...It wasn't a music that had any respect, and I felt that the best way to market the Wailers was to change it from being a singles music to being an album music, and the best way to do that was to market them as a group and to make an album and release an album first...cos in the way Jamaican music was marketed before there was never a group image and we were really at the height of group consciousness (Interview with Chris Blackwell, Capital Radio, 1982).

As Blackwell points out, the reggae industry, both in Jamaica and Britain, revolved around the production and marketing of singles rather than albums. Singles were cheaper to manufacture, had a quicker turnover and required lower levels of investment. By being more responsive to individual choice, they were generally better suited to the consumption habits of reggae's primary working-class audience. The vast majority of albums released within the reggae market, moreover, tended to be "various artists" or "greatest hits" compilations. The rock market, by contrast, was based on album sales by particular artists which, although requiring greater initial investment, ultimately yielded much larger profits. The Wailers' transition from a studio, singles-based vocal group to an album-based touring band signalled an attempt to repackage reggae in a form tailored to the consumption patterns of the rock market. Since the late 1960s, that market had revolved around the sales of albums and cheap, stereo hi-fis (Frith, 1983). Rock albums were designed for consumption by an attentive, stationary audience prepared to sit and listen for a considerable length of time. As Davis points out, the order of songs on such albums was pre-arranged in the production process:

> The European and American audiences that Blackwell wanted the Wailers to penetrate were accustomed to getting their music from albums on which ten or more tunes clicked together in a more sustained atmosphere. Bob Marley was asked to make the first reggae album, which Blackwell would then transform into a record that could appeal to the rock fans who were his principal customers (Davis, 1983, p. 95).

Blackwell's decision to market reggae as an *album* music and to establish the Wailers as more profitable, transnational artists heavily shaped the production and packaging of the Wailers' debut LP for Island *Catch a Fire*. The first important change in the production process was the scale of financial investment made in recording the album. As Blackwell explained:

> In Jamaica they were just making records on a very limited budget. And the records were made very much just for the Jamaican market. And they weren't in stereo. Their early records were great for what they are, but for getting to a wider market they needed more money spent on them (quoted in Gayle, 1975b, p. 13)

Blackwell doubled the customary rates for Jamaican session musicians, enabling them to record for longer than the standard two and a half minutes (Williams, 1972b). In accordance with Island's marketing plans, *Catch a Fire* was recorded in stereo. The latest technical facilities of the recording process were employed to "clean up" the music. The upgraded standards of sound reproduction were designed partly to broaden the music's commercial appeal by undermining the common accusation made by rock fans that reggae was a music of inferior quality. Although the backing tracks for the album were recorded in Jamaica, they were subsequently remixed and edited in London under the supervision of Blackwell (Clarke, 1980). As part of this process, session musicians were brought in to overdub rock guitar, tabla and synthesiser parts over the Wailers' music (Davis, 1983). In addition, Blackwell accelerated the speed of the Wailers' basic rhythm tracks by one beat, thinking that a quicker tempo might enhance the music's appeal to rock fans (Davis, 1983). R'n'b-influenced rhythms and back-up vocals were also employed to lend a more cosmopolitan flavour to the music.

These transformations amounted to a distinct move away from Jamaican music's traditional emphasis on drums and bass towards a more "produced" sound, filled out by keyboards and guitars (Johnson, 1983). The addition and remixing of instruments became a recurring feature in Island's production of all the group's subsequent albums. Island attempted to repeat the production formula of these early recordings with other artists like the Heptones. Such strategies, however, met with mixed success. By adding rock guitar, emphasising the treble and percussion at the expense of the bass, and occasionally increasing the speed of the original rhythm tracks, they tended to alienate both rock and reggae markets.

Unlike most previous reggae albums *Catch a Fire* was retailed as a full-priced LP, and was the first in a series of glossily packaged and well-produced stereo albums that could be promoted, reviewed and consumed in rock terms as complete "works of art". Island's innovatory marketing strategies were most clearly reflected in the elaborate packaging and design of album sleeves. *Catch a Fire's* pop-art sleeve cover, designed in the form of a large cigarette-lighter, was a novel selling-point. The double sleeve of *Burnin'*, the Wailers' second album, opened out to reveal assorted photographs of Rastas in various "dread" poses. The song lyrics on the *Burnin'* album were printed on the inner cover, making them accessible to white consumers in an unprecedented manner. These ploys seemed to confirm Island's intention to sell the Wailers as "rebels" by stressing the uncompromising and overtly political aspects of their music.

By the time *Natty Dread*, the Wailers' third album, was released late in 1974, it was clear that the image of Marley as a licentious, ganja-smoking Rasta rebel was to be a central feature of Island's marketing campaign. The album's sleeve carried an impressionistic and romanticised portrait of Marley which emphasised his hair in a way designed to evoke a sense of eroticism and fantasy in the intended white rock-fan. With the album's release, the key icons of ganja, locks and Rasta colours became firmly established as the symbols most effective in selling reggae to whites. In accordance with this strategy *Catch a Fire* was later re-packaged with the cigarette-lighter cover replaced by a full-sized photograph of Marley smoking a large "spliff".

The company's marketing strategies were further reflected in the occasional alteration of album titles. Hence the third album's original title, *Knotty Dread*, taken from the Wailers' Jamaican 45 release, was subsequently changed to the more ambiguous *Natty Dread* (Davis, 1983). This alteration involved a subtle, but critical, shift in meaning. "Knotty" implied a sense of uncompromising Rasta militancy and black consciousness symbolised by the extolling of locks, while the more innocuous "natty" had connotations of "hip" style and fashionability in white parlance.

Island's intention to promote the Wailers as a rock group was further confirmed when the company organised a concert tour of Britain in 1973. The band's itinerary took in a string of predominantly college and university-based rock venues and included national radio and TV appearances on Radio One's show, *Top Gear*, and BBC 2's *Old Grey Whistle Test*. The staged spectacle of the live gig was one of the mainstays of rock culture both as a promotion medium for companies through which to stimulate record sales, and as an important channel of expression and consumption for artists and fans respectively (Frith, 1983). By the early 1970s the staging of rock concerts had become dependent on a vast technological infrastructure of sound equipment. By contrast, such live spectacles were rare in the context of the Jamaican music industry, based as it was largely around sound systems, studios and a handful of session musicians. The sophisticated hardware and instruments of rock technology, taken for granted by most English and American groups, were beyond the incomes of most of Jamaica's

70

ghetto artists. The economic realities of life in West Kingston militated against the formation of financially autonomous bands, in favour of vocal groups and solo artists who relied on session musicians both inside and outside the studio. Although Jamaican groups had toured British night-clubs intermittently during the 1960s, the leap in the scale of exposure entailed by the Wailers' tour was a major new development in the marketing of reggae. Live promotion subsequently became one of the most important channels through which reggae was made available to a mass white audience.

Despite the media interest generated by the Wailers' British tour, and by their first two albums for Island, the 1972-3 campaign was something of a false start in terms of mass popular acceptance of reggae. *Catch a Fire* sold only a modest 14,000 copies in the first year of its release (Davis, 1983, p. 101). The group's eventual breakthrough came two years later, with their second British tour, undertaken in the wake of *Natty Dread*. That breakthrough was achieved under the new title of "Bob Marley and the Wailers" after the original group had disbanded. The change in title indicated both a reorganisation of the group's personnel and a marketing ploy by Island to push Marley as the band's front man and "star".
As Carl Gayle explained:

> It became obvious to Island pretty soon that Marley was the one to pin the genius tag on. Bob, with his rebel rasta image, was projected as the key figure to the exclusion of Tosh and Livingstone (Gayle, 1975b, p. 13).

The intense media interest surrounding the Wailers' 1975 tour of Britain, together with the escalating sales of *Natty Dread*, signalled Marley's commercial breakthrough to a mass white audience. The tour was the climax of a two-year promotional campaign by Island. The subsequent release of the single "No Woman No Cry", a love-song aimed directly at the pop charts, and the successful *Live!* album of the London Lyceum gig marked the beginnings of Marley's entry into mainstream rock culture. Eric Clapton's Top Ten hit with a cover version of Marley's "I Shot the Sheriff" in 1974 had bestowed a measure of credibility on reggae and paved the way for Marley's acceptance within the rock community. Island's decision to cast Marley in the role of solo star was canonised in the front pages of the rock press from which he was hailed as "reggae's first superstar" (Melody Maker, 26 July 1975).

The release of Marley's successful fourth album *Rastaman Vibration*, for which advanced orders alone totalled 600,000, was the prelude to a whole string of concert tours, chart hits and successful albums in the late 1970s. As the whole machinery of the pop industry swung into action behind him, a flood of Bob Marley ephemera hit the market in the form of t-shirts, posters and scrapbooks. In response to this rapidly widening audience, Marley's music underwent something of a shift in emphasis away from the roots-orientated sound of earlier albums towards a more pronounced pop flavour. Albums such as *Exodus*, *Kaya* and *Uprising* included a greater proportion of love-songs and softer melodies designed to appeal to a wider audience (Johnson, 1977).

By the end of the decade Bob Marley had established himself as a top-selling, international recording artist. His success gave a financial boost to a mid-70s music industry ailing under the impact of the recession and the stagnation of rock culture. In 1981 a London spokesperson for Island estimated Bob Marley's world-wide album sales to be in excess of $190 million (Davis, 1983, p. 228). It was after his death, however, that the true scale of Marley's commercial importance was revealed. The release of the album *Confrontation* marked the beginning of a posthumous marketing campaign designed to make fresh revenue from old back catalogue and unreleased material. That campaign reached fruition in 1984 when the company attempted to remarket Marley as a "legend".

Launched on the anniversary of Marley's death, the *Legend* campaign was aimed at a broad-based, record-buying public. The *Legend* album was a compilation of Marley's greatest hits, and was heavily promoted through television ads and video releases compiled from old film footage. Companies like K-Tel had already proved that television could be a lucrative marketing medium with their successful series of chart-hit compilation albums promoted almost exclusively through television advertising. Island's campaign revolved around the attempt to present Marley as an all-round entertainer and a pop-hero of "legendary" proportions. This strategy was reflected in the seemingly deliberate omission of the term "reggae" from the campaign and in the attempt to surround Marley's music in a posthumous aura of nostalgia. In the video which accompanied the chart hit "One Love", for example, Marley

72

appeared as a cute, lovable father-figure, while full-page press advertisements proclaimed that "the legend lives on". Marley was promoted as a household name on the basis that "everyone should own at least one Bob Marley album". Such was the campaign's success that Island took the second biggest share of the UK market in 1984, *Legend* being one of the company's biggest-selling albums for ten years.

3.3 Oh, What a Rat Race!

The success of Island's campaign with Bob Marley marked the beginning of a period of intense commercial activity in the international marketing of reggae. Island had shown that it was possible to sell reggae to white consumers and had pioneered the marketing techniques for doing so. In the wake of Marley's success, Island expanded further into the reggae market, building up a roster of artists that included Burning Spear, Third World, Inner Circle, Zappow and Max Romeo.

The company's move into film as a promotion medium for reggae signalled a new phase in the commercial development of the music. Island had pioneered the use of film as a marketing tool with *The Harder They Come*. Feature films such as *Exodus*, *Rockers* and *Countryman*, together with the sound-track albums they advertised, formed part of a concerted strategy to market reggae in a form which presented no threat to white consumers. The cinema was an ideal medium through which to promote reggae in ways that avoided some of the contradictions of frequenting live concerts, sound-system dances and reggae shops.

Coffee-table books and pamphlets were further examples of this marketing strategy. Some were little more than promotional vehicles for specific recording companies, while many were simply travelogues or compendiums of glossy visuals which focused on the imagery of locks and ganja, and, as such, formed part of a general strategy to market reggae as an aspect of rock culture.

The success of Island's campaign with Bob Marley tempted other independent record companies to venture into the reggae market. Of these, by far the most significant was Virgin. Virgin had begun as a mail-order retail outlet for progressive rock in the late 1960s, and had subsequently evolved into a national chain of record stores and an independent label specialising in underground rock. The company had begun exploring the sales potential of reggae as early as 1974. In 1976, however, following the collapse of Trojan records and Island's breakthrough with Marley, Virgin's director Richard Branson announced that the company was "keen to break into the reggae market" (Black Echoes, February 1976, p.3). The financial collapse of Trojan, hitherto the biggest distributor and retailer of Jamaican music in Britain, had left something of a gap in the reggae market. Virgin was one of a handful of independent labels which attempted to fill that gap.

The company proceeded in early 1976 to sign up several leading Jamaican artists, including Johnny Clarke, U-Roy, the Mighty Diamonds, the Gladiators and I-Roy (Black Echoes, 7 February 1976). Virgin's intention was to promote such artists to both black and white audiences. For this purpose, it created a specific label, the *Front Line*, as an identifiable outlet for reggae. Under the *Front Line* banner, the company released the first of two compilation sampler albums, intended as cheap introductions to reggae for audiences unfamiliar with the music. Retailing at 69p, and billed in the music press as "a beautiful album for the price of a single", the LP was designed specifically to whet the appetites of reggae's new consumers and to seduce them into buying the full-priced albums that it advertised.

Between 1976 and 1979 Virgin conducted an extensive promotional campaign involving radio plugs, record-shop window displays, fly-posters and press ads (Black Music, May, 1978). A central feature of the campaign was a major concert tour of Britain in 1976 by the Mighty Diamonds and U-Roy (Black Echoes, 14 August, 1976). Island had shown with Marley that live appearances at large rock venues could be one of the most effective means of promoting reggae. Virgin followed suit, making reggae available to substantial numbers of white fans through the concert hall. Extensive national tours by artists like the Gladiators, Culture and Toots and the Maytals became regular events in the late 1970s. Collective promotion of artists, under the banner of slogans like "The Front Line in Music" and "Sounds of Reality" was another common feature of Virgin's campaign, a campaign which appealed, like Island's, to rock notions of "progressive" "protest' music".

Faced with the same marketing dilemma as the one that Island had faced four years earlier, Virgin similarly decided to repackage reggae and promote it as something radically different from what had gone before. Album covers, once again, became a key selling-point. The sleeve of the *Front Line* album, for example, featured a dramatic picture of a blood-stained hand grasping a single strand of barbed wire. On the individual albums, artists were frequently depicted in varying states of stoned, "dread" belligerence. Cover artwork and photography homed in on the, by now, familiar imagery of locks and ganja. The sleeve design of U-Roy's *Dread inna Babylon*, for example, portrayed the artist shrouded in a cloud of ganja smoke, while the front cover of the dub album *Well Charged* featured a close-up, mug-shot of an anonymous, bleary-eyed black face, spliff hanging out of the mouth in a state of apparent stonedness. The sleeve of Peter Tosh's *Legalise It*, in a similar vein, depicted the artist crouched in a field of ganja, smoking a pipe. The intention was to create a specific kind of visual appeal that would catch the eyes of potential white consumers. In Peter Tosh's case that appeal rested on an attempt to represent the artist as a new counter-cultural hero to the rock audience. Thus, as one journalist proclaimed in a review of *Legalise It*, "Tear down your Dylans, your Guevaras, your Maxfield Parishes and your maps of middle earth and pin up your 1976 style hero" (Black Echoes, 31 July 1976, p. 14).

The promotional campaigns mounted by both Virgin and Island played a central role in popularising reggae in Britain in the 1970s. The distribution access of these companies to high-street record-shops, including Virgin's own chain of retail outlets, enabled reggae to be disseminated to a whole new generation of white pop and rock fans. Both Island and Virgin succeeded where other companies had failed in introducing reggae both to mainstream record shops like HMV and Our Price and to national chain stores like Boots, W. H. Smith and Woolworths. In doing so, their marketing strategies were assisted by the retailing revolution that took place in the mid-1970s, with many of these high-street chains moving into record sales. Those strategies helped to create and consolidate the burgeoning interest in reggae amongst white youth. Moreover, by gaining access to mainstream retail outlets they paved the way for other independent companies like *Greensleeves* to acquire national distribution for more roots-orientated reggae releases.

The success of independent labels like Island and Virgin in breaking reggae commercially alerted the mainstream recording industry to its economic viability. With the music's marketing potential secured, there began something of a stampede for reggae amongst multinational companies competing for financial and legal stakes in what was a new, relatively unexplored field (Gayle, 1976b). The mid-1970s ushered in an era of international commercialisation, reflecting the increasingly transnational character of the recording industry generally in this period, with its ever more fluid movement of capital across national boundaries, and its tendency towards greater concentration and vertical integration. Multinational companies like EMI monopolised increasingly large areas of the music business, eventually subsuming independent companies like Island. From 1975 onwards, a number of these multinational entertainment corporations, such as NEMS, CBS and WEA, began to involve themselves in the production and distribution of reggae (Gayle, 1976b).

For these companies, reggae was a rich grazing ground requiring low levels of investment but yielding substantial profits. Jamaica was merely one of several developing countries which represented a source of relatively untapped musical talent for the multinational giants of the leisure industry (Wallis and Malm, 1984). Reggae artists could be bought relatively cheaply with much smaller advances than those demanded by equivalent rock groups. The relative poverty of most reggae musicians made such advances appear large in Jamaican terms, disguising the relations of unequal exchange involved (Clarke, 1980).

Developing countries functioned not only as sources of exploitable talent but as marginal markets themselves (Wallis and Malm, 1984). The growing demand for black music in parts of Latin America and Africa opened up a third side in a lucrative, latter-day "golden triangle" of record production and distribution. Island had been one of the first to recognise and exploit the potential of profitable overseas markets for reggae. By the mid-1970s, however, Island was being rivalled as the main international distributor of reggae by Virgin.

Virgin had reputedly sold £150,000 worth of reggae in 1975, a year in which the company was not yet directly involved in releasing reggae but was exporting other companies' products to Third World markets (Clarke, 1980, p. 167). The trade routes forged by Virgin and Island were followed by other multinational companies like CBS who similarly attempted to meet the burgeoning demand for Afro-Caribbean music in the developing world by connecting their reggae product to lucrative markets like that of Nigeria (Wallis and Malm, 1984).

In contrast to the relatively sustained involvement of companies like Island, most of the majors had a more predatory relationship with the reggae market, shying away from any long-term financial commitments. Larger companies tended to venture into the reggae market only on the basis of an established best-seller. Behind such strategies invariably lay a distribution or licensing deal which enabled master-tapes or release rights to be bought from reggae entrepreneurs in exchange for a flat royalty rate. The result was a cheap deal for the major company who were spared the production costs if the record flopped (Frith, 1983). It was an attractive way of avoiding risks and overheads in an uncertain market like that of reggae, a market which most majors had little knowledge of. The greater relative costs and investment risks were placed on the shoulders of small reggae producers and independent labels who hired studios and musicians, paid for cutting and pressing of discs and were invariably denied the kind of credit facilities that the majors took for granted. This licensing strategy was partly behind the success of records which intermittently "crossed over" from the reggae market into the pop charts. In promoting such records, the majors were able to rely on their national distribution networks and access to the media to ensure their chart success. Examples of such reggae "cross-over" hits were Dennis Brown's "Money in my Pocket", which provided the WEA corporation with a hit on their subsidiary label Lightning; Althea and Donna's "Uptown Top Ranking", also on the Lightning label; Errol Dunkley's "OK, Fred" and Janet Kay's "Silly Games", both on the Scope label, another subsidiary of WEA, and Sugar Minott's "Good Thing Going" on RCA.

Of those major companies that signed reggae artists to their labels, most invariably attempted to repackage and reprocess them for the pop market. Companies such as CBS, RCA and EMI briefly flirted with British reggae groups in the late 1970s. CBS signed the Reggae Regulars. Tradition was signed by RCA and Black Slate and Matumbi by EMI. However, since most majors lacked sufficient knowledge and experience to market reggae effectively, the customary pattern of these contracts was for a group to be signed for one or two albums then dropped.

The majors' international involvement in reggae proved to be equally fickle. CBS typified the multinationals' strategy of quick entry and withdrawal in order to maximise profits. The involvement of some independent companies in Jamaican music ultimately also proved to be transient. It was widely speculated that Virgin, for example, having lost one of their major Third World markets for reggae, Nigeria, because of the introduction of strict import controls, withdrew their investments in Jamaican music as a whole (Melody Maker, 25 October 1980, p. 9). By 1980, Virgin had begun to terminate their contracts with Jamaican artists, many of whom left the *Front Line* label dissatisfied with the company's lack of investment and promotion.

3.4 Reggae and the Media

While record companies such as Island and Virgin were responsible for packaging reggae for a mass audience, certain channels of the media also played a crucial role in popularising the music in Britain. The most influential of these were the music press and radio. Music journalism was an important medium through which popular music in general was presented and interpreted. Music papers represented key channels of promotion and publicity for the recording industry. Their news items, interviews, album and concert reviews were invariably synchronised with the industry's own production and marketing cycles through album releases, tours and publicity campaigns (Frith, 1983).

During most of the 1960s, however, Jamaican music had received scant coverage in the music press. Most of that coverage consisted of hostile and derisory criticism. It was not until the early 1970s that a small number of music journalists began to pay any serious attention to the contemporary popular forms emanating from Jamaica. In this period sympathetic commentators like Richard Williams and Carl Gayle were heavily responsible for introducing and interpreting this "new" Jamaican sound to a white readership. Island's campaign with the Wailers found ready allies within the rock-music press where a handful of journalists picked up on the musical and political shifts represented by the Wailers' first two albums. Richard Williams of the *Melody Maker*, for example, attempted to draw reggae into a familiar frame of reference and justify its status to rock fans as a valid, contemporary popular music form.

Bob Marley was tagged by Williams as the "first genius of reggae" and "the man who's about to give it that big shove out of its normal cultural confinement and into the rest of the world" (Williams, 1973a, p. 13). In his formative review of *Catch a Fire*, Williams spelt out the album's correlation to the rock tradition by pin-pointing those features most likely to appeal to a rock audience. Echoing Island's own marketing predicament, Williams pleaded the album's case to a rock readership of whose hostility he was well aware:

> The problem - how to communicate the excitement of this album to people who are already prejudiced against what it represents . . . I'm taking for granted that most readers of this paper still believe that reggae is a crude form of musical expression with a complete lack of creative potential (Williams, 1973b).

In contrast to the "rubbish" that had hitherto been released in Jamaican music, *Catch a Fire* had upgraded the sound quality of reggae, to the extent that the album could be "enjoyed on headphones". The Wailers had also introduced a radical slant into reggae which resonated with the revolutionary pretensions of progressive rock. As Williams pointed out:

> Many pop fans will be surprised to learn that reggae musicians are writing songs with lyrics as uncompromisingly revolutionary as anything Grace Slick or John Lennon ever penned (Williams, 1972a, p. 37).

Williams' *Melody Maker* articles were amongst the first accounts of reggae in the rock press to attempt to explain its broader significance as a black musical and cultural phenomenon. The interest shown in the Wailers' music by rock journalists like Williams complemented Island's campaign to market reggae as progressive, rebel music. Following the company's breakthrough with the band in 1975, Marley rapidly became a major focus of attention throughout the rock press. Journalists quickly realised that his eccentric appearance and uncompromising life-style could have a novel appeal to a rock audience disenchanted with its increasingly unfashionable heroes, and accordingly placed him firmly within the traditions of rock protest by dubbing him the "new Dylan" and the "black Mick Jagger".

As reggae's popularity burgeoned, lengthier, more analytical articles on reggae began to appear in the rock press, fostered by a series of promotional visits to Jamaica organised for journalists by companies like Island. The importance of the music press as a publicity medium for reggae was such that by the late 1970s journalists were being transported en masse to Jamaica by recording companies to cover the island's music scene. The 1978 "One Love Peace Concert", for example, which featured Bob Marley, was attended by over 160 journalists and cameramen, one third of whom were flown in by Island (New Musical Express, 6 May 1978). As a result of these excursions, certain journalists began to adopt a more sociological approach to the music. A series of lengthy reports on the Jamaican reggae scene subsequently appeared in the rock press, attempting to situate the music within a broader, if caricatured, vision of Jamaican society as a poverty-stricken Third World country, torn by political strife and corruption (New Musical Express, 16 October 1976, 23 October 1976, 27 May 1978, 3 June 1978; Melody Maker, 12 June 1976). Much of the photography that accompanied these articles continued rock culture's preoccupation with the conspicuous and flamboyant aspects of Rastafari and roots exotica. Rock journalists revelled in all the extra copy to be made out of locks and ganja, and terms like "natty" and "Jah". This approach was typified by the coverage of reggae in the *New Musical Express* with its zany, lampooning style of journalism, reflected in its subheadings and picture captions.

The style of rock criticism exemplified by the *New Musical Express* was partly derived from the underground press of the late 1960s (Frith, 1983). As self-appointed guardians of rock culture charged with maintaining its "authenticity", many rock journalists were naturally drawn to reggae as an "uncommercial", "rebel music". This resulted in a tendency to focus almost exclusively on the protest element in reggae, which in turn had consequences for the way the music came to be interpreted by white fans. The emphasis on reggae's political and revolutionary rhetoric, together with the relentless focussing on the imagery of locks and ganja, reinforced the process whereby all reggae became identified with roots Rasta style.

The coverage of reggae in the rock press was a complex mixture of raw enthusiasm, serious commentary, romanticism and

80

undisguised voyeurism. At a time when reggae was becoming increasingly fashionable, that coverage undoubtedly played a significant role in fostering white interest in the music, and consolidated the symbols by which reggae came to be widely identified amongst large numbers of young whites. At the height of their popularity in the 1970s, the four main publications of the rock press (*Sounds, New Musical Express, Melody Maker* and the *Record Mirror*) commanded impressive circulation figures and exerted considerable influence as opinion guides amongst rock fans (Frith, 1983).

As the era of the album-buying rock fan began to be eclipsed by punk, the circulation of the major rock weeklies went into decline. The post-punk vacuum in popular music journalism was filled by a new generation of glossy, colour pop magazines, typified by *Smash Hits*. Launched in 1978, *Smash Hits* catered for a younger audience that cared little for political commitment and artistic integrity, and even less for the tortured analytical prose of the old guard rock papers. Building its popularity around simple, uncomplicated journalism, chart information, song lyrics and full-page colour pictures of artists, *Smash Hits* began to challenge the hegemony of the rock weeklies. By the end of 1984, its circulation had reached over half a million, while that of its nearest rival, NME, slumped from 202,000 in 1979 to 123,192 in 1984. While coverage of reggae artists in *Smash Hits* was restricted to a handful of artists who represented the music in the pop world, such as Musical Youth and UB40, the publishing of lyrics, and the stress on appealing aesthetics and photography allowed for a more diffuse dissemination of black images and styles to younger generations of white pop fans.

The most consistent journalistic support for Jamaican music in Britain came from specialist publications in the black music press. This sphere of the music press had long functioned as an important outlet for the appreciation of black American traditions such as jazz, blues and r'n'b. A number of Jamaican music "fanzines" run by amateur enthusiast-journalists had also appeared sporadically since the early 1970s. The first major national publication to give regular coverage to reggae, however, was the monthly magazine, *Black Music*. Launched in December 1973, the journal, with its glossy presentation and relatively expensive price of 25p, attempted to reach the expanding and potentially lucrative audience for black music in Britain. The magazine's somewhat studious, analytical approach was aimed particularly at the more discerning black music music fan. *Black Music*'s publishers, the press group IPC saw the magazine as a door into this "specialist" market. As *Race Today* speculated:

> IPC are thought to be using *Black Music* as a test operation to see how to most effectively get into the market. They intend to be more popular than the specialist blues and soul magazines and yet retain that particularly black identity (Race Today, December 1973, p. 325).

Whilst the magazine's coverage was oriented chiefly towards black American forms, *Black Music* provided limited scope for more detailed and analytical articles on reggae by freelance journalists like Carl Gayle. Gayle was one of the first black journalists in Britain to write substantially about Jamaican music from within its cultural and political traditions. He pioneered a much-emulated journalistic style that attempted to convey the messages of the music and its artists as far as possible on their own terms and in their own idioms. Gayle's articles were frequently influential in exposing roots artists who were little known outside the black community to a wider audience. His early articles on Burning Spear, for example, were directly responsible for generating interest in the band amongst both record companies and white fans alike (*Black Music*, October 1975a, 1975b). Gayle was one of the few early writers on reggae who were sympathetic to Rastafari, exposing and lending support to its ideals through his own political engagement with the movement.

Black Music was joined in 1976 by a cheaper weekly newspaper, *Black Echoes*, which also employed freelance journalists and gave regular coverage to reggae. By the late 1970s, *Black Echoes* was the only weekly national newspaper that dealt substantively with most aspects of reggae culture. The paper developed into an important channel of promotion for the reggae industry, reaching the growing numbers of whites who were interested in consuming the music in an undiluted form. *Black Echoes* played a major role in consolidating this section of the market through its mail-order advertisements, its charts (compiled from the sales returns of reggae shops) record reviews, feature articles and news about sound-system dances and tours by artists.

Compared to the relatively narrow readership of the specialist music press, the broadcasting institutions of the media tapped a potentially larger, more popular audience for the music. Of these institutions, it was radio that arguably played the most important role in popularising Jamaican music. That exposure, however, did not generally come about through the channels of mainstream broadcasting. During the 1960s, forms like ska and rocksteady faced a blanket prejudice within the mass media. The BBC's monolithic broadcasting structures proved impervious to Jamaican music, and it was left largely to pirate radio stations such as Radio Caroline to give limited air-play to the music. By setting themselves up on installations off the coast of Britain, the pirates had managed to evade the broadcasting laws which gave the BBC a monopoly of the air-waves. The pirates, along with stations like Radio Luxembourg, served as the principal broadcasting outlets for black music in Britain in the 1960s. In 1967, however, the BBC responded by outlawing such stations with new legislation and creating its own top forty station, Radio One (Frith, 1983).

By the late 1960s, the more popularised forms of reggae such as the Trojan material had begun to permeate mainstream daytime listening on Radio One. Most reggae records, however, were automatically disqualified from national air-play by the BBC's methods of chart compilation (Partridge, 1973). Jamaican music was sold predominantly through independent shops whose sales returns were not taken into account by the BBC charts. Since Radio One relied heavily on these charts as its principal barometer of popular taste, most reggae records simply never reached the playlists, despite their ability to outsell rival pop discs. Many Jamaican releases regularly sold tens of thousands of copies in this way, without ever denting the pop charts (Melody Maker, 20 September 1969).

During the 1970s reggae continued to meet with considerable indifference within mainstream broadcasting. The hostility of Radio One's DJs and programme producers was well known in the reggae industry (Clarke, 1980). Reggae was generally considered to be "unmarketable" in most spheres of the music business. Much of it was accordingly filtered out from the mainstream pop market by those decision-makers and taste-arbiters that represented the "gatekeepers" of the industry, such as record company executives, artist and repertoire personnel, promoters and shop-owners (Frith, 1983). For many radio producers, reggae's perceived lack of harmony and unsophisticated musical arrangement failed to measure up to the standards of white pop, while its overtly political or sexual lyrics were regarded as "unsuitable" for mainstream programming. As far as the BBC was concerned, this was a reflection of the corporation's inherent conservatism which was translated into an emphasis on building a mass audience of individual consumers and private listeners. The result was that a premium was placed on "relaxing" and unobtrusive music which meant that only the more palatable reggae records were selected for air-play. Derek Chinnery, former head of Radio One, summed up the BBC's official position on reggae, arguing that:

> It seems to be a regional interest, there doesn't seem to be much of a national demand for reggae . . . there's no strong indication that our listeners want more reggae. And of course there's an awful lot of reggae that's simply not suitable for Radio One. Some of them have strong political content while others are just poor quality records. (Melody, Maker, October 1976, p. 36)

The crudest example of these criteria in operation was the BBC's overt censorship of reggae through the periodic banning of specific records. Max Romeo's "Wet Dream", for example, was banned by Radio One in 1969 for its suggestive lyrics, while in 1975 a dub-toasting record by Rupie Edwards entitled "Irie Feelings" suffered a similar fate as a result of its oblique references to marijuana.

Eschewed by national pop radio, most Jamaican music was consigned to the realms of "minority" "specialist" taste, of interest to black people alone. It was within this sphere of broadcasting, however, that reggae achieved its most significant breakthrough.

The early 1970s saw the launching of several local BBC and independent commercial radio stations. While much local radio proved to be parochial, consensus-oriented and pedestrian in presentation, it did allow scope for a limited amount of reggae programming. BBC Radio London's *Reggae Time* and Radio Birmingham's *Reggae, Reggae* were amongst the earliest weekly reggae programmes to be broadcast. A number of independent local radio stations, set up in the mid-1970s under the auspices of the Independent Broadcasting Authority (IBA), soon followed. With greater needle-time than the BBC, and a legal obligation to satisfy "minority" tastes, such stations provided further limited opportunities for the transmission of reggae music.

The launching of reggae programmes on local radio gave an unprecedented degree of access to Jamaican music for white listeners. While aimed primarily at black audiences, formative shows like *Reggae Time* on Radio London were instrumental in arousing interest in reggae amongst a wider, white listenership. The importance of radio as a medium for the dissemination of Jamaican music was enhanced in the late 1970s and early 1980s with a further expansion of local reggae programming. While in 1976 only four out of the eighteen local radio stations in Britain had weekly reggae programmes, with 2 in Birmingham and 2 in London, by 1980, the number of reggae shows had increased to ten. By 1984 this number had more than doubled, with twenty-four reggae shows dispersed throughout the country broadcasting to virtually every major urban area of Britain.

One of the most well-known and successful of these programmes was Capital Radio's *Roots Rockers*, presented by white DJ, David Rodigan. Rodigan began his broadcasting career in 1977 as co-presenter, with Tony Williams, of BBC Radio London's *Reggae Time*. Moving to Capital in 1979, Rodigan began hosting his own show, with a programme format that was partly inspired by Michael Campbell's prototype reggae show, *Dread at the Controls,* on the Jamaican Broadcasting Corporation. Rodigan combined Campbell's presentation style, which mixed records with jingles, sound effects and patois catchphrases, with a format consisting of interviews with artists, oldies, exclusive music and new releases. With that format, Rodigan built up a large audience throughout the south-east of England. Relying on his extensive personal knowledge of the music, Rodigan managed to present reggae on its own terms while remaining broadly popular with both black and white listeners. As Rodigan explained:

> I don't believe in trying to dilute the musical format. Nor do I ever think "Oh, that's a bit heavy, they might not understand that", despite the fact that a lot of white people might think "well what the hell does that mean". Because the people that make the music know what it means; the black audience who may have been born and bred in this country but nevertheless feel an affiliation because of their blood, roots and culture to that music, they know what it means. Now the odd thing is that I didn't come from that kind of background, and yet I

feel as closely affiliated to that as they do, and I know there are lots of other white people who do as well (Interview with the author, 25 October 1983).

For many white listeners, particularly those living in areas of negligible black settlement, radio provided an ideal opportunity for reggae to be heard and experienced in a more private way. As a key contributor to this process, Rodigan himself was well aware of radio's potential to foster interest amongst those who would not otherwise have the opportunity or inclination to buy or listen to the music:

> I know there are a lot of people that listen that don't go to reggae clubs and don't come out where I'm playing because they think they're going to be inhibited or whatever, but make their presence known through letters . . . you know, people who live in Sussex, terribly quiet sort of residential areas who write in saying this and that about the show and buy their records on mail order, but don't actually go and drink Special Brew, smoke a spliff and buy twenty pre-releases in *Dub Vendor* on a Saturday. They actually do it in a different way (Interview with the author, 25 October 1983).

The broadcasting monopoly of the BBC and IBA was increasingly challenged by the steady growth in the number of independent, community and "pirate" radio stations operating in explicit defiance of Home Office regulations. While black music pirate stations had been in existence since the early 1970s, the early 1980s saw a boom in the number of small, land-based, often black-run stations broadcasting soul and reggae (Hind and Mosco, 1985). Established primarily to cater for the neglected needs of the black community, stations like London's *Horizon* and *LWR* (London Weekend Radio) also gave a major impetus to black music's popularity throughout large sections of the white population in the south-east of England. Birmingham's PCRL (People's Community Radio Link) likewise challenged the dominance of local, BBC and independent stations by building up a mass listenership that extended well beyond the boundaries of the black community. The extent of black music's hidden audience was signalled by the mass popularity of the pirates, demonstrated through listening figures that ran into millions, by their influence on local record sales and by well-attended gigs run by these stations.

The pirates represent a more genuine form of broadcasting democracy, providing an alternative to the bland professionalism of mainstream radio through DJs who shared the musical tastes and interest of their audience. For younger listeners in particular, pirate radio provided a unique means of access to records they would be otherwise unable to hear or afford. Moreover, reggae-orientated stations like DBC (Dread Broadcasting Corporation) by presenting reggae in the language, style and idioms of the dance-hall, disseminated black musical traditions to white listeners in a manner unprecedented in the history of British broadcasting.

The effects of the pirates' popularity caused both BBC and IBA local stations to increase their reggae output, with Capital Radio extending Rodigan's show from two to three hours, and BBC Radio London adding two extra reggae shows to their weekly schedule. The exposure of reggae on local radio, coupled with the steady rise in the music's popularity also brought a gradual acceptance of Jamaican music on national radio. By the mid-1970s, it was possible to hear reggae during daytime peak listening-hours, albeit sandwiched between standard top forty output. The challenge to state broadcasting represented by the pirates forced the BBC to concede to the programming of a national reggae show, *Culture Rock*, hosted by Radio One's first black female presenter, Miss P. (a former DJ on the pirate station DBC).

The dissemination of reggae over the air-waves was undoubtedly a major factor in maintaining and cultivating mass white popular interest in the music. Radio presenters like David Rodigan and Miss P. were in one sense reggae ambassadors. Their programmes, and their many equivalents up and down the country, represented important cultural spaces in which the music was transmitted, celebrated and heard on its own terms and largely within its own traditions.

4 White Youth, Black Echoes

4.1 Club Reggae

From the very earliest days of post-war black settlement, the influence of Caribbean music and culture on young white Britons could be detected through various emerging cultural connections and exchanges. Some of these were played out in the music and dance cultures that evolved in specific London night-clubs. The jazz clubs of Soho had long been pioneering islands of cross-racial social interactions, particularly between white Britons and black US servicemen, both during and immediately after the war. By the late 1940s and early 1950s, however, young whites had begun to intermingle with West African and early Caribbean migrants to the sounds of calypso, highlife, jazz and r'n'b. Caribbean and specifically Jamaican music forms became increasingly prominent in the dance palais and clubs of London in the late 1950s and early 1960s. Following the events of 1958, and the growing visibility of an indigenous Afro-Caribbean cultural and community life, the impact of Jamaican music began to be registered on groups of young whites living in close proximity to areas of black settlement. As a result of the music's exposure through the black club scene and the handful of shebeens that catered for a multi-ethnic clientele, some young whites began to express a fondness for ska. In London clubs like the *Flamingo* and the *Roaring Twenties*, the dance styles that accompanied the music were emulated by young white fans, then popularised and absorbed into mainstream white dance culture (Patterson, 1966).

By 1962, a small number of whites had begun to emulate the musical tastes, speech and sartorial styles of Afro-Caribbean young men. For these early forerunners of the mod subculture, ska, with its raucous instrumentation and unorthodox rhythms, became an alternative to the white popular music of the day.

Amongst the more hard-core mods, ska and rocksteady records like those of Prince Buster, acquired a cult status, their patronage imbued with clandestine connotations (Hebdige, 1974). For many young whites in this period, Jamaican music's appeal lay in its esoteric qualities. For the more committed white fans of ska and rocksteady, part of the attraction of Jamaican music lay in the process of hunting down and discovering what was felt to be an underground music form. For the avid white record-collector, this kind affiliation did not necessarily rely on direct social engagement with, or proximity, to Britain's black communities. As David Rodigan recounts:

> You didn't need to have black friends so to speak, because I lived in a village outside of town (Oxford) therefore I didn't live in the black community...you only needed to go to the record shop and listen to the music that had arrived that week. (Interview with the author, 25 October 1983)

Throughout most of the 1960s, Jamaican music remained something of an underground form. Most white consumption of the music was confined to the clubs and took place at a relative distance from mainstream pop culture. Apart from the success of Millie's "My Boy Lollipop", it failed to break through to a mass white audience.

It was not until the end of the decade that Jamaican music received its first significant acknowledgement in the realms of pop culture. The momentum for this process was initially generated outside the pop world and drew in particular on the patterns of shared social and leisure space, and the forms of interaction between young blacks and whites that had already been evolving in certain areas of Britain. By the latter half of the 1960s, white interest in the rude boy subculture of Afro-Caribbean youth was being cultivated through a number of mixed leisure venues dotted around the south-east. London sound-systems like Sir Neville and Count Suckle, for example, began to play an increasing number of "out-of-town dances" in the suburbs, attracting large white audiences. Elements of the black rude-boy style began to be appropriated by some young whites and translated into an equivalent "white rude-boy" style. White youth could be observed emulating the close cropped hair or *skiffle* of black youth, along with sartorial features, such as short, narrow trousers, the loose-limbed walk and selective phrases of patois. By 1968, these elements had crystallised into the more visible and self-conscious style of the "skinhead" (Hebdige, 1974).

Some of the early forms of skinhead culture evolved in close proximity to the black community. Young whites invaded blues parties and pubs in black areas of south and east London, and "did the reggae" with young Afro-Caribbeans in youth clubs and discos. For the skinheads, it was the danceable, punchy rhythms of rocksteady and early reggae which held the greatest attraction. The skinheads expressed a particular fondness for instrumentals, sing-along tunes and "rude" records with sexual references. The music's rough-and-ready qualities suited the aggressively proletarian sensibilities of skinhead culture. It stood in direct contradiction to the white rock music espoused by middle-class youth, a music devoid of meaning and relevance to reggae's most ardent working-class fans. The equal contempt in which rock fans held reggae and skinheads held the hippies symbolised the class divisions and uneven appropriations of black music within white youth culture during this period. At a time when progressive rock was at pains to distinguish itself from pop and black music, most rock fans considered reggae to be the very height of bad taste. For the skinheads, conversely, reggae was everything that progressive rock was not; easy to dance to, spontaneous, unpretentious, and unmistakably working-class in origin.

The skinheads' patronage of reggae nevertheless played a key role in introducing the music into mainstream pop consciousness in 1969. With much Jamaican music shunned by the recording industry in the 1960s, their adoption of reggae was all the more significant. Records like the chart-topping "Israelites" by Desmond Dekker owed much of their initial success to the support of a large skinhead audience. Such support helped to set in motion Jamaican music's first mass intervention into British pop culture. For two years, between 1969 and 1971, pop reggae managed to capture the attention of a mass white audience with its novel dance rhythms and appealing hook lines.

The dulcet strains of Trojan reggae served to introduce a new musical sensibility to a whole generation of whites. While often buried beneath lavish orchestral backings and over-polished productions, that sensibility was carried into the discos, youth clubs and homes of thousands of young whites, who discovered Jamaican music through a diet of Trojan 45s and Reggae Chartbusters LPs. These records specified musical and rhythmic orientations quite unlike anything that had been heard in mainstream British pop culture. For the mass appeal of songs like "Israelites" rested not on their lyrical discourses, since their patois terminology was largely indecipherable to most white listeners, but on their profoundly

91

attractive rhythms. This dimension of reggae's appeal was confirmed by the success of Dave and Ansell Collins's "Double Barrel" which reached the top of the charts in 1971 and was the last of the flurry of pop reggae hits between 1969 and 1971. Of all the records of this period, "Double Barrel" was perhaps the closest to contemporary forms of Jamaican popular music with its heavy bass, dub overtones and scatted "talk-over" interjections. "Double Barrel" not only marked the end of an era of pop reggae success, but also represented something of a limit case to mass white identification with Jamaican music at this point. For even by 1970, white youths' brief flirtation with Jamaican music had begun to show signs of waning.

The emerging interactions between young blacks and whites in the 1960s had rested on certain implicit tensions, rendered problematic by the effects of racism. By the end of the decade, these contradictions had increasingly begun to place those who identified with black culture in a profoundly ambiguous position. Outside the youth clubs and discos where black and white intermixed, in the spheres of school and work, the predicament of black youth had been steadily worsening, as a result of racism in the job market and friction with the police. White youth were now increasingly to be found thrust into competition for an ever-shrinking number of jobs with their black peers and former class-mates. Divisions and conflicts premised on these divergent experiences increasingly began to manifest themselves in the leisure sphere, in the shifting racial composition of youth clubs, and the re-segregation of those leisure spaces in which black-white interaction had originally begun. McGlashen described this situation in London in the late 1960s and early 1970s as the "great reggae war":

> Black teenagers suddenly found youth clubs attractive. Starved for years of places that would let them in, they travelled across London to anywhere with good sounds. . . White youngsters who had been happy with a one-third black minority, found themselves outnumbered; they fled or called in reinforcements or heavies. The game of musical clubs lasted perhaps nine months. Black teenagers wandered around a shrinking circle of youth clubs that played their music to the accompaniment of clashes, petitions and frantic committee meetings. Most youth clubs chucked their reggae

records in the dustbin. Segregation returned (McGlashen, 1973, p. 21).

The reality of the situation outside the youth clubs, and the Powellist political climate of the period, militated against any deeper appreciation of the music on the part of the skinheads. Hebdige cites the poignant example of a mixed youth club in south London where skinheads reacted to the playing of "Young Gifted and Black" by cutting the wires to the loudspeakers and chanting "Young, Gifted and White" (Hebdige, 1974, p. 40). The realities of racism, together with ideological and political shifts inside the black community, served to exclude the skinheads from the leisure spaces they had earlier shared with young blacks. The sound-system and blues scene recoiled into a more compact and exclusively black cultural sphere in order to preserve itself from the white interest and intrusion which threatened its autonomy. The presence of whites diminished till all but the staunchest few remained. To most young whites, roots clubs, reggae shops, blues parties and sound-system dances became intimidating black domains and no-go areas (May, 1977). Most young white people at this time were unable to empathise with the more conscious lyrics that saturated Jamaican music, and with records that spoke of black unity and which dealt increasingly with the specificity of black experience. The political encounters of Afro-Caribbean youth with the Black Power movement, and subsequently with Rastafari, placed firm limits on the extent of their involvement.

The 1960s interlude was terminated by the impenetrability of the very culture which had attracted white youth in the first place. In national terms, the extent of black-white interaction in the 1960s had anyway been highly uneven and confined to specific areas of urban Britain. In the working-class suburbs of Birmingham, Manchester and Newcastle, for example, the black components of skinhead style were much less present (Hebdige, 1974). In such areas the links with Afro-Caribbean youth were a good deal weaker and often non-existent. The adoption of skinhead style revolved more heavily around the culture of the football terraces and around racism directed towards both Afro-Caribbean and particularly Asian communities with equal venom. By 1972, the fragile relationship that had been built up between black and white youth during the 1960s appeared to have completely dissolved. As Gilroy notes, the terms on which young black and white people related to one another had begun to change:

> The rise of an articulate British racism, often aimed squarely at the distinct experiences and preoccupations of the young, destroyed the possibility of essentially covert appropriations of black style music and anger which had been the characteristic feature of the mod and skinhead eras. 'Race' had to be dealt with, acknowledged as a primary determinant of social life and, in the same breath, overcome. (Gilroy, 1987, p. 172)

The growth of an oppositional black culture amongst Afro-Caribbean youth pushed these relations into a new political phase. It was not until the latter half of the 1970s, however, that many of these implications began to be realised in a realignment of the relationship between black and white youth cultures, albeit on new terms and in new forms.

Up until the mid 1970s, reggae had been commercially available to white British youth only in a popularised form. Island's campaign with Bob Marley, however, rendered accessible a more radicalised yet musically cosmopolitan form of Jamaican music for mass white consumption. Thus, while for some black fans Marley's apparent "incorporation" into mainstream rock and pop culture marked the end of his cultural and political credibility, for white youth it signalled the beginnings of a mass encounter with Jamaican popular music in the late 1970s and early 1980s.

4.2 The Punky Reggae Party

The fruits of Island's campaign with Bob Marley were first signalled by the successful 1975 British tour, during which Marley played to large, mixed audiences in London, Birmingham and Manchester. However, it was not until the following year that the mass gravitation towards reggae by white youth really began. That process must be understood against the backdrop of an increasingly inert and clichéd rock culture. As one journalist succinctly put it:

> The white kids have lost their heroes; Jagger has become a wealthy socialite, Dylan a mellow home-loving man, even

94

Lennon has little to say any more. So along comes this guy with amazing screw top hair, and he's singing about "burning and looting" and "brain wash education", loving your brothers and smoking your dope. Their dream lives on. (Black Echoes, 26 June 1976, p. 12)

In Marley's music a generation of white rock fans rediscovered the oppositional values which so much contemporary rock music appeared to have lost. The marketing campaigns conducted by Island and Virgin caught the eyes and ears of white fans increasingly dissatisfied with mainstream rock. For while Marley made compromises in his musical style, by successfully combining reggae with other international pop forms, his songs maintained a political militancy and a counter-cultural quality which appealed deeply to white youth. In the universal, egalitarian themes which he addressed, they found meanings with which to make sense of their own lives and experiences in post-imperial Britain. The live performances to which Marley regularly attracted large white audiences throughout the 1970s, often witnessed the spectacle of thousands of young whites chanting "Rastafari" in unison and singing "stand up for your rights" along with the band.

The promotion of Marley as a "reggae superstar" by the media and entertainment industries served to encourage his reception as a hero figure amongst thousands of young whites. The projection of reggae as rebel music and the imagery by which many other artists were marketed as counter-cultural heroes, enhanced their political appeal amongst white youth disillusioned with the complacency and self-indulgence of many rich white rock stars.

It was out of similar concerns and conditions that the punk movement emerged in 1976 as a reaction against rock's increasing technological sophistication, the gigantism of its live concerts and the widening gap between audience and artists. Punk challenged the musical orthodoxies and aesthetic criteria of rock which had become dependent on recorded, rather than live performances and on the primacy of albums over singles (Laing, 1985). It was no coincidence that many punks chose to register their rejection of the "dinosaurs" of rock culture through a strong identification with reggae. Reggae had the political edge and the spontaneous, participatory qualities that were absent from so much contemporary rock. Reggae singers, by addressing themselves to the concerns of everyday life, and to themes of poverty, suffering and protest, were felt to have an authenticity that was lacking in rock. In its attempt to shock the morality of mainstream culture, punk found in reggae and Rastafari a rich source of subversive and forbidding qualities, qualities of "dread", conviction and rebelliousness (Hebdige, 1979; Laing, 1985).

There were similarities between punk's discourses ("Crisis", "Anarchy") and those of Rastafari ("Armaggideon Time", "War inna Babylon", etc). Punks drew analogies between their position and that of Rastas on the basis that both faced discrimination as a result of their appearance and beliefs. Such connections were immortalised in Bob Marley's "Punky Reggae Party" which acknowledged the links between the two movements, proclaiming that while "rejected by society and treated with impunity", both were "protected by their dignity". Punk and new-wave groups like the Ruts, the Clash and the Slits incorporated reggae and Rasta rhetoric directly into their music. The Clash, for example, played live in front of a large backdrop of the 1976 Notting Hill riots, wearing stage clothes stencilled with phrases from reggae culture like "Dub", and "Heavy Manners". The Notting Hill riot was itself a seminal event in punk culture which provided the inspiration for the Clash's "White Riot".

At many punk gigs, reggae was frequently played during the interval between bands, as the only acceptable alternative to punk (Hebdige, 1979). Punk artists like the Sex Pistols' John Lydon, moreover, openly declared their enthusiasm for reggae, an enthusiasm which in Lydon's case was pursued further in his subsequent group, Public Image Limited. The Clash also paid homage to the music by recording their own version of popular roots songs like Junior Murvin's "Police and Thieves" and Willie Williams' "Armagiddeon Time". Thousands of copies of the originals, together with cult records like Culture's "Two Sevens Clash" were also bought by punks on import. Besides the Slits, several other female and mixed-gender new-wave bands, such as the Mistakes, the Au Pairs and the Raincoats, also employed reggae rhythms in their music (Steward and Garratt, 1984). Some groups began putting instrumental or dubbed versions of their songs on the B-sides of their singles. This practice, borrowed from the dub mixes on reggae releases, opened up possibilities for new kinds of experimentation with instruments, sounds and voices, through an appropriation of dub techniques.

Reggae was adopted by the punk movement for its ability to signify white youth's own struggles for political and cultural power. In the same way that young white rock musicians in the 1960s found in the blues a means of expressing the collective experience of youth, so the model for punks seeking to recreate rock as a communal music in the late 1970s was reggae (Frith, 1983). Like the organic artists of the reggae tradition, punk musicians insisted on relating musical expression to the mundane concerns and experiences of everyday life. Punk's concern to expose the oppressive nature and boredom of everyday life under capitalism resonated with reggae's antipathy to commodity forms, its emphasis on "roots" and its faithful documentation of topical issues and current events. That resonance was itself partly predicated on white youth's own developing political consciousness of Britain's economic and social crisis, a crisis increasingly experienced through unemployment by the young.

It was in Punk's challenge to orderly consumption and its deconstruction of reified notions of pleasure that the movement intersected most clearly with reggae's own refusal to distinguish between leisure and politics. Reggae's ability to integrate explicit lyrics with musical intensity, its spontaneity, performance-orientation and commitment to improvisation, all proved profoundly attractive to young whites alienated by the predictable musical products of mainstream rock and pop. Reggae's contribution to punk's demystification of pop ideology and its reaffirmation of young people's creative power was everywhere evident; in the movement's DIY approach to music-making, its directness of expression and its attempts to close the gap between artists and audience. The fruits of this connection were realised not only in the democratisation of musical performances and band formation, but also in a widening of access to the means of production and distribution themselves. Here the parallels with the reggae industry were striking, in the emergence of an autonomous network of independent labels, distribution organisations and retail outlets. Such connections were made concrete in organisations like *Rough Trade*, which provided a distribution service and retail outlet for both punk and reggae records.

In these ways the impact of reggae created scope for new kinds of opposition and new ways of being "political" in white youth culture which reflected the continuity of cultural expression with political

97

action in black musical traditions. Many of these connections were made explicit in Rock Against Racism (RAR), an organisation formed in late 1976 by a loose political alliance of musicians, fans, media workers and anti-racist/fascist activists (Widgery, 1986). While conceived most immediately as a counter-response to the racist utterances of prominent rock musicians like Eric Clapton, RAR was also formed against the backdrop of a resurgence of popular racism, and a rise in the tempo of nationalist far right activity, particularly amongst young people.

RAR drew its momentum from the informal dialogue between black and white youth which had sprung up in the shadow of Bob Marley and the punk intervention. By openly acknowledging the political influence of black music traditions in white youth culture, it attempted to politicise the links between punk, the recession and race politics. RAR gave vent to the strong anti-racist feeling and the passionate opposition to fascist violence and police harassment that already existed amongst substantial numbers of young people in Britain. The extent and depth of that feeling was reflected in the letters pages of *Temporary Hoarding*, RAR's publication, which revealed the range of local concerns and personal experiences around racism. Letters of sympathy and protest conveyed both the strength of white youths' affiliation to black music as well as their sense of outrage at the racism of their parents and peers. Capturing the prevailing mood of urgency and spontaneity, the paper's editorial wrote:

> Everyone wants to tell us their experiences, their fave local bands, their ideas about how to fight fascism, about their bigoted families, about mates beaten up, about anger and frustration about their town, about racism in their street, their blocks of flats, about fear – helplessness (Temporary Hoarding, Winter 1977, p. l)

RAR's decentralised structure meant that it was at the local level that the organisation was often at its most effective. At a host of small provincial venues, black and white musicians collaborated under RAR's umbrella in a spontaneous manner that often relied on local, informal friendship networks, in settings wholly autonomous from the mainstream music industry. In less than three years, RAR successfully managed to stage nearly 800 gigs and was instrumental in putting reggae groups into venues from which they had hitherto been excluded. Bands like Steel Pulse, Aswad, Black Slate, Misty and The Cimarons regularly appeared alongside punk groups at town hall gigs and open-air carnivals, giving thousands of whites in provincial areas the opportunity to hear reggae, often for the first time.

The organisation's activities climaxed in the late 1970s and early 1980s in a series of major anti-fascist demonstrations organised in alliance with the Anti-Nazi League. The three great RAR/ANL carnivals were amongst the largest anti-racist political mobilisations that had been seen in post-war Britain. The ANL had been formed a year later than RAR with the specific intention of defeating the National Front at the polls. With its broader social and political constituency, however, and its tendency to lay the problem of racism in Britain exclusively at the feet of the NF, the ANL served to narrow and undermine many of RAR's wider political objectives. For RAR's was a much broader anti-racist vision premised on the collective transcendence of "race" in concrete settings. Under the simple banner of "love music, hate racism" RAR pioneered new sorts of links between politics and music, providing both a broad, *cultural* challenge to racism and an emotional alternative to nationalism and patriotism. With its slogan of "militant entertainment" RAR put into practice the concept of music as a source of both pleasure and political education that was so characteristic of black music in general and reggae in particular.

The political alliances between black and white, and the anti-racist sentiments that RAR helped to foster during its brief history, suggested something of the shared political concerns between different sections of working-class youth. Through the impact of reggae, the punk-RAR experience as a whole succeeded in cultivating an unprecedented awareness of race amongst the most mainstream of white youth. However, while the RAR/ANL intervention succeeded in winning over large sections of those most vulnerable to fascism and nationalism, the process of politicisation spawned by white youth's mass engagement with reggae culture was by no means assured of leading in a progressive direction. The accompanying encounters of young whites with these contradictions showed themselves to be capable also of generating more reactive and explicitly racist responses.

4.3 Young, Powerless and White

Punk was a contradictory and precarious movement as far as the politics of "race" were concerned. While some punks were drawn to the very exclusivity and impregnability of Rasta, for others, the movement's insistence on the specificity of racial oppression and black identity constituted a barrier to any deeper appreciation of its politics. Punk's attempt to subvert the symbols of nationalism, for example in the Sex Pistols' iconoclastic use of the Union Jack and the Queen's figurehead in "God Save the Queen", its attempt to draw parallels between the experience of racism and the position of dispossessed whites, for example in the Clash's "White Riot—these contained ambiguities which were susceptible to manipulation by the far-right. Such contradictions were unsurprising given that punk was born out the same social and economic crisis that had produced the rise in nationalist right-wing activity. For the same powerlessness, desire to shock and sense of anger at official smugness expressed in punk's working-class audience, were precisely the same motives which steered jobless and powerless young whites towards organised racism.

These contradictions began to manifest themselves in explicitly racist forms through the less ambiguous use of fascist and nationalist symbols such as swastikas and Union Jacks by some sections of punk audiences. The coincidence of the revival of skinhead culture with the resurgence in organised fascist activity became increasingly noticeable in punk gigs by bands like Sham 69, who began to attract sizeable contingents of increasingly vocal young National Front supporters. While the connections between nationalist, right-wing organisations and the resurgent skinhead movement were by no means automatic or reciprocal, the skinhead style became progressively inflected with racist connotations, as organisations like the British Movement and the National Front consciously sought to forge a link between its exaggerated working-class imagery and its racist/nationalist agenda.

In the late 1970s both organisations began to concentrate their efforts on mobilising the young during their leisure time, particularly on football terraces, at rock concerts and on the streets (Murdock and Troyna, 1981). The political lessons of RAR were not lost on groups like the National Front and British Movement whose youth wings attempted to match the Left's interventions, measure for measure, with their own mirror organisations such as the *Anti-Paki League* and *Rock Against Communism* (RAC). The youth organisations of the far right attempted to engage with the concrete problems and needs of powerless white youth, by acknowledging and capitalising on the very real sense of boredom and disillusionment that was the frequent experience of the dole for many white youth. They did so by making "race" the basis for working-class unity and coherence; a coherence defined against middle-class authority, the state, "foreigners" and blacks. In the youth-oriented publications of the far right such as *Bulldog* and *Young Nationalist*, youth culture was treated as a battleground and a site of "race war". Bulldog's response to the "arrogant black-power cult" of Rasta and the "Paki-power" of Asian youth was to invert the left political discourse of "black and white, unite and fight" by invoking the need for white youth to "unite and fight". Thus, echoing Bob Marley, *Bulldog* told its readers that the time had come for them to "stand up for your rights":

> We cannot allow ourselves to be pushed around any longer. The time has come for white youths to unite. We must stick together in the fight against black violence. (Bulldog, no. 23, p. 5)

The imagery of black power and violence tapped a deep-seated resentment of black youth culture's autonomy and militancy among some sections of white youth. Such discourses played on young whites' perceptions of black youth as "arrogant" and "intimidating" and on the very real rivalry that existed at street level in some neighbourhoods. They mobilised complex feelings of fear, envy and begrudged admiration for the solidarity and combativity of young blacks, particularly against the police. It was a solidarity and cohesiveness which white youth were seen to lack, and attempted to create through a defensive assertion of white working-classness. The fabrication of imaginary contexts of origin and belonging, through the creation of a mythical white ethnicity, was one way in which this was achieved by those who felt neglected and excluded in terms of their own lack of "culture" and "history" (Hebdige, 1981).

Bulldog's translation of the discourses of reggae and Rastafari into the slogans of "white power" suggested something fundamental about the political resonance of black youth culture. While feared and resented by some whites for its racially specific discourses, its musical and cultural forms remained profoundly attractive. The contradictory nature of that attraction required the far right to struggle constantly against the pervasive influence of black culture amongst white youth. The widespread popularity of black music, style and dance forms amongst the young was recognised as a specific threat to the political designs of organisations like the *British Movement* and the *Young National Front*. In pointing out that threat, Bulldog rejected the implicit "multiracialism" of soul culture, warning its readers that:

> The record and cassette is more powerful than the TV or newspapers, as far as youth is concerned. Disco and its melting pot pseudo-philosophy must be fought or Britain will be full of black worshipping soul boys (Bulldog, no. 23, p. 10).

The far-right's explanation of black dance culture's appeal amongst white youth, as a form of "irrational and emotional frenzy" (Bulldog, no. 23) was a distorted acknowledgement of the powerful pleasures attached to the consumption of black music by white youth. Those pleasures presented a major obstacle to the right's attempts to mobilise white youth around different political and cultural objectives.

Bulldog's *Rock Against Communism* column was conceived as a direct answer to its left counterpart, and attempted to promote an alternative musical culture, purified of black influences. Exploiting the ambiguity in punk's discourses, the RAC column featured a regular chart composed of songs and groups specifically chosen for their racial connotations. Lyrics and song titles such as the Angelic Upstarts' "Brave New World", the Clash's "White Riot" and the Cure's "Killing an Arab" were given explicitly racist readings (Bulldog, November 1978). Some song titles were chosen merely for their colour references, such as "White Noise" by Stiff Little Fingers, a song about British army torture in Northern Ireland. Groups like Sham 69 and "white reggae" acts like Madness and Bad Manners, all of which attracted hard-core skinhead followings and were labelled as "fascist" in the music press, were also adopted by RAC as specifically right-wing bands. Mixed groups like the Specials, meanwhile, were referred to as "The Specials Plus Two" thereby excluding the band's two black members (Bulldog, no. 17, p. 5).

More than any other post-punk trend, it was the music of the *Oi* movement which was claimed as the exclusive property of the far right. Oi was seen as the natural heir to punk, preserving its 'authentic' 'white spirit' (Bulldog, July 1982, no. 28). Oi was defined as an emphatically British form of white working-class "folk" music. Bands like Cock Sparrer, the Cockney Rejects and Skrewdriver projected an aggressive East End working-class identity. Their songs, heavily over laden with football chants, addressed the concerns of a specific section of white, working-class young men. Songs like "Class War" by the Exploited, "Master Race" by the Four Skins and "Blood on the Streets" by the Criminal Class compounded race and class themes from a self-consciously "white" perspective. Through the notion of "white oppression" Oi inverted racism by making whites the victims of "black violence" and "pro-black" police discrimination. In this way, the discourse of Oi fed into the skinhead movement's own mythology about itself as subject to unprovoked assaults by blacks and police alike, denied jobs, spurned by the press and continually forced to the back of the queue (Hebdige, 1981).

While the growth of popular racism and right-wing nationalism amongst the young formed one pole of responses towards black youth-culture in the post-punk era, there were other social and cultural currents in the same period which produced a quite different set of responses. For the same race and class determinants that underpinned these overtly reactive movements amongst young whites were also responsible for generating more syncretic musical and cultural movements that were played out in the very heart of pop culture in the late 1970s and early 1980s.

4.4 Two-Tone Tonic England

One of the legacies of punk had been to stimulate an unprecedented level of interest in reggae amongst young whites, an interest that was signalled most immediately in the flurry of hits that crossed over from the reggae market into the pop charts. Punk's championing of reggae, together with the mass availability and exposure of the music, served to establish it as a central feature of white youth culture in Britain. These developments opened the way to more diffuse popular forms of engagement with Jamaican music and culture, and to the direct incorporation of reggae into white youth's cultural repertoire. In musical terms, one of the most immediate effects of these processes was to encourage the formulation of various rock-reggae hybrids.

Traditionally, most white rock musicians had found Jamaican music hard to imitate. Since the late 1960s a succession of pop and rock artists had attempted to experiment with reggae rhythms, achieving intermittent chart success with near approximations of Jamaican styles. For most rock musicians, Jamaican music was alien to the r'n'b and blues traditions to which they were accustomed. By the late 1970s, however, as a result of punk, a number of groups were drawing openly on reggae music styles as sources of inspiration and creativity. While a number of new-wave artists attempted to produce one-off, popularised versions of reggae, it was the bands of the *Two-tone* movement who were the first to come up with a more convincing and organic fusion of Jamaican music and rock.

The decentralisation of music-making and the boom in local bands brought about by punk paved the way for various regional appropriations of reggae. Two-tone's roots lay in the unique social and geographical proximity that existed between black and white communities in some areas of the West Midlands. The multiethnic composition of bands like the Selecter, the Specials, the Beat and UB40 reflected the unprecedented degree of rapport that had been built up between black and white youth in those areas. Their music was premised on the experience of a whole generation of young people who had been to school together and shared the same streets, neighbourhoods and leisure activities.

Hebdige argues that punk had created something of a "crisis of confidence" within the UK recording industry (Hebdige, 1983). The unpredictability of musical trends that followed in its wake opened the way for more flexible and less cautious signing and management policies which gave more power to young musicians to control their own products, with a greater say over release dates, cover designs, mixes and promotion strategies. This had the effect of removing some of the obstacles and checks which normally slowed down the industry's response to new musical trends, thereby accelerating the process whereby new styles and sounds were generated (Hebdige, 1983). This fluidity in the recording industry was borne out by the speed of Two-tone's intervention into mainstream pop in late 1979.

The Specials' first release "Gangsters" achieved cult status within a matter of days and went on to become the largest selling, independently-distributed single of 1979.

The interest in Jamaican music cultivated by punk had encouraged some young whites to seek out the root forms that preceded the music of reggae artists like Bob Marley. The "ska revival" music of Two-tone provided an opportunity for those white youth who had identified with reggae culture during the punk period to maintain their affiliation to the music. There were differences in style, however, between the various groups. The Selecter were perhaps the most reggae-influenced. The Specials used a more up-tempo fusion of ska and rock, while The Beat drew on a whole range of punk, reggae, calypso and soul influences. Jamaican forms supplied the characteristic upbeat guitar, the keyboard shuffle and the drum and bass foundations that were crucial to the music's danceability. The most characteristic feature of the Two-tone sound, however, was its distinct synthesis of the rhythmic pulse of Jamaican music with the drive and cynicism of punk.

Two-tone music was born out of its exponents' various attempts to reflect the heterogeneous tastes of their mixed audiences. In order to appeal to both black and white sections of the audience, groups like the Coventry Automatics (the forerunners of the Specials) drew on the less "separatist" more up-tempo forms of Jamaican music represented by ska and rocksteady. As Linval Golding, the Specials' guitarist, pointed out, ska had an energetic quality that was more suited to the post-punk mood of white youth:

> I don't think white audiences can enjoy straight reggae so much as ska. Reggae's too heavy, it's too laid back for today's generation who wants to let off steam and energy. They want to jump around a bit (Black Music, February 1980, p. 27)

Two-tone's revival of the music of ska and rocksteady was accompanied by a revival also of the sartorial styles and symbols associated with the era. The Two-tone style was based on that of the 1960s "rude boy" and consisted of tonic suits, loafers, pork-pie hats and cropped hair. Its most distinctive feature, however, was the black-and-white check design found on the band's record label and promotional material. The Two-tone logo suggested the possibility that a new hybrid cultural identity might be achieved through the music. As Hebdige points out, its colour symbolism signified the multiracial ideal of black and white, "adjacent yet separate, different but connected like squares on a chessboard" (Hebdige, 1983, p. 160).

The exponents of Two-tone were united in their hope that the humour and style of both black and white working-class youth could find a common voice in the movement's music and identity. Their hopes were largely vindicated by the mass enthusiasm throughout Britain for Two-tone's unique style, music and cultural politics. A series of extensive national tours undertaken by the Two-tone roster between 1979 and 1981 dispersed the music to the most provincial areas of Britain (New Musical Express, 25 August 1979; 27 September 1980). The Two-tone bands criss-crossed the country, playing to packed dance halls. The rowdy, exuberant atmosphere of the concerts underlined Two-tone's importance as a predominantly live dance music. While the bands addressed serious political and social issues, it was two-tone's infectious dance rhythms which drew in the crowds. Pauline Black, the Selecter's lead vocalist, summed up the music's politics by telling the audience at the beginning of the group's set that "you're here to dance, and then to think" (New Musical Express, 23 February 1980, p. 48). The impact of Two-tone's live performances revolved heavily around this combination of "good-time" dance rhythms and deadly serious lyrics. Taking their cues from the reggae tradition, the Two-tone groups worked in and out of the popular, attempting to merge political sensibilities with the music itself. As Pauline Black elaborated:

> While we're trying to entertain people, we're also trying to give them something to think about...we catch them with the beat, then try to make the lyrics something they can relate to. (Melody Maker, 6 October 1979, p. 20)

Most of the Two-tone bands relied on their own local, shared experience of urban life for the raw material of their lyricism. First-hand experience of racism, police harassment and unemployment formed the basis of songs like "Concrete Jungle" by the Specials and "Black and Blue" and "Too Much Pressure" by the Selecter. Songs like the Specials' "Do the Dog" attacked petty tribal divisions and subcultural rivalries amongst the young, while the Beat's "Stand Down Margaret" captured youth's disillusionment and anxiety about

106

their future in Thatcherite Britain. The latter song was important not only because it offered a condensed, articulate political critique of Thatcherism, but also because of its use of dub techniques. While the album version of "Stand Down Margaret" contained the original lyrics in their entirety, with additional toasting by Ranking Roger, the single release (on the b-side of "Best Friend") featured a dub version of the song. "Stand Down Margaret (Dub)" used a whole range of sound effects and mixing techniques to explore the music's instrumentation and drum and bass patterns. The end result was a novel fusion of punk, reggae and jazz influences with calypso phrasing and dub effects. The song's meaning was enhanced by the selective dubbing-in of the key phrases "work", "whitelaw", "short sharp" and "world war" from the original lyrics. The dub process transformed the song into a series of political statements and puns, around the interrelated themes of unemployment ("work"), racism ("whitelaw"), state repression ("short, sharp, shock") and nuclear weapons/war ("world war").

The Beat's use of dub was far from the only example of the reggae tradition's political and musical influence on Two-tone. All of the bands acknowledged their debt to reggae culture by covering many original ska, rocksteady and reggae songs. The Specials also included the veteran Jamaican trombonist, Rico, in their line-up, while the Beat displayed their commitment to reggae by releasing music by roots artists like the Congos on their own *Go Feet* label.

It was around the issue of *race*, however, that Two-tone made some of its most dramatic cultural and political interventions. The Two-tone bands displayed an active commitment to political organisations like Rock Against Racism and the Anti-Nazi League, playing at various benefit gigs and demonstrations. But the power of Two-tone was in giving shape to a *sensibility* amongst the young, not just a political programme. Songs like the Specials' "It doesn't make it alright" and "It's up to you" reflected the hopes and aspirations of many young black and white people with their advocacy of tolerance and mutual respect. In a more poignant sense, the movement's message could be inferred from the combined presence of black and white musicians on stage. As the Beat's Ranking Roger argued, "Once you've said it, you don't need to say it again or you'd be pushing it down people's throats: All you got to do is look on stage and you see unity" (Black Music, October, 1982, p. 21).

The mere existence of the mixed bands of the Two-tone movement was a powerful signifier in its own right. As one member of the Selector pointed out, "By simply doing what we do, and being who we are, we *are* rock against racism" (New Musical Express, 25 February 1980, p. 7). Two-tone's political ideals were founded on common anti-racist values which were given expression in the music itself. Its exponents variously described the movement as a "non-separation of things" using music as a "common ground" and language through which to bring people together (New Musical Express, 23 February 1980). By acknowledging and reflecting some of the contradictions of race, the movement attempted to straddle the cultural and political differences between black and white, without permitting them to become a source of division.

The Two-tone bands attempted to use the stage as a platform from which to confront the increasingly vocal racist groups amongst sections of their audience. Contingents of young fascists had been present at the earliest Two-tone gigs. The Specials, and Madness in particular (the only all-white band in the early Two-tone entourage) regularly attracted nationalistic and racist elements of the skinhead revival who saw in the Two-tone style an accurate historical reflection of themselves. The chanting of racist and fascist slogans and the sporadic violence at gigs was a constant reminder of the forces which threatened to undermine Two-tone's fragile unity. The effects of racism, far from being banished by the music, were reproduced in the concert hall, where they enhanced the already fraught and tense atmosphere characteristic of Two-tone gigs.

The synchronisation of the Specials' chart-topping "Ghost Town" with the summer rebellions of 1981 was a fitting climax to Two-tone's brief reign of success. Within days of the riots, the Specials were topping the bill at the Leeds anti-racist carnival. The cultural drawing-power of their music was confirmed by the massed legions of young Two-tone fans who attended the rally, of whom a significant proportion were Afro-Caribbean and Asian. "Ghost Town" held the number one position in the pop charts during the week in which black and white youth clashed with the police in Britain's inner-city areas. Its sharp evocation of crisis conditions and urban decline provided an apt soundtrack to the summer riots. The song itself employed a straightforward reggae-based rhythm, much slower than the band's customary up-tempo ska beat, suggesting the sombre nature of its subject-matter. Its political message, enhanced by the toasted interjections of Neville Staples, suggested that black and white youth might find common meanings in their shared post-industrial predicament.

Two-tone's legacy lay not only in the popular character of its anti-racist politics but also in its projection of black musical traditions into the heart of pop culture. Its use of dub, toasting and reggae rhythms, and its fusion of musical "entertainment" with political realism, all reflected the profound influence of Jamaican music's characteristic political and cultural traditions. Over the course of Two-tone's short-lived history, those traditions occupied a central position at the heart of pop culture for a period of two years.

Two tone's success paved the way for other groups to intervene in mainstream pop with musical styles more closely related to contemporary reggae. The most immediate benefactors of this process were UB40. Whereas the Two-tone bands synthesised black and white musical forms, UB40 attempted to reproduce reggae as faithfully and accurately as possible. Following in the wake of Two-tone, UB40 emerged in the early 1980s as the most popular and successful purveyors of reggae within mainstream pop. Like the Two-tone groups, UB40 owed much of their initial success to their ability to retain a measure of autonomy from the established music industry. Their debut album, *Signing Off*, was the first number one album to be recorded, pressed and distributed entirely through independent channels. This level of independence and control over their music enabled the group to release and popularise their own political material. *Signing Off* thus contained songs about Thatcherism ("Madame Medusa"), imperialism and apartheid ("Burden of Shame") and black civil rights ("King", "Tyler"). The band, moreover, declared their specific intentions to encourage a wider appreciation of reggae by producing a popularised version that could open up the pop market to Jamaican music. As Robin Campbell pointed out:

> We actually set out in the first place to popularise reggae.
> That was our intention . . . Originally, we saw ourselves as
> ambassadors but I don't think we do anymore, because to a
> certain degree we've been successful. (New Musical Express,
> 3 September 1983, p. 6)

109

UB40's characteristic sound was tailored to the pop market through the use of softer melodies, greater instrumentation, more polished vocals and songs with strong hook-lines and choruses. The band saw this as a deliberate ploy to convey the music to a larger audience, thereby creating interest in more roots-orientated reggae. As Campbell argued:

> I wouldn't ever claim credit for every success that reggae's had in Britain, but I think we've played no small part in it. Our success has no doubt helped people like Black Uhuru and Gregory Isaacs who now have chart albums and singles. Our success has opened a lot of people's ears to reggae. (New Musical Express, 5 September 1983, p. 6)

While in the minds of many young whites, UB40 were the be-all and end-all of reggae, they nevertheless provided a marker for the music in mainstream pop. The band themselves maintained a commitment to the reggae tradition by supporting local artists and by paying homage to their sources of inspiration on the album *Labour of Love*, a collection of cover versions of old reggae hits. In subsequent releases they managed to sustain the political flavour of their music by focussing their songs around issues such as unemployment, race, ecology and nuclear weapons. The consistency of their chart success, moreover, suggested the continued relevance of reggae amongst mainstream white youth as a rhythmic counterpoint to mainstream pop.

The spaces in pop culture carved out by Two-tone and UB40 enabled black groups like Musical Youth to reach a mass white audience with musical styles and forms firmly rooted in the reggae tradition. Musical Youth's meteoric rise to fame in 1982 with "Pass the Dutchie" was a seminal event in reggae's pop history. The song was a version of a well-known roots hit "Pass the Kouchie" by the Mighty Diamonds, itself a version of a classic Studio One rhythm. The replacement of "kouchie", a ganja pipe, with the more innocuous "dutchie", a cooking pot, was a calculated move to widen the song's appeal by minimising the possibility of media resistance. Even before the band's record company, MCA, had finished grooming them for pop promotion, "Pass the Dutchie" had already forged its way to the top of the charts. In the first week of October 1982 it was reported that the record was selling twice as many copies as its nearest rival (New Musical Express, 9 October 1982). By the end of that week the single had sold over half a million copies, making it the year's fastest selling single.

The band received unprecedented media coverage for a black reggae group. In the space of four days Musical Youth appeared on *Top of the Pops*, *Blue Peter*, *Razamattaz*, the *News at Ten*, the *Nine O'Clock News*, the *Late, Late, Breakfast Show* and Radio One's *Roundtable*, while also making the front page of the *Daily Star* and the inside pages of the *Daily Mirror*, *The Sun*, *The Daily Express* and *The Daily Mail* (New Musical Express, 9 October 1982). With an average age of 13, the group's mass appeal clearly rested on their status as a novelty act within the mainstream media, and on their projection as the acceptable face of black youth. The group, for their part, showed themselves to be well aware of this contradiction. As Junior, the band's drummer astutely observed:

> I think a lot of people still think we're a novelty. Some of them probably don't even care about the music. They see us on Top of the Pops and go "Aaah, the lickle kids are doing so well". And they go out and buy the record. (New Musical Express, October 1982)

While these endearing images of black adolescence were crucial in understanding the band's popular appeal, "Pass the Dutchie" nevertheless opened up the cultural politics of reggae to a whole new generation of young whites through its exposure of Rasta symbolism, patois and toasting traditions. By shrewdly co-opting contemporary Jamaican rhythms and employing the DJing styles of the moment, Musical Youth rendered black forms available to a mass audience of largely uninitiated young whites.

The video that accompanied "Pass the Dutchie" played a crucial role in this process, receiving several successive plays on *Top of the Pops*. Filmed partly inside a court-room and partly on the banks of the River Thames, with the Houses of Parliament in the background, the video used the icons of Rasta and reggae culture to signify a semantic "turning of the tables" on the British power structure and legal system. The group's tender age, moreover, and their image in the media as school kids/pop stars created an immediate point of identification for younger whites. Through its opening proclamation that "this generation rules the nation" the record created its own immediate youth-specific audience. For the "musical youth" specified in the group's title referred as much to the political culture of which the band were junior ambassadors, as to the generation of young fans who were able to relate to that culture through their music.

Musical Youth's intervention was a significant moment in the mass dissemination of Jamaican music through mainstream pop. In the post-punk era of the early 1980s, however, such breakthroughs were few and far between. In the melee of trends that followed in the wake of Two-tone, reggae and Rasta culture were frequently reduced to one of many "ethnic" styles that were plundered and selectively recombined into musical forms which, while clearly drawing on reggae, owed little to the principles of the reggae tradition. The playful and stylised use of white dreadlocks was a prime example of this relocation of black symbols into contexts drained of any connection with black cultural and musical traditions. Jamaican and black British reggae artists were overlooked by the recording industry in favour of more marketable white pop acts that employed reggae as a stylistic ingredient in a successful hit formula. It was highly ironic, and somewhat symptomatic of this post-punk sensibility, that Musical Youth's "Pass the Dutchie" should be toppled from the number one spot by Culture Club's "Do You Really Want to Hurt Me" (Rimmer, 1985). Compared with Musical Youth's evocative anthem to the reggae tradition, Culture Club's was an altogether more bleached affair, complete with white toaster, which distanced itself from its black, specifically Jamaican musical sources.

Black reggae artists continued to make sporadic forays into pop culture in the mid-1980s. Smiley Culture's "Cockney Translation" and "Police Officer" indicated the potential of black British reggae styles to attract a new generation of young whites to whom Bob Marley was but a distant "legend" encountered through slick TV commercials. The intermittent success of artists like Smiley Culture reaffirmed the power of mainstream pop to disseminate the images and styles of black music in general, and Jamaican popular forms in particular, to a mass white youth audience. Reggae's presence in the heart of mainstream rock and pop, and the forms of popular white identification that it generated, were sufficiently extensive in this period to foster an awareness of "race" amongst the most mainstream of young white people. While providing an important entree to black British culture for young whites living in areas of negligible black settlement, these processes were also crucial in providing an ideological and cultural barrier to the political incursions of the far-right into white youth culture in this period.

Part II Ethnography

5 Birmingham Version

5.1 Northfield, Birmingham (October 1986)

The time is roughly 2 a.m., during the indefinable zone between Saturday night and Sunday morning. The Birmingham suburb of Northfield has shut down, its pubs closed many hours ago. Most of its inhabitants have long since retired to their beds....most, but not all. For in a dilapidated block of flats behind the giant Longbridge car plant, something is happening...music is playing and people are moving to a particular rhythm, with a different sense of time to that embodied by the adjacent monolith to British motoring. Tonight, *Scientist Hi-Powa*, champion sound system of south Birmingham, are playing a "musical meltdown", as the flyer announces, to which "all posses are welcome" (photo 4). Approaching the flats on foot, the faint reverberations of a bass line can be felt, carrying through the buildings and along the pavement. As we enter through a broken-down doorway, the DJ's voice becomes audible above the now rumbling bass patterns. Moving swiftly up the stairs, we knock on the door, greet the gateman and enter...

The session is *ram* tonight, the air is hot, smoky and filled with the scent of perfume and ganja. Squeezing past the tightly-packed bodies, the crowd seems especially young. All posses are indeed present, for the balance between black and white, male and female, is strikingly even. The blues' young patrons intermingle freely with one another, dancing and talking, joking and smoking (photo 7). Desmond, the MC sends out "big requests" and "special dedications" to all sections of the audience, drawing them in, promoting "strictly niceness" (photo 5). "Played-by-the-champion-sound-in-the-whole-wide-world" he exclaims in one rapid breath, introducing a new selection; "Musical-ting-like-the-Rambo-by-the-cat-called-Super-Black". The needle drops on the record. On hearing the familiar intro, two white girls standing by the speakers in smart evening dress, handbags over their shoulders and cigarettes in hand, begin to sway to the rhythm..."Haul and pull it mi selector" calls the DJ. As the needle is brought down on the dub, the excitement moves up a notch. Shorty takes up the mike and begins to chat (photo 6). After a few standard opening salvoes and bombastic claims to be the "hardest whiteman inna England" he moves into his own improvised lyrics. The crowd erupts with vocal encouragement. Whistles blow all around; "Listen-Daddy-scientist-a-go-gi-dem-betta-cos-a-we-rule-the-country-area." As the record comes to an end, Shorty winds up his rap, relinquishing the microphone with a parting "level vibes, seen?"

And "level vibes" it is, at least for a while, in this small pocket of interfusion deep within the heartland of white working-class Birmingham. The blues continues into the night with the sound system pumping out a crucial selection of soul and reggae right through till dawn. As Saturday night melts into Sunday morning and the drab grey surroundings of the south Birmingham suburbs become faintly visible through the window, an inkling of a contradiction begins to suggest itself.

Photo 4: *Scientist* Sound, handbills and flyers, Birmingham 1985-86

Photo 5: Desmond, Emeris & Scooby, *Scientist* Sound, Butetown, Cardiff, 16th December, 1986 [Jon Girling]

Photo 6: Shorty on the mic'(L), Robbo Dread (R), *Scientist* Sound, Butetown, Cardiff, 16th December, 1986 [Jon Girling]

Photo 7: *Scientist* dance, Birmingham, 1986 [Jon Girling]

5.2 Urban Encounters: Inner-City and Outer-Ring

"Race" has long occupied a paramount but contradictory position in the political and social history of the West Midlands. Birmingham in particular was the site of a particular conjuncture between the decline of its manufacturing base, its changing employment structure and patterns of population replacement. These provided the backdrop to a series of politically charged and racialised confrontations around housing, employment and settlement patterns in the 1960s and 70s. This history, combined with the city's strong traditions of white working-class conservatism and the activities of far-right neo-fascist groups such as the National Front, served to establish it as the unofficial "capital" of racist reaction in Britain.

And yet, out of this same regional history an unprecedented degree of rapport had evolved between its different ethnic communities, and a more dynamic encounter between their respective cultural and political traditions. This rapport was founded on decades of close living and interaction in certain areas of the city. Examples of such close living were to be found in most of Birmingham's inner-city areas, but most notably in Sparkhill and

Balsall Heath. Balsall Heath in particular was renowned for its relatively unsegregated character. As one of the oldest areas of black settlement in the city, migrant workers and families of Asian, Afro-Caribbean, Irish and English working-class origin had settled and coexisted there since the early 1950s. The links between these communities had been strengthened by time, and by a common experience of privation. Despite having undergone successive phases of slum-clearance and redevelopment, the area had managed to retain a strong community spirit.

A study of housing patterns in Manchester's inner-city community of Mosside, had shown that slum clearance, and the process of residential succession in the area had taken place in such a way as to have a communalising effect on its residents (Ward, 1979). As a result, racial distinctions received less emphasis than in other inner-city areas, and gave way to joint political action around common housing interests. To a certain extent, a similar process had occurred in areas such as Balsall Heath where the process of population replacement has positioned black and white communities in close proximity to one another.

As a result of these local social ties and links, the cultural lives of black and white communities had become harmonised around the shared spaces and cross-cutting loyalties of street, pub and neighbourhood. Multiracial kinship and supportive neighbourhood networks, produced by cross-racial friendships, relationships and marriages, had progressively eroded the more pronounced ethnic and racial boundaries. Leisure activities clustered around a similar set of focal points and shared institutions, including cafes, restaurants, grocery stores, pubs, gambling houses and betting-shops. The leisure spaces and institutions of the Afro-Caribbean community, such as dances, blues parties, record shops and various social functions, were also inhabited by other groups in the local population. In an area like Balsall Heath it was not uncommon to find significant numbers of young whites who had grown up within, or in close proximity to, the black community. Pre-adolescent intermixing between black and white children was the norm rather than the exception in such areas, and invariably began at infant school and in local play-areas.

This juxtaposition of black and white working-class communities was by no means unique to Birmingham. Equivalent communities and organic multicultures were to be found in many other parts of Britain. Similar forms of close living and shared experience existed in many urban inner-city areas with significant multi-ethnic populations. Liverpool's Toxteth, Cardiff's Butetown and Bristol's St Paul's were perhaps the most notable examples of long-standing, mixed communities, all of which had existed for several generations. In looking at the different contexts in which black-white youth interactions occurred in Birmingham, the inner-city environment was one of two broad settings in which those interactions were enacted. Each context had a distinctive social geography and was characterised by specific patterns of leisure space, schooling and housing that shaped those interactions. The other setting was comprised of predominantly white working-class suburbs in the outer-ring of Birmingham. These areas included Northfield, Rubery, Kings Norton, Longbridge and Bartley Green, amongst others. The social geography of these areas, with their large post-war housing estates, contrasted markedly with that of the inner city. The black population in these areas was far smaller and more dispersed. Many Afro-Caribbean families were council tenants who had been moved to the suburbs during Birmingham council's inner-city slum clearance and rehousing programmes in the late 1960s and early 70s. These areas where referred to generically as "country" in black British patois vernacular. The term "country" was a specifically Jamaican taxonomy that referred to rural areas, but had been adapted in local vernacular speech to refer to the suburbs or any town smaller than Birmingham.

Predictably, these outer-ring areas were characterised by much lower levels of black-white interaction, and by more pronounced forms of informal and organised local racism. White youth's experience of Afro-Caribbean culture in the outer ring was accordingly more distanced and diffuse. Most young whites in these areas did not experience the same levels of intimate contact with the black community from an early age, as those in the inner city.

Despite this profile, however, pockets of shared experience and cross-racial contact nevertheless existed in the outer ring. The local council's housing policy of dispersing black families across large areas of the suburbs, while placing those families in a more vulnerable position, also generated specific patterns of black-white interaction and mixed relationships.

Of the sixteen people interviewed in the study, five had grown up in an inner-city environment, while the remainder were from outer-ring, white working-class backgrounds. These resulted in two different routes of introduction into black cultural and community life, and, accordingly, two sets of distinct, but related, life experiences.

Jo-Jo's background was representative of the small, but growing number of young whites who had been brought up in mixed family households in inner-city neighbourhoods, alongside black family friends and "relatives". In Jo-Jo's case, cross-cutting kinship ties had generated an intimate level of familiarity with black community and family life from an early age. Born and raised in Balsall Heath, Jo-Jo had an Irish father and Scottish mother who had settled in Birmingham in the early 1950s. Like many Irish families in the area, they had developed close ties with their black neighbours, sharing the same living spaces, supportive child-care networks and survival strategies. Jo-Jo recounted the experience of being brought up in these kinship networks:

> You see, I was brought up by mainly black people. I was passed around about three different families…'Cos when my mum and dad first came to Birmingham they lived in the same house as this old black woman. And my mum used to look after her, you know, give her lots of things and say "look after the kids". Cos my mum was still young then and she wanted to go out and whatever, and there was always some West Indian granny in the street that would do it. So my mum kind of kept her as a regular person to look after all of us [Jo-Jo was the youngest of seven brothers]. And I was left in this house on Durham Road with this black lady named Granny and she knows everyone of us right down from the oldest . . . I tell you there was five [black] kids I ever played with [names them individually] . . . and we all played together, and like, you know, we used to make mud pies together. And it was like I just grew up with them man. That's the way it was. It was just a natural thing . . . I grew up with everyone in Balsall Heath.

In contrast to Jo-Jo, Jon had spent most of his childhood in West Heath, a white working-class suburb on the outskirts of south Birmingham. For Jon, as for many young whites from outer-ring areas, it was secondary school that provided their first important point of contact with young blacks. School was a key site in which black and white youth first encountered one another outside their immediate neighbourhoods, and an important space where mixed friendships and peer groups were first formed. For Jon, and for others with similar backgrounds, school was a key site in which one-to-one "best-friendships" were initially formed with individual black pupils. Jon recounted how he had struck up a close friendship with one of his black classmates at secondary school, and how football figured prominently as the initial basis of the friendship:

> The only thing the world went round till I was eleven was football, and Clive was the best footballer in our year. So that's why a lot of people liked him and wanted to be his friend. And it just so happened that Clive was black and he came from Balsall Heath, like tougher areas from where I come from and from where most of the other white kids come from.

Shared enthusiasm for football was a common mechanism of friendship formation between black and white male school friends and peers. This was unsurprising given the centrality of football in adolescent boyhood culture generally. The role of street football has long been important as a way in which young male adolescents have learned a distinctive kind of class sociability and masculinity. Respect for young blacks as "good footballers" and admiration for their sporting abilities and masculine qualities was a common basis of attraction and friendship formation in cross-racial male adolescent relationships.

Some young whites developed especially close relationships with their black school friends, relationships which led to intimate involvement with individual black families. These adolescent routes of introduction seemed to progress through a common sequence of events, from "playing together", through "stopping for tea" to "meeting the family". For those with no pre-adolescent contact with the black community, these processes were an important means of initiation into black cultural and family life. For Jon, his black friend Clive became something of a mentor in this regard. Jon recounted how he held Clive in high esteem as an inner-city youth well-versed in black youth culture, and how Clive had introduced him to previously uncharted cultural spaces, such as record shops and youth clubs:

I can still remember the day when I first met him, cos I was really happy that day...and he was kinda different from us, because he came from Balsall Heath, and he was kinda hard [cool] like, and everyone respected him. But he was really influential, like. We used to go all places together like Bournville [youth club] and buying records and that. I used to go to Don Christie's [local reggae record shop] with him all the time ...and that's when I started getting reggae and going to blues.

These kinds of adolescent best friendships could act as important mediators of cultural and musical influences for both white boys and girls, albeit in gender specific forms, as discussed in the next chapter. Through their initiations into black youth culture, and through practices such as listening to music and borrowing records, music forms such as reggae were brought to the attention of young whites in a highly personalised way. It was often through their friendships and peer-group affiliations that most of the respondents were introduced to the leisure spaces where reggae was most salient.

5.3 Club Mix

In Birmingham, reggae was disseminated and available through a network of media and commercial leisure channels, including local radio, live music venues, and both mainstream/high street and independent record shops. In addition, reggae was encountered through a wide range of youth- specific leisure venues in which young black and white people came into contact with one another. It was in these spheres that the mass-marketed forms of black culture and music became enmeshed with, and mediated by social interactions between black and white youth. The specific contexts in which these encounters were enacted were continually shifting, from particular pubs and night clubs, to specific shopping precincts, parks, skating rinks and amusement arcades. However, the most consistently important of these contexts were youth clubs, discos, live-music venues and those leisure spaces situated within the black community, including blues parties and sound-system dances.

Non-commercial leisure provision for young people in Birmingham's voluntary sector encompassed a range of different institutions. Youth clubs, for example, varied tremendously in their cultural composition, from the exclusively white youth clubs of the suburbs to inner-city clubs where the clientele was predominantly black. Some of these latter institutions catered specifically for the Afro-Caribbean community and were often attached to local community centres and voluntary organisations.

A more integrated milieu was to be found in the youth clubs of south-central Birmingham in areas such as Highgate, Balsall Heath and Sparkbrook. The clienteles of these clubs were comprised of Afro-Caribbean, Asian, white and mixed-race youth, their composition reflecting the relatively fluid intermixing between young people found in local schools and the surrounding neighbourhoods. Their multicultural character mirrored the extent to which an organic youth culture had evolved in these areas, one composed of diverse elements and influences under the hegemony of Afro-Caribbean forms.

A handful of mixed youth clubs also existed temporarily in the suburbs of south Birmingham in the late 1970s. These clubs, held in church halls and local schools in areas such as Rubery, Northfield and King's Norton, were well known at the time for their relatively unsegregated character. One such club in particular, in the Bournville area of south Birmingham, acquired considerable notoriety during the late 70s, both as a site of interaction between black and white youth, and as a source of conflict with local racists. Its history was fairly typical of other multiracial youth clubs in the Birmingham suburbs.

The club began as a heavy rock and pop disco frequented mainly by local white youth. The relative abundance of youth clubs in the white working-class suburbs of Birmingham contrasted with a lack of equivalent leisure provision for black youth in inner-city areas. This situation encouraged young blacks to look further afield for leisure venues that could accommodate their musical tastes. A similar situation had existed in London during the late 1960s and early 1970s (see chapter 2). Groups of young blacks in search of such venues accordingly began to frequent youth clubs in the outer-ring, transforming them in the process from pop/rock into soul/reggae discos. Lisa, a local-white girl who frequented the Bournville club in her early teens, described how this process came about:

When I first went to Bournville it was all white people and heavy rock. There was only a few black people at the very back in the corners but then it just changed completely. Cos all of a sudden, Bournville became the place to go for a whole set of youth from up town. And from when one posse moved in, all the others began to infiltrate the place. And obviously they didn't want to listen to heavy metal all night, so they brought their own records down with them . . . And so what happened was the black people gradually worked their way down to the middle, with all the rockers at the front and the rest were just neutral, normal, people. And then it worked its way to an absolute majority of black people, and white people that wanted to mix with them. Cos a lot of the heavy rockers just run when they saw loads of black people coming in.

Other youth clubs and discos in Birmingham underwent a similar process of cultural reshuffling described here by Lisa. The ratio of black to white, and male to female, differed from venue to venue. In some youth clubs young white men and women attended in roughly equal numbers, while in others the clientele was composed largely of black boys and white girls. It was clear from talking to those who frequented such clubs that they were important courtship settings in which mixed dating patterns were initiated and played out. Pat, another white girl who had regularly attended a similar youth club in Northfield described this process:

See, what happened, is we all used to go to the same youth clubs when we were school kids, and we all used to mix together. And then people from different areas started going to them clubs, 'cos they was the only clubs on in the week . . . It was like all the guys from up town just discovered there was life up *country* [the suburbs] and girls too. So they used to come down. And that's how everyone got to mix together, sort of, this one's going out with this one, and that one's going out with that one.

For those from white working-class areas these local youth clubs and discos were important sites of interaction with young blacks, in which many were first exposed to black youth culture, music and

126

style. Cross-racial courtship and dating relationships were a central element of this process. While black male/white female mixed relationships were still the dominant pattern in many areas, the race and gender balance of mixed dating showed signs of shifting during the research period towards a notable increase in the numbers of white male/black female relationships. It was noteworthy that seven out of the ten young men interviewed had black girlfriends, either currently or in the past. The crucial role played by dating patterns was apparent right across the leisure sphere where courting relations and sexual encounters between young blacks and whites were played out.

Having outgrown the youth-club scene, many subsequently graduated to commercial forms of leisure provision in the form of city-centre night-clubs and discos. Reggae had always survived in a small number of leisure spaces that had been carved out of Birmingham's city-centre night-club scene. Black music clubs, however, had always sat uneasily within the city's commercial entertainment network. Such clubs had something of a chequered history, continually undermined by local licensing laws, police harassment and underworld manoeuvrings. In the early 1980s black youth continued to face exclusion and discrimination from those venues which operated racist door policies and quota systems and which enforced dress restrictions aimed specifically at barring Rastas. Despite these racially segregated patterns of leisure space, however, the city's night-club circuit had intermittently played host to a handful of integrated venues. One of the most well-known and long-running was the *Rainbow Club* which played reggae and soul to mixed audiences of black and white young men and women for a number of years. In addition, some clubs adopted a policy of opening their doors to reggae on certain nights of the week. Most of Birmingham's mainstream discos had, at some point, held "reggae" or "soul" nights. Whether in the form of particular pubs, wine bars or discos, such venues had always managed to survive in some part of the city's entertainment network, their locations, like their musical and stylistic inflexions, continually shifting and evolving.

For some young whites, the youth club and disco scenes served as stepping-stones to music and leisure institutions that were situated within the black community. For those who had built up friendships with young blacks in the contexts of school, neighbourhood and youth club, this was seen as a natural progression. The accessibility

127

of the black community's music and leisure spaces to white participation varied considerably, however, by neighbourhood. Blues parties, night-clubs and sound-system dances in some areas were effectively closed to all but a handful of local white residents, while in other areas, such as Balsall Heath, it was not unusual to find whites regularly inhabiting such spaces in significant numbers. For those brought up in such areas, these institutions were invariably encountered at a relatively young age through the neighbourhood, kinship and friendship networks described above. However, whites from adjacent areas, including the suburbs, were increasingly also to be found in these spaces.

In the suburbs of south Birmingham, sound systems could be found playing regularly at church halls, pubs and house parties. While catering primarily for the small black population in these areas, such events also attracted considerable numbers of local whites. The music at these events was increasingly provided by a growing number of local sound systems based in the suburbs.

Originally, most of these local sounds were small "hi-fi" sets run by older blacks living and working locally and playing at private house parties and family celebrations. Neighbouring whites of all ages were often to be found in these spaces. A number of the respondents had gained their first experience of the black community's leisure activities by being invited, through their black friends, to events such as these. With the consolidation of the black community in the outer ring, many of these "big people" sounds began to be challenged by larger, more powerful youth sound systems, such as *Scientist* (see photos 5-8). By the mid 1980s, the scale of white involvement and participation in this local youth-oriented sound system culture had expanded to such a degree that it was not unusual to find white participants comprising over half of the audience at some events. In addition to playing in private dwellings, sound systems were also to be found playing in traditionally white working-class pubs in outer-ring areas on specific nights of the week. Here, an often extraordinary mix of black and white patrons could be found, with sound systems entertaining regular white interlopers in the local reggae culture, as well as older, white working-class drinking fraternities and other local white peer-groups. The social geography of the outer ring lent these suburban sound system sessions and "country" blues parties a distinctive cultural character. Building on the mixed friendship patterns that already existed in the outer-ring, many of these spaces had evolved into unique suburban, multicultural spaces.

The noticeable increase in levels of white participation in these local black musical and leisure spaces was precipitated partly by changes in black British musical culture in the early 1980s. The growing convergence of soul and reggae cultures served to bring about a unique crossover of musical and cultural influences between black and white youth. While that convergence broke down some of the barriers between soul and reggae factions amongst black youth, it also opened up new routes into reggae culture for white youth. Young white affiliates of soul, funk and hip-hop began to encounter reggae through their black peers, and by frequenting the increasing number of leisure spaces where both soul and reggae were played. The growing popularity of new forms of British reggae, such as fast-style DJing, also became visible, not only on the dance floor, but in the increased white patronage of reggae record shops in the city centre.

Running alongside this local sound system culture was Birmingham's live music scene which had also long been an important channel for white youth engagement with reggae. Live music-making was both a key medium through which reggae was encountered and experienced by white audiences, as well as a space in which musicians themselves from different musical cultures intermixed and exchanged traditions. Local reggae bands played to mixed audiences on the circuit of pub and club venues in Birmingham where both live rock and black music were regularly featured together. In areas like Moseley and Balsall Heath the rock and reggae communities had traditionally been closely connected, with a casual basis of exchange having long existed between black and white musicians. Many of these connections were given concrete political expression in the local RAR movement, which frequently played host to punk and reggae bands on the same bill, and helped expose reggae to a generation of young whites.

The proximity of black and white communities, and the networks of shared social and leisure space characteristic of these areas were particularly conducive to the formation of multiracial reggae and rock bands. In the pubs of Balsall Heath and Moseley, black and white musicians of all ages and backgrounds could be heard jamming together on a regular basis. Something of a similar integrated music scene also existed in Coventry around the city's pubs and working-men's clubs. Most of the multiracial groups that emerged from the West Midlands in the late 1970s, and went on to form the core of the Two-tone movement, emerged from these settings. UB40, for example, came together in the Moseley/Balsall-Heath area of Birmingham as neighbours and former school friends who were unemployed. Countless other, if less successful, mixed reggae and rock bands were formed in similar ways out of their respective members' shared experiences and common enthusiasms for Jamaican music.

The cross-racial appeal of Two-tone music locally was reflected in the often highly eclectic, mixed audiences that some of the bands attracted to their live gigs. Birmingham gigs by Two-tone bands like The Beat, for example, drew a wide cross-section of youth, including young Asians, Rastas, black "beat girls" and young white rudies. The West Midlands as a whole was the centre of a vibrant subculture that grew up around Two-tone music. At the height of the movement's popularity, Birmingham's Top Rank night-club staged regular mod and rude-boy revival discos which attracted a large, young multiracial clientele. The Two-tone movement and the live reggae music scene in Birmingham generally, played a key role in popularising the music to a wider mainstream audience. For many young white affiliates of Jamaican music, their interest in Two-tone, and in other, more popular exponents of reggae, such as UB40 and Bob Marley, were important routes of initiation into the wider culture of which it was a part.

6 Black Culture—White Youth

In the early 1980s, across large parts of inner-city and outer-ring Birmingham it was evident that a multi-ethnic youth culture was evolving in which many of the dominant components were Afro-Caribbean in origin. In some areas, the extent of this process was such that the culture and politics of young people exhibited a seamless and organic fusion of black and white sensibilities. Black youth culture appeared to exert a gravitational pull on significant numbers of young white people, including those living in areas with a small black population. But what was it that attracted these young whites to the expressive culture of their black peers, its style, music, language and political philosophies? What was the basis of their affiliation to reggae and their adoption of black speech patterns? Having looked at some of the key contexts in black-white youth interaction occurred, in this chapter I want to look more closely at some of the individual responses that resulted from these encounters.

6.1 Style and Patois

In Birmingham, as in most major urban areas with significant black communities, the influence of sartorial styles derived from black youth culture was widespread and detectable amongst suburban young whites who had little or no contact with young blacks. These styles of dress and appearance had acquired such a common currency amongst the young generally that it was often difficult to determine their precise origins, let alone their symbolic meanings. While the selective adoption of hairstyles and clothing items associated with black youth culture was commonplace, these appropriations were continually changing in response to the ever-turning cycles of youth fashion. Thus, by the mid-1980s, the styles associated with reggae culture and Rastafari had become outmoded, and were being subsumed by styles associated with soul and hip-hop culture. The dominant aesthetic in these emerging styles was a predilection for casual "designer" clothes and sportswear, including trainers, baseball caps and sports anoraks, and black American hairstyles such as the *jheri-curl* and *flat-top*.

The enormous diversity of stylistic influences exhibited by white youth in Birmingham, and the many different levels of appropriation of black style, made any general reading of their symbolic significance difficult. Within specific contexts of black-white interaction, however, the resonance of these stylistic influences became visible and significant. It tended to be amongst those who had large numbers of black friends, and close affiliations to black youth culture, that the cultural and political meanings of "style" could be observed.

Most of the interviewees admitted to having passed through a "phase" of overt affectation of black styles of dress and appearance in their earlier youth. Some told of how such styles had "rubbed off" on them during the course of their everyday interaction with their black friends. Maureen, for example, explained that she and her white friend Lisa had unconsciously "picked up" certain dress and hair styles in their early teens as a consequence of "going round" with their black peers:

> We did go through a stage when we dressed like them, but not because we wanted it to be known that we went out with black people. We had our hair crimped, but that was only because you liked crimped hair, it wasn't because other people done it. We used to wear all the clothes like red pleated skirts, Jesus boots [sandals] and leather coats and all that. But that was only because we was going around with the people and picked up certain fashions.

Ian also admitted that he had consciously adopted straight trousers, in preference to baggy ones, after observing the sartorial styles of black boys at a local youth club:

> I remember when I first went to Bournville, baggy trousers was the in-thing and I'd wear my best pair of baggy trousers, but I remember like, all of a sudden, I narrowed up my trousers. That was a direct influence and I'll admit that. Cos you'll find that the baggy trousers was largely a white fashion thing and the narrow trousers comes from the sixties rude boy era, and the black kids was still going on with it. But I never thought about it much at the time. I just wore

these narrow cords because I liked them and because my friends was wearing them.

For those, like Ian, with large numbers of black friends, adopting a particular style of dress was a visible way of expressing an affiliation to their peers. As Ian told me: "It just made me feel more part of what they were dealing with". For others, experimentation with styles of dress and appearance was taken a stage further into an attempt to reproduce a complete roots-style look modelled on Rasta aesthetics. In Shorty's case, he saw this as part of an adolescent stage of identification which included the adoption of black clothing styles and Rasta colours, as well as patois speech patterns, standing postures and walking styles:

> I'd be more into the styles and fashions in them times, around 13,14...like the way I used to talk and dress...like Gabbicci tops [a popular make of cardigan amongst young blacks] and cut trousers, and the way you walked, it all played a big part, cos like four years ago I'd say most of the black guys who were Rastas were really bouncing. And a lot of people, especially white people, identified you as a Rasta if you wore a hat and bounced up and down, that was as good as being a Rasta.

For some, the attempt to emulate a carbon-copy dread style was motivated by a strong attraction to locks. Pete, for example, candidly admitted that he had passed through a phase of wanting to be like the Rastas he saw in his neighbourhood and at his local school:

> I loved 'em when I first saw 'em...cos I used to see them at school and round by where I lived. I used to just look and think "yeah man, its hard", I just wanted to be like them. I thought it was brilliant. I used to think they looked hard when they walked down the road with their heads in the air, with their big hats on.

The feeling of wanting to be "different" from their white peers was a common motivation for these youthful white appropriations of black style. Pete had gone to the lengths of growing his hair, and using Vaseline to make it entwine into "locks". I was told of other white youth who had also put Vaseline or wax in their hair to speed up the relatively slow process of locksing straight hair. When I asked Pete why he had decided to grow his hair, he offered the following candid explanation:

> I don't know ... It just come... it just grew... it was like to be different . . . when I was that age I thought I'd love to have been a black man . . . I've changed my mind now though . . . But if I was black now, I'd have big long locks all down here [points to his waist] . . . I'd look the part then wouldn't I?

Bizarre as Pete's admission might appear, his wanting to "be black" was, in one sense, merely a logical extension of his wanting to be like his black peers. While Pete's experience represented a particularly intense form of white adolescent identification, it was just one moment in an evolving process of affiliation with black culture. Similar overt appropriations of black dress and hairstyles were not uncommon amongst young whites with large numbers of black friends. Reflecting on these appropriations some saw them as part of a "naïve" adolescent phase of affiliation and a product of growing up with black friends who were themselves going through a particular stage of their youth. White adolescent participation in black youth culture, in this sense, involved a measure of complicity and encouragement from black friends. Colin, for example, admitted that this tacit approval had encouraged him in his early teens to continue emulating his black peers: "I carried on doing it..." he pointed out "..cos none of my black friends seemed to mind, and like, most of them supported me."

"Style" was only one dimension of youthful white engagement with black youth culture, however, and arguably not the most significant. A more telling and concrete register of that engagement was the adoption of patois speech patterns. Roger Hewitt, in his formative study of the linguistic dimensions of black/white interaction and interracial adolescent friendships found that the acquisition of patois or *creole* by some young whites occurred almost involuntarily in school and street contexts (Hewitt, 1986). By their mid-teens, patois was being used unselfconsciously by those young whites with a high proportion of black friends as part of their normal conversations and peer-group banter with their black peers. Hewitt found that the levels of creole use amongst young whites varied from the use of selected words and phrases to full-blooded fluent usage. The forms and contexts of such usage followed familiar Afro-Caribbean patterns. Patois was thus used as a means of conveying specific tones and emotions (such as sarcasm, joy, anger, irony, humour and drama). It was also used in association with expressions of prestige and personal excellence, in reference to the opposite sex and, most commonly, as a form of abuse.

Hewitt suggested that under certain conditions creole was employed as an interactive strategy between young blacks and whites. Its use could assist in processing the political and ideological discontinuities between black and white within small pockets of interracial friendship. In some contexts, white creole usage could also be instrumental in shaping such friendships, and in mediating black-white relationships across a wide range of social contexts. Such use, however, did not automatically signal friendship. It was required to rest on close, pre-established ties if it was not to result in condemnation from young blacks. Indeed, imitation and insensitive or jocular use of creole could potentially be read as a way of conveying or displacing racist attitudes towards black youth, as much as a means of identifying with them.

All the young whites interviewed displayed varying degrees of creole influence in their speech. All, equally, admitted to having passed through a phase of regular patois usage in their early and mid-teens. Most described their acquisition of patois in terms of having simply "picked it up" from black friends through the course of everyday conversational exchanges. Patois was adopted as a way of identifying with their friends, as much a bid for inclusion and acceptance by them as an expression of affiliation to black culture in general. Paul, for example, regarded his ability to use patois as an essential and normal part of communicating with his black peers:

> I feel sometimes that when I'm talking patois to some people I'm being understood better. If I talked to them, say, like "urr, know what I mean like" [affects a drawling Birmingham accent] they might think "Oh God, what's this guy". So sometimes you gotta meet them on the level and chat the way they chat, like.

While many regarded their experimentation with black speech patterns as being part of an earlier, adolescent phase, it was clear from informal discussions with the respondents that patois continued to influence their everyday speech. Although its full use was reserved for specific contexts such as those outlined above, patois phrases and words cropped up time and time again in conversations both with myself and with others. As Maureen admitted: "To tell you the truth I still use bits of slang like "slack" and "extra", like words that you come out with because you're so used to hearing them around you all the time."

Others similarly confessed to occasionally "lapsing into" patois and had clearly incorporated Rasta terms like "seen" and "dread" into their everyday vocabulary. Indeed, words like "man", "whole heap", "hard" and "wicked", together with terms of ridicule like "shame" and swear words such as "raas" had acquired a general usage amongst young whites throughout Birmingham as a whole. Fashionable catchphrases amongst young blacks were continually being picked up by young whites. Reggae records were key sources of such terms and expressions. Phrases used by certain reggae DJs had found their way into the speech of many white youth, while the styles popularised by more mainstream artists like Musical Youth were often to be heard being employed by pre-teen young whites.

Many creole lexical items and grammatical features had crept unconsciously into the everyday speech of white youth, forming part of a generalised local vernacular spoken by all young people. On any weekday afternoon these items could be heard being openly used by white youth in their daily interaction both with each other and with young blacks, whether on buses or in the street, on their way home from school.

While patois functioned as a cultural mediator of black-white interaction, it was also used by young whites in contexts from which blacks were largely absent. With its high cultural prestige, patois could be employed in all-white company for display purposes or as a mark of difference from other white peers. Shorty admitted to occasionally using patois in this way:

> Sometimes I might go to a pub and there's no black guys there and they might say "what do you think of that" and I'll go "yeah, seen, seen!"...or on the bus, when it's really full and I'll be having this conversation with Flux [black friend] and we'll be sitting at the back just DJing for ages and having a laugh.

The association of patois with conflict and assertiveness made it particularly amenable to use in oppositional modes by young whites. Nowhere was this more apparent than in the school context where white usage often paralleled that of young blacks. As a vehicle of resistance and an emblem of cultural difference, patois could be used to exclude and confound teachers. Shorty, for example, recounted an incident at his secondary school where he was allegedly expelled for "answering back" to one of his teachers:

> It was a history O-level class, and there weren't any black kids in that class and this teacher, right, I kept arguing with him all the time in patois. I started swearing and cussing him down and he couldn't understand it like, and he'd be really mad, he'd say, like, "stop mumbling, stop that mumbo jumbo".

Jo-Jo told of a similar school incident in which he had used a particularly crude form of patois abuse to defy his teacher in the classroom:

> I used to walk into school every day in flash clothes, long leather [coat], brand new shirt and a gold chain. I was twelve years old, man. I was walking into school with a quarter of weed in my pocket and I'd just be sitting there and the teacher'd go "blah, blah, blah" and I'd say "I'm not fucking doing that" you know what I mean…"You do your work!" [shouts] and I'd go "fuck off" [mumbles belligerently]. So he comes up and he says "Get your face in the corner." I says "Who do you think you're speaking to?" He says "You hear me *now*!" [shouts louder]. I says "go and get fucked man!" An old saying I used to use was "Go fuck pussy and breed a dog!", an old patois saying, one of the wickedest things you could say…so I said that to him, and he slapped me right across the face, man! So from then on I was marked….bad!

Both these examples vividly demonstrate how language was often one of the most graphic means of registering opposition to schooling and teacher authority. But patois could be deployed in a similar manner in any number of contexts to challenge adult authority

137

figures in general. The sense of pride in both Shorty's and Jo-Jo's ability to confound their respective teachers suggests something about the oppositional resonance of black cultural forms for some young whites. This oppositional borrowing was a common feature of white appropriation which extended beyond the school context. For many young whites, black speech and style became vehicles through which to express their own experience of domination.

The two cases above also suggest how these appropriations could involve the adoption of a surrogate "black" persona which could be used to bolster individuality and prestige in relationships with other white peers. Such identities, as we saw earlier, could draw upon a range of linguistic and stylistic elements. These appropriations, however, were gender-specific and corresponded to the gendered differentiations within black youth culture itself. Thus in the case of some of the young male respondents, their use of black aesthetics tended to be underscored by a specifically masculine attraction to black style as "cool". In this sense, Colin confided that he would "dress the way he dressed" because it made him feel confident: "It was like being a stepping razor, you know, you feel dangerous, like the way you feel when you're going out and you're dressed criss [smart]."

In some cases, however, this appropriation of black male style could slip into a more openly masculinist and oppressive form of self-projection in relations with young women. Black style was valued, in this sense, not for its aggressive "hardness", in a white working-class sense, but rather as a way of approaching and "handling" women, socially, that reflected the importance placed on individual skills with the opposite sex in black male adolescent cultures. Shorty, for example, admitted to adopting black style and speech patterns in his mid-teens specifically for the purpose of attracting girls:

> I might have had about four or five girlfriends at one time when I was about fifteen, sixteen, you know, I just kinda hit it off with all the girls, with the talks and things...the way I used to talk and the styles and that, and perhaps the girls used to like it, but like, now I don't really go on with things like that no more. I'm more humble in a sense.

138

These perceived models of masculinity provided by black boys were strong points of attraction for some young white men. This was confirmed by Jon who admitted that some white boys were attracted to what they perceived as black boy's "freewheeling" attitude to relationships with girls. Jon, however, felt that such appropriations were shaped more by the general power relations of gender than by any specific cultural elements:

> The whole business of moving with more than one woman, that rubs off on everybody . . . like, relating to it through a sort of cool style which says, like it's OK to deal with more than one woman . . . But that's something that some white guys do anyway.

While the impact of black style on young white men could be employed to bolster their masculinity, the evidence suggested that, amongst young white women, black female styles could be appropriated, conversely, to project a confident femininity and to resist gender subordination. This was again particularly apparent in the school context, where mixed female peer groups, pitched against male adolescent culture, could form along gender lines, temporarily undercutting racial divisions between black and white girls. There was a suggestion also that white girls were drawing on aspects of black femininity to defy school rules and undermine dominant conceptions of feminine passivity. This was achieved through a whole range of strategies that included the courting of deviant and exaggerated images of femininity, the use of patois speech patterns and various forms of vocal and "unfeminine" behaviour stereotypically assigned to young black women.

For some young white women, black feminine culture could also provide more "adult" models of womanhood. Elements of this culture could be appropriated to resist gender-stereotyping within the school system. This could take the form of a semantic "guerrilla warfare" against school dress regulations, involving the use of make-up, or the flagrant ignoring or subtle reappropriation of school uniforms. These same strategies and uses of black feminine culture and style could also be deployed outside the school context in public spaces. Here, black feminine styles, particularly the "chic" styles of dress favoured by many young black women in the mid 1980s, could be adopted by young white women to boost their self-confidence and sense of dignity in relations with boys.

6.2 Sweet Reggae Music Playing,

Reggae music had a central cultural significance for all of the young white people interviewed. It was through music and reggae in particular, that the political culture of Afro-Caribbean youth exerted its greatest influence. But this did not occur solely through the music's lyrical discourses, important though these were to the music's overall symbolic significance. Reggae's impact and power was felt, at least initially, through its sonic structures, rhythms and textures. The importance of rhythm, bass, and non-verbal sounds to reggae's meaning and affective power was borne out by the interview responses. As initial points of attraction, and sources of pleasure, the lyrics of reggae songs were often secondary to the music's non-verbal sounds and sensibilities.

For most of the respondents it was these elements, and its bass in particular, which initially engaged them. It was by these features, moreover, that reggae was distinguished from other forms of popular music. Reggae's appeal was not solely dependent on the literal meanings of its lyrics, but on the capacity of its vocal and instrumental sounds to hold their own specific meanings and pleasures.

This relative unimportance of lyrics, as an initial basis of attraction to reggae, was clearly apparent in discussions with the respondents about the music's appeal. Jon, for example, on first hearing reggae at a local youth club disco, confessed that the lyrics had no particular relevance or meaning for him:

> When I first went along to Bournville I didn't really think about the lyrics or the artist. I just took it for what record I liked on the night and what I didn't . . . It took me ages to find out what certain records meant.

Paul suggested that it was the "reggae beat" that was the main point of attraction for younger listeners:

> I see why some of the youngsters like it when they hear it, when they're about 14, 15, especially if they've got black

friends in them ages. They hear the constant beat of the music . . . it gives you an uplifting feeling, it makes you feel on a natural high.

For some young white people, as Paul suggests, reggae's appeal was intimately bound up with both the pleasures and the frustrations of adolescence. It was not only that the music articulated feelings of boredom and powerlessness associated with youth and adolescence, but also that it provided a physical grounding and sense of self-identity through which to combat and survive those feelings.

Responses to questions about why reggae was so appealing suggested that the music was able to evoke certain emotions within its young white listeners which transcended specific verbal meanings. Reggae, first and foremost, produced feelings and sensibilities. Its power lay in its capacity to capture particular moods or sentiments through a combination of both verbal and non-verbal sounds. As Paul observed "sometimes when I want to express something I can say to a person "listen to this record, that's the way I'm feeling". In a similar manner, others appraised particular records as "saying something" purely on the basis of an expressive dub, a powerful bassline, or an evocative horn section. Particular "rhythms" were also enthusiastically endorsed for their communicative potential in terms similar to those used by young blacks.

For many of those interviewed, the syncopations and textures of reggae's drums and bass patterns had a capacity to produce certain kinds of sensual pleasure not tapped by other forms of popular music. Jon saw reggae's unique musical and rhythmic properties as being the direct antithesis of white rock music:

> The thing about reggae is that it's easier on your ears. 'Cos the one thing that bugged me about heavy rock, was that it was just a lot of noise . . . just high frequency sounds, which gets to your ears a lot faster, whereas reggae's more bass-oriented. You can listen to it all night 'cos it's less aggravating.

Reggae's power rested on its ability to act on both mind and body simultaneously, and its capacity to literally *move* the body, both physically and emotionally.

Of all the music's characteristic features, it was the physical power and prominence of reggae's bass which seemed to hold the greatest attraction. While for some, the bass captured the eroticism and overwhelming sensuality of reggae, others felt that it epitomised the music's "rebel" sensibilities. This dimension of reggae's appeal was further specified by Pete who confessed that the it was "the music" that was initially more important than "the singing". When I asked him to clarify what he meant by "the music", he was unequivocal in his response: "It's the bass, man! The bass!...It gets you in the gut, like. Most times I don't listen to the singing. The singing's, like, going on and that, but I listen to the bass."

Reggae was felt by some to communicate something subliminal in its down-to-earth rhythms. Ruth, for example, described the bassline of one of her favourite records as "subterranean" while Jane heard echoes of the body's own pulses in reggae's rhythms:

> Its heart music . . . music of the heart, it just gets you right there [lays her hand on her chest] . . . Reggae's like a heartbeat; it's the same kind of rhythm. There's something very crucial about rhythm and I'm not sure what it is.

It was in the "live" context of consumption that reggae's drum and bass rhythms, and the sensual feel of the music were at their most powerful. Through its characteristic modes of transmission, via the technical hardware of the sound system, reggae was materialised at the site of the body, to be felt, as much as heard. The experienced pleasures of its affective power were enhanced in the dance or blues party where the bass provided an immediate material relation to the music. As Ruth graphically described:

> At first, right, when I went to the blues, all I could hear was the bass, I couldn't hear the words . . . I just loved the music, and the dub plates, and the whole feel behind them. I just used to listen to it, right going "tss, tss, tss, tss" [imitates the sound of the tweeters] and "durr, durr, durr, durr" [imitates the bass] and I thought how do they make it sound like that? Have they got mixers on it or what?

In these contexts, the pleasures of reggae music were closely bound up with dancing. Through dance, such pleasures were realised in the movement of bodies. It was here that the sense of self-emancipation articulated in reggae, through its celebration and freeing of the body became most apparent. These qualities were uppermost in genres such as Lovers Rock where the music's direct courting of sensuality generated a heightened sense of self and body. The close couples-style dancing that accompanied the music was particularly popular amongst the young women that were interviewed. Some like Maureen proclaimed "we just dance like that anyway...it's our way of life"

Most of those interviewed admitted to having experimented with reggae dancing styles. The more enthusiastic affiliates incorporated the styles they had picked up from their black peers into their own repertoires of cultural expression. Jon, for example, reminisced about his initial enthusiasm for "skanking" and "steppers", both popular dance forms amongst young blacks in the 1970s. He described how he had begun experimenting with these styles himself, after witnessing them at a local youth club:

> That used to amaze me, right, 'cos a lot of the youth were just starting to knot up [grow locks] and they used to get in this circle right and you'd hear a whole heap of noise coming from this circle, so you'd just bustle up and see two guys in the middle challenging each other with some wicked form of skanking, right. And that fascinated me, and ever since then I've loved skanking. I picked up on it real fast and I'd practise the moves at home while I'm listening to my records. And we'd all sort of mess around, me, my sister and my cousin. And they'd show me the dances they were learning.

While some were attracted to the more popular and fashionable reggae dance moves, for others, the music's appeal lay in its simplicity as dance music, a simplicity which Shorty contrasted with the specific steps and movements required in other forms of music:

> With reggae it's just the beat, the beat and the dancing that I'm accustomed to. Reggae's just perfect dance music. Like with reggae you can just do anything...you just move. Whereas to Funk you have to do this, and to New Romantic

you have to do that. But with reggae, you know, you can get away with, like, just nodding your head.

For those who maintained their allegiance to reggae into adulthood, the music, in this way, came to stand for a sense of cultural stability amidst the ebb and flow of youth cultural styles. Reggae was seen as having an integrity and lack of pretentiousness that was counterposed to the transitory and superficial fashions of mainstream pop culture. This was evident in Ian's strong enthusiasm for sound-system culture, and the entertainment principles on which it was founded. Ian felt that the "dead atmosphere" of some city-centre night-clubs was no match for the drama, spontaneity and excitement of a sound-system dance. He contrasted sound system culture's participatory and democratic structures with the regulated and depersonalised forms of leisure represented by mainstream commercial discos:

> They're a ten till two, start-stop entertainment. You go there and they say "You can't start until you're through the door and then you have to stop when you come out". It's like a factory-run entertainment. But with a blues or a sound, there's something there. You're not churned in and out, 'cos the people who's running the entertainment are in the same position as the people coming through the door. You go to Faces [one of Birmingham's elite night-clubs] they couldn't give a shit. As long as they can clock up three, four hundred people a night, they couldn't give a shit. They'd kick everyone of 'em in the face if they had the chance! . . . They're not concerned with people! It's just a business, and all they wanna do is just suck you dry with the bar there.

Ian's enthusiasm for sound system culture was echoed by other respondents. Both Pat and Anne also contrasted the leisure institutions of the black community with "mainstream" and "official" forms of youth leisure provision.

> The blues was hard cos it was different from a disco, you could do what you wanted and it was all night, something what young people want instead of shut at 12.00 or 1.00. (Pat)

144

Being English people, and living in Northfield, it was just boring to me. I used to go to discos up Shenley, but it was just boring. They played a bit of reggae and I liked it. But the blues was so different, it was just brilliant, the music had so much more feel to it. (Anne)

For those like Anne, it was precisely because the black community's leisure practices and institutions were perceived as "different" to "normal" white English leisure activities, that they were so profoundly attractive. The strength of that attraction was such that some respondents felt a powerful sense of belonging to reggae music and its traditions. It was the sound system that most powerfully symbolised and embodied those traditions. Through it, reggae's unique practices and conventions articulated a collective spirit and sense of community that was able to draw in and include some young whites.

All of the interviewees felt there was more to reggae than other forms of popular music. As Pat explained: "Each record tells a story about things that have gone on, like". Jane, similarly, found in reggae songs, a source of both personal and collective spiritual nourishment:

It's telling people something through music, through something that most people like and enjoy. It gives you a lot of wisdom. Cos in your heart, you know you feel that way, and when you listen to it, you know that other people are thinking on them same kinda ways, and it kind of gives you more strength.

Reggae was felt to be most powerful when it worked through the pleasures of consumption to suggest values, sensibilities and perspectives on life. Its ability to chronicle the feelings and life experiences of these young whites, to "tell stories" and impart wisdom, was particularly evident in their identification with the music of Bob Marley.

For many young white reggae affiliates in the study, as in Birmingham generally, Marley was the music's chief ambassador, more responsible than any other single artist for generating a wider interest in Jamaican popular culture. While not all those interviewed saw Marley's music as being important in their initial attraction to reggae, most considered him to be a figure of immense importance.

145

The effects of Marley's projection as a "reggae superstar" by the entertainment industry were clearly visible in the symbolic status accorded him by many of the respondents. This echoed Marley's position as a "hero figure" in the popular consciousness of white youth, and showed how the mass-marketed iconography around Bob Marley had become meaningful in the most intimate spheres of their domestic and personal lives. In some cases Marley was viewed as a figure of mythic proportions, particularly after his death. As Jumbo declared:

> That man was dread, 'cos it's just the truth he's talking and he's showing you facts as well. I check him as a prophet. It's like he had to die 'cos in a way he came for that purpose to show that Rasta is worldwide.

Some, like Michael, expressed a close, almost mystical affinity with Marley: "Any time I want to see Bob Marley I just close my eyes and I can see him there in the flesh, singing any song I want him to".

A number of the respondents had acquired a considerable knowledge of Marley's lyrics. That knowledge was gleaned from the close scrutiny of lyrics printed on album covers and from hours of careful listening. The degree of familiarity with his music shown by some was a clear demonstration that his songs, while developing primarily from a Jamaican working-class black experience, were also open to other interpretations and readings. For, time and time again, Marley was held up as a purveyor of universal and non-race-specific messages who "spoke for everybody".

The themes and metaphors employed in much of Marley's music carried a certain looseness of meaning which permitted universal and class-based readings to be extracted from them. The terms of address used in such songs, through the subject positions of "I", "we", "they" and "you", gave Marley's songs a double-voiced quality that made them relevant to different contexts and identities. Through these terms, the calculated ambiguities of songs about Jamaican politics and African liberation could be made relevant to young whites in Britain. Many of those interviewed directly applied Marley's song lyrics to their own life-situations. As Paul pointed out: "A lot of white people relate to Bob Marley, and I can see why you know, 'cos a lot of the things he sings about I've been through myself." In a

146

similar way, Colin was able to apply the theme of "sufferation" in Marley's music to his own particular experience of school:

> I could relate very strongly to sufferation and sufferers' music even though I wasn't black . . . you know, "stop pushing me Mr Boss Man", loads of them songs...And the ones about freedom too. Cos I hated school, I felt I was captive by school, and by people in authority.

These kinds of class-based interpretations of Marley's music were made possible by the selective appropriation of key lines and lyrical fragments from particular songs. For example, songs like "Get Up, Stand Up", "Babylon System" and "Them Belly Full (But We Hungry)", or key lines like "brainwash education to make us the fools", or "they don't want to see us unite" were open to class-based and universalist interpretations. The relative ambiguity of their lyrical discourses rendered them capable of holding a range of non-race-specific meanings. If this was true of Bob Marley's music, it was no less true of reggae as a whole. The lyrics of many reggae songs could be inflected with meanings that accorded with different needs and experiences. Part of reggae's appeal lay precisely in the lack of any straightforward singular meanings in its song lyrics, and the susceptibility of those lyrics to selective modes of interpretation. The commonplace discourse of "unity" for example, with its call for black people to unite amongst themselves, or protest against racial inequality, could also be taken to mean "black and white unite". The abundance of anti-racist songs in reggae music could be made meaningful to situations of interaction between black and white youth.

Such songs could provide a common language through which black and white youth were able to share their parallel experiences. Reggae was seen to have the capacity to draw people together and unite them in their feelings. Joanne provided concrete evidence of this, while reminiscing about the youth clubs and parties she had frequented in her earlier youth. She recalled those occasions when black and white would respond enthusiastically to the theme of "unity" expressed in some song lyrics:

> You went along to listen to the music and you thought it had some meaning . . . It'd say something about 'black and white

people must unite' and everyone'd be really chanting it at the top of their voice, really meaning it like.

While the multi-accentuality of many reggae songs enabled different readings to be extracted from them, others were directed more specifically at a black listening audience and appeared less open to such readings. The use of patois sayings, Rasta metaphors and religious symbolisms often made the immediate comprehension of some lyrical discourses difficult for white listeners. Those songs which addressed cultural, historical and political themes around the experience of blackness, moreover, could problematise the listening process. As a way of gauging their responses to such lyrics, I asked the respondents how they felt about songs which dealt with such themes. Some, like Pete, were typically ambivalent in their responses:

> I don't listen to records like that, I just don't bother for them... they sound prejudiced to me... I suppose they're not in a way, some of them, 'cos they're telling you, like, how they suffered and all that . . . But it can still make you feel bad.

Most of those interviewed expressed a strong empathy for reggae songs that dealt with issues of racial oppression, and many had gained knowledge of, and respect for, such issues through their critical engagement with such themes. This much was evident from the responses I received when I asked some of the other interviewees whether they agreed with Pete's view that lyrics aimed specifically at black listeners were "prejudiced against whites":

> Nah man! That's stupid. How can they be prejudiced! They show the history man . . . what's happened, and all the tribulations that black people's been through. Nah man! I like them kinda lyrics. I'm dealing with it on a different level from people that say that. (Colin)

> I can understand what they're saying to a black person. Like if it's a friend of mine, I can see how it might be a solution to a problem that he might be going through. (Jumbo)

148

Looking at it from their eyes I suppose we was really a wicked set of people, to come and steal their land, rape their women, take what we wanted from their country and do what we did. So I don't blame them for looking at everything like that. (Joe)

I like them records. I understand them, 'cos it's from a black man's point of view. It's not a scheme to fight down white people or whatever; it's just something that happened. (Shorty)

The sensitivity to such themes partly depended on bringing wider cultural knowledges to bear on the listening process, knowledges gleaned from personal interactions with black peers, with the black community generally, and its musical and leisure institutions. Personal engagement with reggae, in this sense, could become something of a didactic process, which involved learning about the music's political traditions and about the historical and social conditions which had produced it. It was through the act of consumption itself, through listening critically to the music in specific contexts, be it a blues party, live gig or a more private, domestic space, that such awareness was acquired.

The double-voiced symbols of reggae and the diversity of themes addressed in its lyrics made them meaningful to young whites in different ways. Reggae was relevant not only as a form of "reality" or "rebel" music, but also through its celebration of leisure, sexuality and love. Many of the Rasta-informed discourses which pervaded roots music were available to white youth as accounts of their own lives through themes such as "Truths and Rights", "Police and Thieves", "Hard Time Pressure", "Tribulation", and "Poor and Humble". Notions of "freedom" and "justice", and songs which addressed the pressures and contradictions of everyday life provided young whites with discursive and symbolic resources to interpret their own life-situations and predicaments. Lyrics concerned with issues of unemployment ("No vacancy"), capitalist/state authority ("Bobby Babylon") or the law ("To be poor is a crime") were available as tools of critical analysis to make sense of their own experiences of worklessness or police harassment. Some like Jo-Jo, were attracted to what they felt were the "sound arguments" expressed in many reggae lyrics, and the practical common sense

149

which they dispensed through their metaphors and proverbial sayings:

> I like the common sense of the lyrics, man. They've got a logic to them, on all kinda subjects . . . It's just like simple ideas, simple morals, like "the cow never know the use of its tail, till the butcher cut it off". You know, don't take things for granted, man, don't be greedy.

The level of critical awareness conveyed in such responses suggested particularly intimate forms of involvement with reggae. Such awareness was invariably acquired only after a period of close engagement with the music. What these responses demonstrated, however, was a capacity to identify with reggae music in all its characteristic forms, and to make universal and class-based readings of its discourses, as well as anti-racist and cross-racial readings of black experience. The discovery and recognition of these broader meanings was itself part of a transformation process from adolescent forms of affiliation to more informed, reflective modes of engagement. It was the recognition that there was more to reggae than the pleasures and frustrations of youth, and that its historical and political traditions were not defined specifically by age, that enabled young whites to deepen their affiliation to the music and carry it through into their adulthood.

6.3 Jah no Partial

Given reggae's saturation with the political philosophy of Rastafari, it was perhaps inevitable that some of these young whites should become involved, in some way, with the movement. As a result of their social interactions and relationships with young blacks, and their presence in the black community, all had come into direct contact with Rasta. As Jon explained, Rasta was already a significant presence in the lives of those white youth who had a strong attachment to reggae, large numbers of black friends, and were exposed to the movement through their everyday experience:

> It was gonna click eventually, from being at dances and seeing certain man and man [Rastas]...and from seeing the colours [red, gold and green] on album sleeves and seeing

150

guys at school. It was all there in front of me right from the start, if I wanted to pursue it . . . It's just how long it took me to tune in.

While some young whites' encounters with Rasta were fleeting and relatively superficial, others maintained a more intimate involvement with movement into their late teens and early twenties. For these young white Rasta affiliates, reggae was an important point of departure. Some like Michael claimed Bob Marley as a major source of inspiration: "He has played the most influence in my life, and it's through his music that I came into Rasta." Michael frequently cited key lyrics from Marley's songs to justify the basis of his affiliation to the movement. One of these lines was taken from the song "War", a song based on a speech by Haile Selassie which was a militant commitment to the struggle against racism and colonialism. By highlighting one particular line, Michael used the song to justify his identification with Rastafari as a white person:

> The first time I listened to Bob Marley and the Wailers, I couldn't understand a word of it. The only bit I understood was a part of one song when he said "until the colour of a man's skin is of no more significance than the colour of his eyes, there will be war" and my friend said "look, he's showing you there that anybody can be dread".

This same lyric was quoted by three other respondents, independently of each other. In some cases, the original line was abbreviated to "the colour of a man's skin is of no more significance than the colour of his eyes", or "the colour of a man's skin is of significance to all but a fool". By this semantic reworking, anti-racist lyrics in reggae songs were taken as evidence that anybody, including white people, could be Rastas.

While an elementary knowledge of the core tenets and principles of Rasta philosophy could be gleaned from listening to certain records, or reading books about the movement, it was invariably through interaction with individual black affiliates that a deeper understanding was acquired. Here, white involvement depended critically on the support and tolerance of sympathetic black Rastas. Most pointed to a key friend or mentor who had instructed and encouraged them. Michael, for example, acknowledged his debt to an older black Rasta friend:

> The first dreadlock I ever met was Dexter. He was very influential. He showed me a whole heap of things. That dread, you could just sit in a room with him all day and listen to everything what he's saying. He really knew what he was dealing with . . . Every move he made was perfect, no lie, he strived for perfection. And I looked at that man and I said, that is what I want to be, that is my idea of a Rastaman. The things that he said are still in my mind. I'll never forget them.

Michael's admiration for Dexter suggests the importance of older, black role models in inspiring young whites to become involved in the movement. These relationships were by no means unique to young male affiliates. Some of the young women who had become involved in Rastafari expressed similar desires to follow the examples set by their black female friends. Pat, for example, told of her Rastawoman friend, Juliette, who had been an important guide and confidante to her:

> I got interested in it 'cos she was doing it, and it was like, I looked at Juliette, right, and the way she does things, she seems to be doing them properly. She's a lot of help to me though, if I've got a problem concerning black people, if I want to know something, she'll try and explain it to me.

It was quite common for female affiliates of Rastafari to become involved through their black boyfriends or partners who were already, or subsequently became, Rastas. This was the case for Anne:

> I suppose just living with him, and him showing me just influenced me greatly, because I believe that actions speak louder than words and his actions and way of life proved a lot to me. I started to check for what he was dealing with and he was reading a whole heap of books at the time, but I'm not really into reading so we'd usually sit down and talk and he'd show me. And then I started to wear a wrap [headcovering worn by Rastawomen].

Similarly, in Jane's case, she cited her boyfriend as a major influence on her deepening involvement in the movement:

> He came into it before me, but that's what spurred me on a bit, 'cos he was a Rasta and I knew him like I know myself...He was the first guy I really went out with and he's learnt me a lot...You have to go out with someone, if you're white, before you really get to know about it. You don't know nothing till you get into it like I have.

In the same way that the key tenets and principles of Rastafari were subject to different interpretations amongst black Rasta affiliates, so too were they open to different appropriations by whites. While at first glance it might have appeared inconceivable that these young whites could identify with a pan-Africanist political philosophy, it was clear that many of the movement's main themes could be made relevant to their own experiences. Rites and practices such as vegetarianism or Bible-reading were perhaps the most accessible and non-contradictory points of access for white affiliates. Rastafari's insistence that "Jah no partial" and that Rasta did not have a colour provided discursive spaces that could be inhabited by them. On specific issues, such as growing dreadlocks, some argued that locks were simply a sign of "natural living". Thus, for Jon, locks were not only an expression of blackness, but more fundamentally a sign of "righteous living": "It don't matter whether it look like a black man's hair or not, as long as you're dealing with the same thing...righteousness...it locks, no matter what nobody else want to say."

Similar kinds of universalist reasonings were made around the seemingly thorny issue of repatriation to Africa. While the notion of a white person wishing to go "back to Africa" might have appeared somewhat absurd, repatriation was nevertheless considered to be a viable goal, and great significance was attached to Africa as the birthplace of humanity. Africa was variously seen as "the place where we all come from" (Ruth) or the place "where life began" (Michael). Jon appealed to historical evidence to support this particular line of argument:

153

We're all coming from the same place. This civilisation come from Africa via Rome which was via Greece which was via Egypt and where's bloomin' Egypt?...Argument finish and done! And the people are coming the same way as the civilisation, everybody's moving away from Africa.

Some, like Colin, saw "Africa" in symbolic terms as a representation of all nations and peoples, quoting Black Uhuru's song "The whole world is Africa". Repatriation was understood as a spiritual movement towards a universal Utopia or "Zion" involving all humanity. "Zion", however, was not just a mystical vision, but was seen as an actual social and political state of affairs to be strived for. It symbolised a goal of universal freedom and equality and offered a sense of hope in a future world that was yet to come.

For those young female affiliates in long-term relationships with black partners, Rasta represented a whole "way of life" and an alternative form of social reproduction. They saw their commitment as a long-term one, a commitment which, in Jane's case, was interwoven with the process of raising a family:

> For me, it's just everyday living, like some people put Rasta in the same category as mods or punks, but it's not...it's not a fashion. People believe in Rasta and, for me, it's a way of life. I take it seriously 'cos I've got kids and they're gonna grow up.

While Rastafari was recognised by most as a force for radical change, some, like Ruth, were more sceptical about its ability to liberate women. Ruth was more conscious than most of the contradictions within Rasta philosophy around gender issues, and remained critical of the more patriarchal aspects of the movement.

> I can't really check for Selassie. A man?...God?....No! No way!...I can see corruption within the Bible too, the Bible has been written and rewritten by white men, so there's all their prejudices and biases in it.

Ruth's arguments clearly owed something to the interventions made in Rastafari by black women. Anne was also aware of the debates within the movement around theological and dress restrictions on women. She felt that Rasta women should "dress how they feel" not how they were expected to dress by men. Jane was similarly critical of suggestions that women should be subordinate to male Rastas:

> I feel that I'm equal to a man and I can walk anywhere with my man. I don't like to put myself in a second place. I don't believe a woman should restrict herself 'cos I think women have got a lot more potential. They're stronger than men, 'cos everything is from within.

Ruth had taken these arguments a stage further and drew on various oppositional elements in Rastafari and reggae culture to signify her independence and autonomy from men in general: "I stopped dealing with men for a time completely, because all they were bringing me was problems."

Ruth was involved in a local sound system and played bass guitar in an all-female, reggae band, and recognised the taboos which restricted women, both black and white, in these male-dominated spheres. For Ruth, the discourses of "tribulation" and "pressure" were particularly relevant to her oppression as a white woman in a male-dominated society:

> I get a lot of pressure. I get hassle just for what I am. I'm a woman for one thing, which gives me hassle. I can't walk on the street at night. Because if I walk on the street at night and anything happens to me, I'll be told it's my own fault. This is a man's world! And if you check it further, it's a white man's world. Women don't have any say; white women don't have any say.

The implicit comparison in Ruth's response between the experience of being black and that of being a woman suggested the potential of Rasta discourses to resonate with distinct but related forms of domination. This was also evident in the appropriation of Rasta notions of "naturality" by white female affiliates which paralleled the interventions made by black Rastawomen around black femininity and standards of beauty. Rasta aesthetics, through their opposition to glamourised images of women as sex objects, had acquired a particular resonance. Jane, for example, rejected cosmetics as a form of "vanity": "I don't deal with vanity. I just know better than that,

155

you know, you can't judge a book by its cover". Ruth had arrived at a similar position after years of what she saw as being "groomed" into a particular image of femininity by authority figures like teachers and parents. When asked why she had decided to grow dreadlocks, Ruth replied:-

> Because it's natural. The system is there to say, yes, smooth shiny hair is the thing, you know... so like, it's kind of a rebellion on the system's concept of beauty which they jam down your throat and which, as a woman, I feel very aware of because of the hair-care, or rather hair-mashing [destroying] products, you know, aimed at women.

Ruth's adoption of Rasta aesthetics suggested the possibilities of feminist appropriations of black culture, appropriations through which young white women could resist dominant ideals of feminine glamour and commodified beauty, and express alternative conceptions of womanhood.

These responses revealed the power of Rasta philosophy, through reggae music in particular, to shed light on universal, as well as class, age and gender-based forms of oppression through its core themes and discourses. The same egalitarian and anti-capitalist principles which also pervaded reggae were available to young whites as accounts of their own lives and experiences. Rastafari's critical insights were relevant to any number of political issues, from unemployment and the law, through food production and the natural environment, to its critique of the systematic nature of capitalist and state oppression in the form of "Babylon". Jon showed how the discourses of Rasta could be interwoven into a total world-view, by connecting its critique of "Babylon Destruction" with its conceptions of ecology and the natural world:

> It's natural living, it questions things like make-up and food and the environment, and the way it's being wrecked. It's saying, you know, we're men and women who live off the land, and because the land keeps us alive, if you kill the land, you kill yourself. And that's the moral of Babylon. Babylon was a system and a civilisation which went beyond its means. It created its own downfall.

7 Living a Contradiction

The cultural processes described in the previous two chapters did not take place in a social vacuum. They were underpinned and problematised, at every turn, by the wider realities of racism. These realities were especially pressing in Birmingham, given the high profile of "race" in its political and social history. They were most visible in the activities of far-right nationalist groups, and in the local black community's own political struggles against organised racism, the police and the local state. Cross-cultural interactions and affiliations occurred within this local historical and social context as much as they did within the broader terrain of "race" politics and black struggle in Britain. The ubiquity of racism, and the structural relationship between black and white working-class communities, placed these young whites in a contradictory social position. Racism was an unavoidable social fact which hung over these processes. It acted to proscribe cross-racial friendships and complicate white appropriations at every turn, imposing limits on the extent and forms of white involvement in black culture.

7.1 The Limits of Appropriation

We saw previously how adolescent white involvement in black youth culture was sustained by a large measure of complicity from young blacks. In the more intimate social contexts, young whites' appropriation of the style, speech patterns and music of their black peers could assist the formation of mixed friendships. However, while such appropriation may been tolerable and actively encouraged within such friendships, beyond their confines it could become a sensitive and politically charged issue. Since white youth's appropriation of these forms invariably followed, or paralleled black youth's own political engagement with them, such complicity could not be taken for granted. The foundations on which it rested became increasingly tenuous with each step in awareness made by young blacks, politicised by their own experiences of racism. It was at this intersection between individual friendships and wider, group allegiances that these contradictions began to manifest themselves. The dialectic between shared class positions and perceived racial divisions was played out incessantly in a dialogue of response and counter-response that fluctuated between inclusion and exclusion, similarity and difference, acceptance and rejection.

Given the wider realities of racism, it was perhaps unsurprising that white attempts at claiming oppositional cultural signs and spaces should be met with a degree of black suspicion and disapproval. That disapproval could be brought to the fore in a number of ways, and in a variety of contexts. It invariably took the form of a symbolic "policing" of white encroachment on black cultural territory, and was often provoked by particularly flamboyant appropriations of black style and cultural artefacts such as items of clothing, headgear or hairstyles. White appropriation of such items was liable to be seen as a form of cultural expropriation by young blacks, and could accordingly become the object of considerable hostility.

Such hostility often took the form of verbal castigations, or "cussing", directed at the legitimacy of the appropriation in question. At other times it was felt to be expressed through "bad looks" or "bad vibes." White appropriations were taken to be an implicit reinforcement of stereotyped images of blackness and black culture. Hostility most frequently took the form of "cussing",. All those young whites who had adopted black styles of dress or appearance at some stage had experienced such incidents.

As Paul pointed out, such confrontations seldom erupted into violence: "Most times they don't hit you with physical violence; they hit you with words...Words you can feel more than violence." Young blacks would occasionally home in on particular cultural items and confront the person concerned. Joe, for example, told me of one incident in which he had been accosted in the Bull Ring shopping centre by a group of Rasta boys for wearing a red, gold and green badge:

> What they were basically coming off with was that it was a badge that I shouldn't be wearing 'cos I was white . . . so the badge wasn't mine. But all I could say was "but I bought it", I just missed their point totally.

Young white women who displayed their affiliation to black culture by adopting black styles of dress could also incur hostility. Anne remarked that she had received "bad vibes" from black Rastawomen for wearing a wrap.

White patois use was an especially sensitive issue that was particularly liable to provoke hostile reactions. As a language of solidarity and resistance amongst young blacks, and one of the most important boundary signs of blackness, patois was invested with considerable symbolic meaning. Its use by some young whites as a source of amusement, through caricatured voices for example, could be interpreted as a form of derisive, racist parody. While the use of patois by young whites could assist the formation of cross-racial friendships, attempts to extend that usage beyond the friendship base could be fraught with difficulty. Paul, for example, admitted to having "toned down" his patois use since his mid-teens because of its potential to provoke hostile reactions in certain situations: "I don't chat it as much as I used to, cos I know some people don't like it." Paul's criteria for patois use depended on the strength of his prior friendships and familiarities with the conversants in any given context:

> When I don't know people that well I just drop it, till I get in there and get to know some of them, then I'll talk . . . Anyhow I get in a situation when some are talking and some ain't, I just listen for a while and suss it out. Its gotta be the right atmosphere.

Learning these informal rules meant being sensitive to the broader social implications of using patois. Knowing when and when not to speak patois required a certain understanding of the social contexts in which its use was, or was not acceptable. Failure to appreciate the possible interpretations of using patois could have serious consequences, and some had been roundly condemned by their black peers for inept or insensitive use. As Maureen suggested, white girls who made a self-conscious display of their affiliations were liable to be severely reproached by black girls: "If they found out you were into reggae and you went around with black kids, they either liked you or they hated you. They could get really nasty with some girls, especially when they tried to talk like them."

Problems of a similar kind could be encountered as a result of inhabiting cultural and leisure spaces within the black community where black people were in the majority. Given that some of these spaces were bound up with a particular kind of territorialisation of black identity, and charged with political meaning, the mere presence of whites could be a sensitive issue and one subject to proscription. One site where these contradictions could be encountered was in the context of the record shop. Reggae record shops with their predominantly black clientele, often located in inner-city areas, could present obstacles for white record buyers. As Jon pointed out, for white people unfamiliar with this environment, the process of entering a reggae shop for the first time could be an uncomfortable experience:

> The first couple of times I went down there, I felt really uneasy, 'cos when I went in there, for at least the first year or so I never seen anybody white go in there. You'd get the odd white person walking past and sort of turning their heads, like, as if to say, "mmm that sounds alright" . . . but not having the nerve to walk into a shop full of black people . . . which is often half the hang up.

Similar contradictions could arise through frequenting the spaces of blues parties and sound-system dances where the audience was predominantly black. For some of these young whites this could be a fraught and problematic process. As Shorty's first impressions of the blues suggest, this transition involved its own specific problems and tensions:

> By the time I got there the blues was ram [packed]—and everything was really dark and hot, like all the windows steamed up. And, going in, all I can remember is this reddish light, but I just had to black everything out, 'cos if I'd have took it in, I'd have just died on the spot. I can't remember seeing anybody white in there, there was quite possibly, but I didn't really think about it . . . I just didn't look. When you're in that situation you don't look, you just walk and pray you don't bump into anybody. And I just found a space on the wall, and stayed there, you know, looking at the ceiling like . . . and then these guys rushed me for some cigarettes, and asking me if I wanted to buy a draw. And I was only young you know! I was just going 'yes" and "no", I couldn't understand a lot of them.

160

While similar feelings of apprehension were expressed by others, for most, the strength of their attraction to the music and the atmosphere of the blues were sufficient to dispel these reservations. It was clear from the ambivalence of these responses that these experiences invoked a complex mixture of trepidation and exhilaration. As Ruth explained:

> I wouldn't go to the blues for ages. I was really scared to go . . . 'Cos I'd heard about dread things that happened down there . . . Anyway, one day we actually got down to the blues . . . and I couldn't believe it! I couldn't believe the blues! It was just speakers everywhere and music like. . . Wow!...I'd never heard anything like it.

The process of listening to reggae in the context of a blues or sound-system dance could also be a problematic experience. In such spaces, the contradictions of engaging with songs that dealt with the experience of blackness could be more acutely felt. Shorty, for example, explained how he had felt particularly awkward when a popular roots tune about the dangers of "informers" infiltrating the black community was played:

> It can make you feel bad, especially if you're the only white person in there. Like there was this blues in Balsall Heath not so long ago, and it was Alloy I think [Duke Alloy, a local sound system] and they played "Informer", you know, "Informer inna de area" [sings] and I always thought they looked at me when they played that record. 'Cos everytime I turned around they'd be looking at me, man, thinking I'm an informer like.

Jon recounted a similar experience:

> They played this Linton Kwesi Johnson record down Jenkins Street [a community centre in Small Heath] you know, the one that goes "we're gonna smash their brains in" and I just didn't know where to put myself! I nearly died! I just said...No, finish this record! Can't cope with this! Certain records like that I used to really struggle with at first, like "Whip them Jah" and that Trinity one that goes "White man

come and him lick them with a whip"....Cos you'd be standing in a dance and everybody else in the room's responding to that record and it kinda separates you off from them, cos in one way it can be looked at as being said against *you.*

The process of engaging with such contradictions was not limited to the context of sound-system dances. These challenges could also be experienced in personal, private listening contexts. But in the blues or dance hall, the boundaries of the political culture of which reggae was a part, were all the more tightly drawn. The sound-system dance was a space of such symbolic significance within black youth culture that white involvement was considered to be a threat to its autonomy and integrity. The flaunting of black style in such politically-charged contexts could be especially fraught with contradictions for those unaware of the potential consequences of their actions. This was evident in one particular incident that occurred at a sound-system dance in Balsall Heath in 1981 attended by myself and Jon.

The dance featured Jah Shaka, one of the most popular and militant sound systems at the time within black British youth culture. Shaka was well known for playing "steppers" reggae. The sound attracted a group of loyal young black male followers who would control a space in the middle of the dance-floor to engage in highly animated and acrobatic steppers dancing. As noted earlier, Jon had acquired a passion for such dancing, and so it came as no surprise when he moved into this centre space and began dancing. Jon's high visibility as a "white Rasta" and his presence in this coveted area of the dance floor signified a degree of white appropriation and encroachment that was politically untenable to the young black people around him. This was confirmed when shortly after Jon had moved into the centre space, two other black dancers came either side of him and jostled him off the floor.

By pushing up against the threshold of acceptable levels of white involvement, the incident highlighted the very real boundaries which constrained young whites' inhabitation of black youth culture. As far as Jon was concerned, it was only sometime after this incident, as the result of feedback from black friends also present at the dance, that he had begun to understand what had transpired:

I could feel people around me didn't like what I was doing, that was made obvious from those two guys ringing me up and cramping me...But at the time I was just inspired to dance and I couldn't see what was wrong with that. But looking back on it now I can see that I was out of order and that I made myself bloody vulnerable, because I was white...I was invading areas which those guys didn't want me to invade.

The problems and barriers encountered by young whites as a result of their affiliations presented them with a number of personal dilemmas. These generated a range of different responses, one of which was to instigate a period of self-doubt and questioning. Amongst some, this resulted in a relinquishing of the more flamboyant signs of affiliation. Shorty, for example, recounted a particular incident which had "brought him to reality" and induced something of an awakening process on his part:

One of the earliest times it hit me was when I was ice-skating in town. I was only about 14 and this black guy turned round, like, and he could see I had my trousers up my legs and the way I was walking and going on like, and he sprayed me, so I sprayed him back, and he sort of turned on me and I said something stupid like "But you're my bredren!" or whatever, and this guy just looked at me. And that really sort of knocked me down, like, even though it wasn't really hassle. It kind of just opened my eyes. There was me thinking we were on a oneness [equal] or something, but we wasn't. Cos you can say that black and white people are on a oneness but they're not really...and then come 16, 17, it just started to hit me you know. I just thought well, you're not this, you're not that, and you can't do this no more...like I mean I started thinking that clothes didn't mean so much.

Such incidents could have the effect of sensitising young whites to the potential implications of their actions. Developing an awareness of the possible interpretations that might be placed by black people on those actions, individually or collectively, was a key part of this process. In Jon's case it was the criticisms from close black friends,

163

combined with the experience of collective group closure, which brought home the wider implications of the dancing incident described above:

> All the pressures and hassles just did me in...they really cut me up. I was too young to understand the implications of what I was doing. I was a bit unaware and insensitive on certain levels. It got to the stage where I couldn't justify my presence within certain circles. I thought what I was doing was right, and then something came along which showed me I was all wrong. So I had to sit down and rethink the way I operated, 'cos you can get to a stage where you just ignore everything, but if you don't consider people, they'll thump you down if you get out of order . . . and I was, 'cos I appeared to be taking something away from black people that was theirs, and it could have been seen as kind of arrogant to do what I did. Cos if you take in the whole situation, there's still that dividing line between black and white, and I'm kind of caught in the middle. I'm caught in my own contradiction.

These lived contradictions between individual friendships and collective identities became increasingly apparent as young blacks and whites entered their late teens. The difference between black and white youth's experiences, and the fact that young whites did not go through the same pressures as their black peers, remained an anomaly even in the closest of friendships. The disparities between such relationships and the wider realities of racism were played out and reproduced incessantly within everyday interactions, Ian, for example, explained that his friendship with his Rasta friend, Roy, required constant reaffirmation as result of these contradictions:

> Because he sticks by me, I get more confident, but I know there's always that bit of doubt in his mind and I'm constantly having to prove myself to him...'cos, like, from his point of view, I'm bound even less than a black guy, 'cos its easy for me to opt out, chop off [his locks] and go and get my Ford Cortina, 2.5 kids and bank accountant's job tomorrow. Whereas no matter whether he chops off, he's still

black same way. It'll only be years of experience that'll take away that doubt.

For young black people, as Roy's "doubt" indicates, white affiliation to black culture could neither guarantee anti-racism nor warrant uncritical acceptance. For Ian, conversely, and others like him, there was no final resolution of their contradictory position. Even though their involvement might have been called into question less frequently, there was no point at which their identities ceased to be the object of critical assessment. Some mixed friendships, as a result, existed in a state of flux. The contradictory responses of young blacks themselves to the behaviour and practices of their white peers caused the prominence of racial boundaries to be continually brought in and out of focus. For the very practices that were condemned by some young blacks in group contexts continued to be endorsed by others in more intimate situations. The result was that a situation of considerable inconsistency, and occasional confusion reigned, in which some young whites could be observed continually lapsing in and out of their involvement in black culture, adopting black styles, dropping them and taking them up again.

It was at this point, as a result of these experienced pressures and personal dilemmas, that some young whites "backed out" of the culture and revoked their involvement entirely. Others took up a more peripheral position, withdrawing from the more intimate and proscribed areas of participation. While it was rare for young whites to relinquish their liking of reggae, for those unwilling to engage with the domain of the reggae record shop, more accessible alternatives were sought out. Others taped their music from the radio or commandeered their black friends to buy their records for them. Some also began to consciously avoid particular leisure venues because of previous "bad experiences" or apprehensions about potential hostility. In Jumbo's case, for example, attending dances organised by the more nationalistic Rasta groups was an unthinkable proposition:

> If I go to one of them dances, and it's pure Blackheart man, war is gonna start in that place and it's probably me what's gonna get chop up anyway, so the best way to avoid that actually happening is not to be there in the first place.

Groundless or otherwise, such fears kept many young whites away from the larger sound-system events and functions. Those that did attend such dances restricted themselves to functions organised by groups like the Twelve Tribes of Israel which were felt to be "safer" and more accessible spaces for white Rasta affiliates.

One of the most immediate responses of young whites to the reproaches of their black peers was to modify the more overt signs of their identification, such as patois use and flamboyant dress styles, in favour of more subtle registers of affiliation. This was invariably part of a general process of self-awareness in which many of the respondents came to regard the persistent use of patois as "false" or "immature". By their late teens, most of the respondents had accordingly begun to restrict their use of patois to selective phrases in specific contexts. Some, like Michelle, condemned flamboyant and self-conscious displays of patois: "I think it sounds terrible I do. It always makes me think they're trying to prove they're someone that they're not, and I don't have to prove that I go out with black people."

Developing an implicit understanding of the limits to white appropriation and the reasons for those limits was part of a learning process which involved separating stylistic emulations from expressions of cultural affinity with black people and black culture. For some young whites, particularly those from inner-city backgrounds, this lesson was learnt early on. Jo-Jo, for example, was critical of those young whites who attempted to project a mirror image of black identity and style:

> I used to see these white guys standing in the corner at the blues you know, with the big Rasta hits on, man, and I'd say to myself "fucking idiots" you know what I mean . . . I know what they're trying to put across, that's why they're in the same room as me. They're there because they're getting the same thing out of it as me, enjoyment! They feel as if they can express themselves. But I don't see why I have to stick on a hat, man, and go out and prove to people that I feel love, and I believe in God. 'Cos you're letting them judge you by your cover, and they will never really know you as a white guy, as a person…you know, I'm putting on an identity that does not fit me.

166

Despite such scepticism, the more committed Rastas in the study maintained their allegiance to the movement. Some engaged with Rasta's political discourses around blackness by making their own interpretations of Rasta philosophy and reggae lyricism. Both Jon and Shorty, for example, showed how they were able to negotiate their earlier difficulties of identifying with the more militant and nationalistic themes in some reggae records by drawing out other readings from the lyrics:

> In time I've been able to interpret those records and say to myself they weren't made directly at me, they were made at the people that were oppressing and now it's our turn to lick the slave-owner back, which I could quite agree with. I'd made up my mind that the guy was justified in what he was saying (Jon)

> It's like if someone come up to me and said, like, "Africa for the Africans", and you're not an African so bat out, I could always find something in the song to argue them down, like "they don't want to see us live together" or "stop the fussing and fighting", you know, there's always another side to it (Shorty)

A common response to the question of black self-determination was to emphasise the divisiveness of racial politics and the insignificance of "colour". Thus, for Anne, a person's skin colour was of no relevance to their identification with Rastafari:

> Rasta's for black and white. They can't say to me I shouldn't be dealing with it 'cos I'm white, because of the colour of my skin, 'cos that's all they're checking, my outward appearance, nothing else . . . like a book.

Michael appealed to higher morals of "good" and "evil" and "right" and "wrong" to justify his continued affiliation to the movement, and thereby attempted to transcend "race":

> If people ask me am I a white Rasta? I'll say no 'cos you're contradicting yourself by saying *white* Rasta, because Rasta is no colour, Rasta is like water, clear! . . . God has no

partiality. God has no respect of person. A black man or a white man isn't better than anybody else. The only thing that makes one person better than another is whether they're living right or not, not what colour they are . . . My skin's white, but that's just my physical form, inside I don't consider myself white. The only thing that makes me aware of my colour is when I look in the mirror, or when people tell me, and I realise I'm a material thing, otherwise I try and live spiritual.

It was not entirely clear whether Michael, by denying his "whiteness" was also attempting to deny the existence of racism. For Michael also stated that he had experienced discrimination for being a Rasta and having locks, and therefore knew something of what it was like to be black. In pursuit of this question, I suggested that he could not experience racism as a white person, nor know what it was like to be black. Michael replied angrily that I was "speaking shit", arguing that:

From when you grow dreadlocks, you will feel the pressure whether you're black or white, you will feel like a black person. You will feel the pressure they might feel. You might not get the full brunt of it, but you can understand how they feel, 'cos you'll get it from black people as well as white.

Michael's response was particularly revealing about the ways in which some young whites attempted to construct an equivalence between their own experiences of "sufferation" and the racism experienced by black people. Others attempted to forge an identity through parallel forms of ethnicity, such as their Irishness, or by pointing to equivalent forms of oppression based on class or gender. Ruth, for example, vehemently argued that she experienced "pressure" as much as black people simply through being a woman (see her earlier response in the previous chapter). The cost of making such parallels, however, was a tendency to deny or downplay the salience of racism. Amongst some respondents this took the form of a denial of the legitimacy of black militancy and anger, or in Jumbo's case, a denial of the historical connection between the racism of the past and that of the present:

Some of them man there, they go back to the times of slavery and that hate is still inside them. You can see it from their point of view, but it's wrong to carry it on, cos, it weren't this person's fault, or yours or mine that it happened.

Paul similarly attempted to diminish the contemporary scale and significance of racism, and thereby deny any complicity in it: "Prejudice is from a bygone age, it stems back from the period of slavery. The people that was there in slavery and the whites back there are no longer the people that are in it today."

Ambivalence about the political basis of black autonomy was particularly apparent in responses to the more militant and nationalistic elements of the Rasta movement, such as the Ethiopian World Federation (EWF). Ruth, for example, dismissed such organisations as "separatist" and a form of "reverse prejudice": "Revenge is not what we're dealing with. If they judge white people by the colour of their skin then they're as bad as the original people that did it in the first place." Shorty's view of the EWF was also ambivalent:

> They got a point, but I class them as a foolish organisation. 'Cos some of the deeper ones are a bit like the National Front, maybe not as bad. I don't think they'd wanna shoot all white people, really...I was speaking to one the other week and, like, there's a lot of difference in there, 'cos one might say if you're white and God thinks you're righteous then you could reach [i.e. Zion]. Whereas a next Federation man might say "No! you're white! you can't come!".

Shorty pointed out that he was still able to reason with militant Rastas who were often curious to know what he was "dealing with". Joe, while criticising the EWF for "fighting down colour" nevertheless respected them for being "organised", and having a strong argument. Indeed, many of those I interviewed, while disagreeing with the political positions of militant black organisations, were able to acknowledge the relevance of their politics. Pat, for her part, felt that the activities of such organisations were not comparable with those of white fascist organisations:

169

You can't really moan about them, white people got the National Front and the Ku Klux Klan, and black people suffered them. I mean they're not really doing much to us. Black people don't come up to white people and say they're gonna stab you and hang you.

The attitudes of these young whites to the vexed questions of race and black politics were typically ambivalent. While various reasonings could be invoked in verbal exchanges with young blacks to justify their position, the realities of racism remained as awkward problems and contradictions to be negotiated. And yet behind these often bizarre metaphysical ramblings there lay a genuine attempt to cut through the material world of appearances and the ideologies of "ism and schism" of which "race" was a part, to a higher, spiritual, plane of existence.

The distinctive subjectivities inhabited by these young whites, through their cross-racial friendships and affiliations with black culture, generated a particularly acute awareness of the boundaries and dynamics of race. For most, that awareness was often painfully acquired through personally experiencing the contradictions of engaging with black culture and people in specific contexts. It was through these experiences that they came to understand the social implications of white appropriation and the racism that constrained that appropriation.

These young whites, as a result, found themselves caught in the middle, in a no-man's-land between "black" and "white" collective identities. For those with close black friends and intimate experience of black cultural and family life this was a commonly experienced dilemma. Jon, as we saw earlier, was perhaps more aware than most of his contradictory position. As Jon explained, however, that position that was rendered contradictory not only by the responses of blacks, but by other whites too:

You're caught between everybody, 'cos you're constantly getting the hassle from the black people that disagree with what you're doing and you're constantly getting it from the white people. At first, you get it mainly from other black people who are outside your friends, but from when you've been around a while, you start getting it from white people, 'cos they start to notice that you're a bit odd, and you get put into situations where the ones that are racist associate you off with black people.

7.2 "Race Traitors"

For those young white people interviewed, it was the responses of other whites that seemed to throw the issue of "race" into especially sharp relief. Such responses came through white friends and acquaintances, family members and peer groups in the local white community and more, anonymously, from individuals and groups in public spaces.

In the inner-city context, with its multiracial demographics, its greater preponderance of mixed relationships, and its general absence of overt, collective racism, support for cross-racial friendships and allegiances tended to be stronger and more widespread. The parents of those young whites from inner-city backgrounds often had their own relationships and interactions with the black community, and were mostly unopposed to their children mixing with black people. However, the families of those from white working-class areas viewed their sons' and daughters' activities, at the very least, with scepticism and disapproval, and in some cases with vehement antipathy.

Most of those from outer-ring backgrounds had vivid stories to recount of family conflicts over their relationships and affiliations. These conflicts were invariably more severe for young women and tended to be focused on the issue of cross-racial dating. Such was the strength of feeling aroused by this issue that for some, like Maureen, having a black boyfriend became a covert act to be kept secret at all costs. In at least three cases, it had been the cause of bitter conflicts and had led to deep family divisions. Jane's family, for example, had been split along gender lines, with her mother and sisters on one side, each of whom had black partners, and her father and brothers on the other. Jane told me that her father had disowned her: "He doesn't have anything to do with me anymore. He thinks I'm mad, completely mad."

Relationships between white women and black men, the age-old litmus test of white racism, seemed to provoke the most intense and sometimes violent responses. Anne, for example, had been on the receiving end of a particularly brutal patriarchal reaction when she was discovered to have been dating black boys:

I had a big cultural clash with my family when they found out I was going out with black guys. I left home 'cos I wanted my own independence. My dad was really prejudiced then. It was a really heavy time, 'cos I was only 17 and they made me make a choice between my man and my family. And I chose my man, so my brothers beat the hell out of me, and burnt all my records. They were very influenced by my father at the time. They made me leave home in the clothes I stood up in.

Maureen was also forced to make a similar decision about her allegiances when her mother found out about her black boyfriend:

There was a big argument and she started laying the law down. She said "choose between the niggers or the whites". So I turned round and said "well I'll have the niggers then!" and she kicked me out! And I went to live with Carl's [her boyfriend's] family.

While some of these family feuds had healed with time, others remained irreconcilable. Tensions and frictions continued to simmer beneath the surface in family relations. Relatives and family friends kept their distance or remained implicitly hostile. As Maureen pointed out: "Even our brother's still funny about it. He goes "can't you find somebody white to go out with", you know, "can't you find something better" and you think, well what's better than that?"

Many of those from outer-ring areas who had black friends but continued to associate with other young whites had experienced varying degrees of disapproval and hostility from their white peers. Some of those responses took the form of a "two-faced" attitude towards their black friends. Lisa and Maureen were particularly critical of the way some of their white peers would grant a nominal acceptance to their boyfriends while maintaining a racist attitude towards black people in general. As Lisa complained:

What gets me is when they say "Oh Carl's different" or "Keith's different" you know. Ever such a lot of people who say they're not prejudiced *are*, underneath. You wouldn't believe how two-faced some of them are. There's always something there when it boils down to it.

This double standard of accepting black people on the surface while preserving racist attitudes at a deeper level was perceived as a familiar white response. By maintaining a "colour-blindness" at the level of inter-personal relations, these contradictions could be elided by accepting individual blacks as "one of us" or "not really black". Maureen suggested that this kind of covert prejudice was especially prevalent amongst white men in their attitudes to dating between white women and black men. Lisa and Maureen cited a number of incidents in which young white men who had claimed not to be prejudiced had revealed racist attitudes when discussing this subject. Maureen, for example, told of a white ex-boyfriend who had objected to her dating black boys, even though he himself mixed with young blacks:

> Even this kid I went out with, now he's gone round with black kids and everything, and he's gone out with black girls too, and he used to say "don't go out with black kids, bab, they're no good like", you know "you're too good" and "they'll only ruin you". And he said "you tell me if ever a black kid beats you up or touches you and I'll kill 'em!".

As Maureen's experience suggests, racist forms of patriarchal control that operated in the "private" context of the family could also be reinforced by white males in more public contexts. White male antagonism to interracial dating, while closely bound up with questions of masculinity and sexual competition, was also part of a more general rivalry over cultural space. While such competition had been partially blunted in some areas and counterbalanced by the noticeable increase in white boys dating black girls, such relationships, as Maureen's experience makes plain, offered no assurances of undermining the double standards of gender-specific racism.

It was clear, from a number of recounted incidents that these young white people occasionally became the objects of a "deflected" racism as a result of their relationships with black people. Conspicuous displays of affiliation to black culture could make them particularly vulnerable to hostile reactions from other whites. Such

173

reactions were more prevalent in outer-ring areas, and were often expressed by older white male peer groups. Where group allegiances were thought to be in doubt, the boundaries of racial affiliations could be vigorously reinforced through such peer-group pressure. Pete had suffered in this manner at his, predominantly white, secondary school in the suburbs. He told of the abuse he had received both from his teachers and his older white peers:

> These older kids used to beat me up, man, and call me "nigger, nigger", "you black bastard" and all this. Even the teachers used to say things like "where's your tea cosy today Peter?" It was a good school like, if you were into the whites. If you weren't, forget it!

Jo-Jo told of a similar experience at a detention centre, where one of the wardens regularly taunted him as a "white nigger" for associating with the young black detainees:

> I used to stay with two black kids called Gladstone and Wallace and one time this screw came up to me and said "you know something, you ought to have been a fucking nigger, in fact I am going to call you a white nigger from now on". I just laughed at him, man.

By demonstrating how racist social constructions could be fashioned against young whites themselves, such incidents served as a reminder that, in such circumstances, "race" was a relational concept that did not always have fixed referents. In these situations, the discourse of "tribulation" could take on a vivid reality for those on the receiving end of such abuse, and the notion of suffering for one's principles and affiliations became grounded in concrete experiences.

Being identified or publically known as someone who associated with black people could have especially serious implications for young white women, who risked being the objects of particularly vitriolic, gender-specific forms of racist condemnation. All the young white women respondents had experienced varying degrees of such hostility, ranging from "bad looks" and innuendos to explicit confrontation. Those women who displayed visible signs of affiliation to black culture or Rasta were immediately vulnerable to this kind of abuse. Pat, for example, felt that it was white boys in particular that were liable to "cause trouble":

> I get it from white boys mainly. I don't get it from white girls. But then you get some white boys who are nice. But I've had a whole heap of trouble from boys round here, calling me "wog lover" and all this...and, like, when you get on the bus; they look on you as if you're dirty or something.

The most serious cases of harassment were experienced at the hands of local white racists and nationalist far-right groups. The threat of such harassment was often greater for those, like Lisa and Maureen, who dated black boys yet lived in white working-class areas. Maureen told of one particular incident in which they had been openly confronted by a group of white men while on their way home from a youth club in south Birmingham:

> We were waiting in Cotteridge for a bus and there was all these National Front about. And these two white guys come up and asked us "Do you go out with black kids?" and "Do you go to bed with them?" and me being really cocky, I said "so what if we do, it's none of your fucking business!" and then they started calling us names like "wog-lovers" and "sluts" and "slags" and all this. And they was going "you're just wogs' meat, you disgrace us, you shouldn't even be alive", and I was really arguing on them. I was really going mad I was. And fortunately for us, there was a police car there which was probably the only reason they didn't beat us up. But it's still as bad now.

Lisa and Maureen's experiences were connected to a whole series of events which took place around certain youth clubs in the South Birmingham area in the late 1970s. The Bournville youth club, in particular, with its large black clientele, became the object of a racist moral panic amongst local white residents who campaigned to have it closed down. Local members of far-right political groups from surrounding white working-class areas were said to have regularly harassed and intimidated members of the club and those of similar venues in the South Birmingham area. One particular youth club, which was reputedly besieged by a group of white racists, needed

175

special transport to ferry its black members safely out of the area. The Bournville club, in particular, became a focus of racist activity with black patrons being attacked in surrounding areas while returning home from the club. Young white women who frequented the club also became the targets of an organised campaign in which leaflets were distributed in the vicinity of the club by far-right groups, and threatening letters were sent to the houses of those who were known or suspected to be dating young black men.

In the context of such activity, young women who continued to frequent white working-class leisure venues risked being ostracised socially if they were discovered to have black boyfriends. Maureen told of an incident at a local pub disco where she and Lisa were confronted by two white men:

> We're just in the middle of everyone 'cos we go about with white kids too. Like we go down this pub, and it's mainly white people up there. And these white kids come up and started an argument, they said "we've been told not to dance with you two, 'cos you go out with wogs and you're trouble" and they were really threatening us. We couldn't believe it, they were almost attacking us in the pub.

The pressures of being "in the middle of everyone" were particularly acute for those from white working-class areas who had black friends, and who moved within inner-city and outer-ring circles, but whose immediate peers were mostly white. The risks of undertaking mixed relationships, together with intense peer-group and family pressure, could lead some to veer away from their black friends, and retreat from their involvement in black culture. As young whites entered their mid-teens, the pull of group allegiances and wider collective affiliations increasingly began to exert themselves on friendship choices, leisure activities and music tastes.

While a withdrawal or lessening of involvement was one potential consequence of these experienced pressures and contradictions, another was to strengthen and transform existing affiliations. The process of engaging with the problems and obstacles posed by others, both black and white, was one of the most powerful ways in which social facts about racism were learnt and a grasp of its wider implications acquired. In the immediate post-school period, the outcome of these processes hung very much in the balance, however, and depended on a number of other contingencies and conditions. The significance of these is explored in the final chapter.

8 Level Vibes

This final chapter looks at how the cultural processes described in the preceding chapters were shaped by conditions and forces that were significant in the lives of these young people, particularly schooling, unemployment, and relations with the police and other state institutions. How did these conditions structure the various cross-cultural appropriations, affiliations and relationships outlined above? What possibilities did they open up around the politics of race?

8.1 The Politics of Shared Experience

Schooling, as previously noted, was one of the most important shared institutional spaces in which young people from disparate communities and ethnic backgrounds were brought together. The local education authority's modification of catchment areas and its comprehensive education policies played a key role in bringing black and white pupils together within the same institutional sphere. As a paramount reality, shaping the lives of both young blacks and whites, the schooling process could therefore function as something of a levelling experience. School was an important backdrop to the formation of racially mixed peer groups and friendships. As we saw earlier, the oppositional borrowing of black youth cultural forms by white youth was particularly evident in the school context. In inner-city secondary schools like the one attended by Jo-Jo, mixed peer groups could be formed out of a shared opposition to teacher authority:

> I used to hang out with these black guys, you know [names them individually] and we used to go to the toilets and get blocked up [smoke marijuana] and listen to music. 'Cos the teachers weren't interested in us, man. As far as they were concerned, we were the wolves, we were all in the same class 'cos we were bad.

Similar mixed peer groups of black and white youth also existed in outer-ring schools with relatively small numbers of black pupils. An example of how educational policies had fostered the interaction between young people from different communities was provided in the case of Shorty. Having been expelled from his first secondary school in the suburbs, Shorty had been transferred to a special school where the majority of the pupils in his class were black:

> They sent me to this centre for expelled kids and that. And that was like the final touch 'cos there was only two white kids and nine black kids, and six of them had natty [locks] like and this was when it really started setting in. Like they used to smoke weed in this school . . . weed! When the teacher went out for dinner, they used to lock the door from the inside and the teachers would be shouting from the other side but you'd just pretend you couldn't hear, turn the music up and just smoke weed in there.

This was a further example of how the oppositional symbols of black youth culture could become resonant for young whites as modes of resistance to school authority. As such, they add another dimension to Paul Willis's work on white working-class youth's experience of schooling (Willis, 1977). They point to the existence of racially mixed counter-school cultures in which black cultural forms played a hegemonic role and served as paradigms of resistance for young whites. School, then, was a site not only of racial division and antagonism, but one of cultural mediation in which more collaborative forms of interaction also took place. Moreover, the shared reality of what were felt to be increasingly irrelevant and valueless forms of schooling could provide a common denominator of experience amongst black and white pupils.

This shared experience of institutional contexts extended well beyond the boundaries of compulsory schooling into other spheres of control and regulation of young people. Other forms of institutional domination shared by young people included the growing number of youth custodial centres, secure units and residential homes, as well as prison. Such spaces could also be sites of collaborative as much as antagonistic relations between black and white youth. Graphic examples of this were provided by two of the respondents, Jo-Jo and Jumbo, both of whom had spent time in detention centres. While racial boundaries could be even more sharply drawn "inside", the shared experience of custody could provide a context for the formation of mixed friendships and alliances between young blacks and whites.

While the sharing of institutional contexts like schools and detention centres played a major role in shaping black-white interactions, it was in the immediate post-school period that some of the most significant shifts in the balance of relations between black and white youth had occurred. The escalating levels of unemployment which hit Birmingham between 1980 and 1984, following the collapse of its manufacturing base, had a particularly severe impact on young people. While the unemployment rate in the region as a whole almost doubled in that period from 10.3% to 19.4%, amongst 16-18 year-olds it was nearer 50% by 1984-85 and in certain inner-city areas it was three times the national average (CBI, 1984).

While unemployment levels were, on the whole, much higher for young blacks than for young whites, in certain parts of the city they showed signs of being more evenly distributed. It was clear that the predicament faced by some groups of working-class youth in the outer-ring, was little better than their inner-city counterparts. Official preoccupation with the problems of the inner-city had eclipsed the rising unemployment levels in these areas, together with the steady decline of housing and living conditions. The experiences of young people living in these areas, particularly in the large council estates of south and east Birmingham, were set against a background of decay and neglect often comparable to that of the inner city. Large numbers of young whites from both areas suffered from the same lack of options, and the same impoverishment, boredom and powerlessness as a result of being unemployed.

Few of the respondents had been in regular employment since leaving school. Some had taken various temporary or part-time jobs only to relinquish them because of poor pay, intolerable working conditions or slender prospects for advancement. These were often "youth jobs" in the distribution and service sectors, such as Ian's at Asda and Shorty's at MacDonald's (both big employers of part-time youth labour). In Shorty's case, he had left his job at MacDonald's because of its regimented and hierarchical nature: "It was just like school again. It was really disciplined and I just couldn't accept it." Jane had given up her job as a shop assistant in Birmingham city centre for similar reasons:

181

> It was dead boring. I just felt like a machine, you know. You gotta get up at a certain time, you gotta go to bed at a certain time, then you gotta get up to go to work again. Your whole life is just set round that one job.

With the state's expanded and increasingly direct political orchestration of the school-work transition, training schemes had become another institutional sphere through which young blacks and whites were both being channelled in the post-school period. Four of those interviewed had been on such schemes. There was, however, a common sense of dissatisfaction with the quality of training and the levels of income that they provided, and their inability to lead to permanent employment. While the majority of those interviewed wanted well-paid and rewarding jobs to fulfil their basic ambitions, some had turned their back on such goals and had rejected waged labour completely. In Colin's case, for example, there was a clear link between this rejection and his engagement with Rasta. Colin had worked as a shop assistant for three years after leaving school at 15. His growing dissatisfaction with the job had coincided with his deepening involvement with Rasta. Colin told me that he had finally left the job on his eighteenth birthday, and had subsequently abandoned any idea of working permanently:

> If I ain't being paid a decent wage for a job, I ain't doing it. And all the kind of jobs that's going don't offer a decent enough wage for the kind of work that's being done.

Colin's attitude to waged labour was indicative of how the transition into the labour market was being subverted and refused by white youth in ways similar to black youth. Such cases pointed to a similar rejection of wage discipline in the forms that it was offered, and a similar questioning of the sense of investment in waged work as it declined both qualitatively and quantitatively. Indeed, for many young whites it appeared that the experiences and cultural knowledges of their black friends were shedding light on their own ambivalent relation to waged work.

It was in the shared predicament of unemployment that this intersection of cultural responses had become most visible. The rise in structural unemployment amongst the young had a number of

182

important implications for the post-school experience of black and white youth. As Ian observed:

> Because of the dole, right, you've got a lot of black and white youth going around together that would have probably, after school, split apart more easily and gone their separate ways . . . And the whites would have gone up their ladders, you know. But that's not happening now. As the opportunities get less and less for white youth as well, the dole's becoming more important . . . It's like, I'm reminded from time to time that I can opt out if I want 'cos I'm white. But as the numbers of unemployed increases, that question comes up less and less.

As Ian points out, while white youth might have previously had greater access to "escape routes" from unemployment, the levelling experience of the dole was acting to decrease the likelihood of mixed friendships disintegrating in the post-school period. For many of these young whites, unemployment was one of the major common denominators linking their life situations with those of their black peers. As Jon observed, the common experience of the dole could act to cement friendships in situations where young blacks and whites were sharing the same leisure spaces:

> It means you gotta support each other. Like say when no one can afford to buy a draw [marijuana] so everybody helps, everybody chips in, and it encourages a bond of friendship, because the only way to survive is to help each other.

While for black youth a repertoire of cultural strategies already existed for the negotiation and survival of wagelessness, increasing levels of unemployment amongst young whites, and the growing disjuncture between the cultural goals of consumption and the means of achieving such goals, were beginning to pose political questions with which blacks had long been faced. The imperatives of day-to-day economic survival, the negotiation of poverty, and the use and meaning of "leisure" were problems that increasingly confronted large sections of unemployed white youth who did not have access to the "youth" economy of part-time work. For some young whites, survival strategies developed within the black community had become meaningful ways in which non-work and dependency could be mediated and some sense of cultural autonomy preserved. Such strategies ranged from an active participation in the community's cultural and leisure institutions, to an involvement in various forms of "hustling" and independently-won incomes. As Ian remarked:

> When you've been there a year on the dole, and all your friends are still there, everything starts to slot into place, you know what I mean . . . Because if you're on the dole, you can't really afford to go to the night clubs up town. And, like, goin' blues is one of the few things you can.

For young whites like Ian, the lack of regulations involved in sound system culture and their distinctive cultural and musical practices proved particularly attractive and relevant to their predicament. Such practices could function as survival strategies in similar ways as they did for blacks. Evidence of this existed not only in the growing levels of white participation in sound system culture, especially in outer-ring areas, but in the emergence of multiracial and white sound systems. Frequenting local sound system events was one solution to the exclusionary practices of the city centre's commercial entertainment network.

Involvement in the local music economy, through selling tapes and records, building hi-fi and sound-system equipment, or music-making, also provided a source of material income for some. The shared experience of unemployment provided a basis for many of the multiracial reggae and rock bands that existed in the Birmingham area during this period. The formative history of UB40 was typical of many such bands. Formed out of their shared enthusiasms for Jamaican music, its members came together, in Robin Campbell's words, "to make reggae music and get off the dole" (New Musical Express, 3 September 1983). The democratisation of music-making that occurred through the increased availability of digital music-making technologies also saw a growing involvement of young whites in the recording of local reggae, using DIY, custom-built recording facilities operating out of converted spaces in private homes.

For the unemployed, reggae culture could become an important source of spiritual strength through which to negotiate and survive their wageless predicament. For some, it offered a cultural and psychological defence mechanism against the dispiriting effects of unemployment on their everyday lives.

The crisis of consumption induced by the impoverishing effects of unemployment was negotiated in a range of other material ways. Home-taping of music, for example, was a strategy directly tailored to recession conditions. With many unable to afford records on a regular basis, cassette tapes had replaced them as a principal currency of music consumption, exchanging hands back and forth between young people. Some had collected large stores of tapes in this way; tapes of friend's records, tapes of live sound-system dances, tapes of radio programmes and tapes of tapes. Economic imperatives had, for some, necessitated an involvement in various hustling and survival "runnings". In Shorty's case this was simply a matter of economic expediency:

> The dole's a waste of time . . . they try and make you live off a cut and dry situation. It's like hand to mouth, you know, a loaf of bread a week. And that's fucked up. How can you do that from year to year? So you need to do some runnings to survive.

"Runnings" embraced a range of economic and cultural practices premised on street knowledge and initiative. It amounted to a form of economic self-management, a way of getting by through odd jobs, bartering, various forms of primary production (including clothes, art and craftwork) and other semi-legal incomes outside the wage relation. These activities extended into white working-class areas and were part of a wider underground economy that included selling and distributing ganja, and various forms of petty crime, ranging from small-time "nicking" and fiddling to more organised criminal activities, such as shop-lifting sprees and handling stolen consumer goods.

For many, the predicament of wagelessness was just one of a combination of circumstances that included lack of regular accommodation, lack of transport and leisure options. In certain parts of the city, these circumstances were showing signs of impinging on the experiences of all young people. In both inner-city and outer-ring areas, both black and white inhabitants were increasingly to be found sharing the brunt of crisis conditions and expenditure cuts in the form of deteriorating council housing, declining public services and lack of leisure facilities.

Through this common experience of privation and survival, working-class loyalties could merge into a shared ideology of "community" that included both black and white inhabitants. Some, like Jo-Jo, saw this community in terms of a set of basic values of everyday life; values of cooperation, mutuality and reciprocity: "People rely on one another in Balsall Heath, people survive with one another. It's a community! You know, you do good, you get good; you get good, you do good!"

The strong symbiotic ties and traditions of black–white collaboration that existed in some inner-city areas could be called upon to challenge dominant notions of racial antipathy and conflict. This could take the form of counter-mythologies of community which highlighted precedents of cooperation or non-racialised conflict. Thus, as Jo-Jo proudly stated: "I've only ever seen two fights in Balsall Heath, and one of those was between two white guys, and the other was between two black guys."

While these strong community ties could be used to challenge racist interpretations of everyday social experience, they could also be mobilised to express shared opposition to "outsiders" in the form of middle-class professionals or representatives of local state institutions. Here, the shared experience of similar struggles and concrete grievances against discernible state institutions such as housing authorities, social services and the DHSS had served to generalise social disaffection amongst both black and white. This intersection of grievances had become most noticeable, however, in common perceptions and experiences of the police.

Increasingly deployed as agents of control and surveillance over the everyday activities of the young, for many black and white youth the police had become the most visible representatives of state control and authority. The colonisation of shopping precincts, parks, public transport and streets by the young unemployed had become a source of increasing conflict with the police. With young people's mobility, and their use of public space subject to ever greater restriction, white youth were finding themselves increasingly drawn into conflict with the law. Many of the respondents, like Jumbo, had their own personal experiences of police harassment to recount:

186

I've had a whole heap of pressure off policemen round here. I can't walk the streets after 11 o'clock. They've grabbed me up, flung me in the car, threatened me...for what? Because they caught me with a draw [marijuana] one time, so they spot me as some kind of drugs man. They make out herbs is some big drug. They're idiots, man! They don't know what they're talking about.

The depth of anti-police feeling amongst the young was particularly marked in inner-city areas where instances of police malpractice were common knowledge and central to the concerns of all young people. Areas such as Balsall Heath already had a long history of police intervention into local community and family life. Amongst large sections of the young, however, perceptions of the police as a common source of oppression and an unwanted intrusion into the community had become increasingly apparent. Jo-Jo was perhaps more aware than most of the long traditions of resistance and common mistrust of police in working-class communities like Balsall Heath:

There's one race I hate and all black people hate and that's the police...that's what we all have in common in Balsall Heath. I can meet a black kid and I don't have to ask if he doesn't like police, I *know* he doesn't like police. No one likes police in Balsall Heath, police are not needed in Balsall Heath. When does anything bad ever happen? All the young generation of Balsall Heath is saying is just leave us alone, man! You give our mums and dads all this stick, you're not giving it to us! 'Cos I tell you something, we won't take it!...You know, we smashed Liverpool, we smashed Birmingham, Manchester, London! It can be done again, and we don't mind 'cos we're only unemployed, so we got nothing to lose.

As Jo-Jo's defiant exhortation suggests, the riots which reverberated throughout urban Britain in 1980-81 and 1985 were partly the result of a long history of mispolicing in working-class, inner-city areas. While fed and sustained by well-established traditions of black struggle, the fact that substantial numbers of white youth joined in the rebellions was a measure of how police coercion had spread of its

187

own volition, as through law and order discourses, to include the white working-class inhabitants of such areas. Studies of the Handsworth disturbances of 1981 showed that while approximately one in five of those involved were Asian, and one in three Afro-Caribbean, one in two were white (Field and Southgate, 1982, p. 43). Equivalent figures for the 1981 riots in Merseyside revealed even higher levels of white participation, preliminary statistics of court cases showing that 108 out of 125 defendants were white (Kettle and Hodges, 1982).

Those young people I talked to who had witnessed or been involved in the riots spoke of their celebratory atmosphere. The sense of temporary victory over the police, and the winning of street control from them, revealed something of the strong feelings of collective empowerment and shared participation that underpinned the riots. In a different sense, the combativity of black youth in inner-city areas also provided an impetus to white youth living in areas of often negligible black settlement who, in 1981, took to the streets in nearly every major urban area of Britain. In the media's rush to portray the 1981 disturbances as 'race riots', the scale of white participation was grossly underestimated. An indication of the symbolic drawing-power of the riots was provided by the events that followed the 1985 Handsworth disturbances. While only a small number of local whites were involved in the initial protests, the ensuing two days saw groups of young whites flocking into the area from all over Birmingham after extensive media coverage. The magnetic attraction of white youth to the riot areas revealed something of the signifying power of urban disorder amongst young people that was more than simply "copycat" antics. For white youth too, "rioting" and "looting" could acquire a symbolic importance as defiant gestures against authority, motivated as much by the desire for excitement and relief from the boredom, as for material gain.

The riots of 1980-81 in particular represented something of a watershed in the evolving political relationship between black and white youth in Britain, pre-empting as much as precipitating a shared sense of purpose born out of common predicaments. The growing resonance of experiences between different groups of powerless young people was an indication of how these commonalities could provide the basis for collective forms of consciousness and action across racial and ethnic boundaries. Perhaps more than any other social or political events of the 1980s, the riots were a spontaneous and visible demonstration that shared local experience premised on unemployment and institutional domination was a reality in some areas of urban Britain.

8.2 Stop this Fussing and Fighting

The cross-racial affiliations and patterns of shared experience described in this and preceding chapters offered no guarantees of generating anti-racist sensibilities amongst white youth. Tolerance did not automatically flow from white engagement with specific forms of black culture. Indeed, the tensions in some of the responses above suggest that it was entirely possible for young whites to maintain common-sense racist attitudes, while continuing to associate with young blacks and appropriate black culture. A striking example of this was provided by a white friend of one of the respondents who was an ardent reggae fan and mixed with young blacks, yet was also a member of the National Front. Powerful feelings of attraction to black culture could coexist with perceptions of that culture as threatening and with resentment and fear of black people. One potential consequence of the proscription of white involvement could be the withdrawal of such involvement and more reactive racist positions being taken up.

It was in the crucial post-school period that responses premised on more generalised feelings of racial hostility could start to harden. Such outcomes were more likely in the outer ring, where the levels of cross-racial interaction and white exposure to black culture were lower, and where collective racial antipathy was still massively present. In these settings, white youth's own experiences of powerlessness could generate greater rivalry with black youth. Similar predicaments could be offset by divergent cultural responses and racialised interpretations of experience. These were articulated amongst young men through aggressive assertions of white working-class identity. Here, the premium placed on notions of masculinity, loyalty and group pride in male peer-groups could make it easier for racist ideas to attach themselves to the values of ritual insult and territorial chauvinism found in white, male, working-class culture. The concern with the boundaries of class, expressed in the language of territoriality, and "us and them", could be voiced in explicitly racist terms where black working-class communities were seen to possess rival credentials.

White involvement in black culture also offered no assurance of generating positive forms of identification with all non-white people. Racism could be displaced or expressed in other forms, particularly against South Asian communities. The familiarity of young whites with Afro-Caribbean cultural forms, because of their greater commercial accessibility, and their perceived similarities with white working-class culture, could serve to highlight common-sense perceptions of Asian culture as "different" and "alien".

Relations between white and Asian youth were specific to different locales of the city, and dependent partly on the relationships between Asian and Afro-Caribbean communities. In outer-ring areas where the vast majority of young whites had little contact with Asian youth outside of school-based friendships, anti-Asian hostility remained acute, and white perceptions of Asians as "different", culturally, linguistically and religiously, were commonplace. The relative distance between Asian and Afro-Caribbean communities in the outer ring, moreover, with its smaller, more fragmented black population, together with the lack of a "visible" Asian youth culture in such areas, enabled young whites to appropriate and identify with Afro-Caribbean forms while maintaining racist attitudes towards Asians. Such attitudes could coalesce around a shared resentment of Asian entrepreneurial and professional success amongst both Afro-Caribbean and white youth.

The situation in the outer ring contrasted somewhat with that in the inner city where a slightly different balance of relationships between white, Asian and Afro-Caribbean communities existed. Those young whites who had grown up in inner-city areas such as Balsall Heath had invariably done so in close proximity to Asian communities. Many had made their own friendships with Asian youth in both school and neighbourhood contexts, and it was not unusual to find mixed peer-groups comprised of Asian, Afro-Caribbean and white youth. Here, closer Asian-white interactions, characteristic of some inner-city areas, could undermine the culturally specific racial imagery that pervaded the responses of outer-ring white youth. For in contexts where white, Asian and Afro-Caribbean youth shared the same leisure practices and music tastes, the stereotyped notion that Asian youth "kept to themselves" could be rendered palpably false. The wider surface of Afro-Caribbean-Asian contact in the inner city, moreover, resulted in distinctive cross-cultural influences between Asian and Afro-Caribbean youth.

Examples of such influences existed in abundance, not only in specifically Asian appropriations of reggae, patois and Rasta culture, but also in the mass participation of young Asians in dance music and hip-hop culture.

The resonance of Afro-Caribbean culture for young Asians was partly premised on the commonality of political interests around shared experience of racism, which had led to a number of tactical alliances produced by local circumstances. The "unity" that existed between Asian and Afro-Caribbean youth in certain parts of the city placed those young whites who identified with reggae and Rastafari, and yet remained hostile towards Asians, in a contradictory position. It did so by exposing their racism, and by rendering the appropriation of black forms less attractive. In situations where Asian and Afro-Caribbean youth relied on common definitions of themselves as "black", the affiliation of young whites to Afro-Caribbean culture could be put in doubt, and the coherence of racist responses challenged. The growing self-confidence and militancy of Asian youth, moreover, and the evolution of their own specifically youthful cultural forms and traditions, could undermine common-sense notions of Asian passivity. Asian youth's ability and willingness to defend themselves against verbal and physical attack had precipitated a respect and mutual tolerance from some young whites. The bottom line in many inner-city areas was that the balance of power at street level was ultimately in favour of young Afro-Caribbeans and Asians. Their numerical strength meant that overt displays of racism were dangerous and risked reprisals. This state of affairs tended to produce a "live and let live" attitude amongst the more isolated sections of the local white community, and prevented racism from becoming fully activated at a collective level.

The unevenness of white attitudes towards the Afro-Caribbean and Asian communities was symptomatic not only of the specificity of different forms of racism but of the deeply contradictory nature of white responses. In struggling to resolve the contradictions that resulted from their friendships and cultural/musical allegiances, young whites constantly had to battle not only against the weight of peer-group pressure and racist common sense, but also against more general, ideological influences. National media discourses and representations, for example, were continually available as sources of racist stereotypes, assumptions and opinions. They provided discursive frameworks through which the perceived problems that

191

arose out of everyday interaction with black people could be selectively interpreted and explained. Racialised divisions and class continuities amongst the young were continually being reproduced and negotiated against the backdrop of shifting forms of popular racism.

The reproduction of these racist discourses was nevertheless constantly being undercut by cross-racial social interactions, inter-mixing and local forms of shared experience. At the very simplest level, these processes could act as an ideological blockage to the mass success of far-right nationalist politics amongst young whites. Working-class white youth's everyday experience of state authority, police harassment and life on the dole did not square up with the more authoritarian nationalist doctrines of "law and order". The shared experience of concrete social grievances against local state institutions provided a base-line of common predicaments which could strain the coherence of racist logic. The cultural allegiances and musical enthusiasms of some young whites highlighted the ambivalence of their commitment to ideas of "race" and "nation".

For this particular group of young white people, it was the specific forms, and experienced contradictions, of their engagement with black culture and black people that generated insights into racism. One of the most potent ways in which this awareness was acquired was through direct personal encounters with the racism perpetrated against their black peers. Through their relationships and experiences, most had witnessed such racism first-hand. In Jon's case this had occurred while entering a city centre disco alongside a group of black friends who were refused entry:

> From when you move with black people it becomes obvious.
> They'd go through tribulation and you'd be alright, and you'd
> wonder why they always got the bum end of things. Like
> going to clubs in town, you try getting into a club without a
> shirt and tie on. Not me, I could waltz past, but I wasn't
> going in no club that operated like that.

In a similar manner, some had directly witnessed incidents of racial harassment and intimidation. Ian, for example, told of how he had seen a black boy being attacked by a gang of young whites while waiting at a bus stop:

That really opened up my eyes a lot that did. Them's the times that made you really stop and think about racism and things like that...and after that I started to see what George and that lot [his black friends] meant when they talked about the National Front.

From accounts of similar incidents which had occurred around the south Birmingham youth club scene in the late 1970s, it was clear that these events had made a considerable impact on the political outlook of those concerned. It was through local experience of racial violence, together with personal observations of the day-to-day abuse and harassment suffered by black friends, that many became acutely aware of the activities of far-right nationalist groups. Others connected their own experiences of police harassment and the law with institutional racism. Jumbo, for example, had seen at first hand the "pressure" undergone by some of his fellow black detainees during his incarceration at a detention centre:

> If you think it's bad outside, right, I'll tell you, inside it's ten times worse. You can see why the Rastaman inside don't like white people when they come out, the kind of pressure they go through from the screws.

Through their close proximity to the black community some had acquired a personal knowledge, based on direct experience, of the repressive mechanisms of institutional racism. Countless stories were narrated of black friends mistreated by local state agencies and by the police. Jane told of how her Rasta boyfriend had been assaulted by two police officers in her presence, before being arrested and forcibly detained in a psychiatric institution:

> From when they see Rastas, they think you're mad. If they see you on the street, they lock you up, put you in a mental hospital and pump you full of drugs and injections. That's what they can do to you, 'cos that's what they did to Jimmy. And if that's the kind of system we're living in, if that's the way the country is run, then I don't wanna live in that system with those kinds of people.

193

It was through such direct experience with the racism suffered by their partners and peers that some of those interviewed had gained a deeper understanding of its social effects and consequences. While these experiences were powerful ways in which these young whites were sensitised to racism, it was the reactions of other whites which drove home its full significance. For many, racism was most sharply experienced through family, peer group and local social networks. It was in these contexts of white-to-white interaction that some of the most penetrating insights into racism were made. It was here that some of the social facts learnt from close engagement with black cultural and community life could be brought to bear to disrupt some of the assumed constituencies on which white-to-white racist discourses often rested.

For those from white working-class backgrounds, it was in the context of family life that such discourses were most keenly contested. Through their experiences, many had come to understand the crucial role of families generally in the social reproduction of racist attitudes. Lizzy, for example, had become particularly aware of the role of parents in the inter-generational transmission of racism:

> It's like they really try and get you as prejudiced as they can, they used to rub it into you, you know. Like someone like Rachel [white friend], it was just all drummed into her head. She'd never even actually talked to black people or anything. It was just passed down from her mum and dad.

In some cases this kind of parental racism could occasionally backfire by pushing those concerned into a closer identification and involvement with black friends and partners. For Lisa and Maureen it was clear that one aspect of their relationships with black boys was the deliberate transgression of parental values and patriarchal control. For Maureen, dating black boys had become an act of defiance:

> I used to hear our dad all the time. Like he'd go "bleedin' wogs…someone wants to put a bomb under them" and all this. It was like you were brought up so much not to like them, that you just did the opposite to what everybody told you to do…you know "don't do this!" and "I won't allow it!"….So you just went and did it anyway.

194

In these contexts, dating black boys was a way in which some young white women registered their sexual autonomy and independence by deliberately subverting the patriarchal restrictions which placed such relationships out of bounds. While the consequence of such actions tended to be more serious for young white women, young men also experienced intra-family conflicts over their allegiances. Jon, for example, described his ongoing battle with his father's racist views. Jon had acquired an intimate experience of black family life as a result of his friendship with his black class-mate, Clive. By drawing on that experience, Jon was able to contradict his father's racism:

> When my dad should have been influencing me, like most dads influence their boys, I'd already got out, gone to school, met Clive and met his family. As my friendship got stronger with Clive I became aware of what my dad's comments meant when he referred to certain people...all this "coon" and "wog" business and "they're all the same". And I'd think, well, Clive don't do that! Clive's family don't do that! Clive's mum did not come out of a monkey tree! She didn't come over on the last banana boat, any of that crap! You name a comment, I disagreed, 'cos I knew better, 'cos I was friends with Clive and I knew his family.

Through their close relationships with black people, a fundamental disjuncture was opened up for those like Jon, between common-sense racist reasoning and concrete personal experience. This acted to to undermine the insinuation of racist common sense by prising open the gap between one set of personal experiences and the racialised interpretation of those experiences

These various social encounters could provide some young whites with a base of knowledge from which to challenge the more diffuse forms of racism in society at large. Many of these young whites connected their own personal knowledge of racism with the more public and institutional forms which they recognised in the wider society. In Jon's case, his opposition to the views endorsed by his father had broadened out into a general rejection of racism:

> I quickly came to the conclusion, from what my dad and all his friends were saying, that that part of society was a load of

195

crap! And as you became more aware of it from school and from other sources like TV, it got to the point where you had to make a choice of either going along with that, or not....and I felt better relating to what Clive's family was dealing with rather than what my dad was dealing with.

The cultural knowledges acquired by some young whites through their personal engagement with the black community provided them with alternative explanations of social and political events to the prevailing discourses. This was particularly apparent in responses to media discourses, where these knowledges were used to deconstruct some of the racist assumptions circulated through television and newspapers. Thus, some complained about racially-biased news coverage, superimposing their own interpretations on the dominant discourses. Others displayed a critical awareness of the representation of black people in the media, particularly in television. Lisa, for example, complained about a particular documentary programme on Jamaica for its portrayal of black people:

It looked as though they were all looped [mad]. They just made everybody look looped, and people watching that'd probably think "my God", you know, "they're like that round 'ere" you know. They'd probably think the whole of Jamaica's like that. And the fact they was all really dark, so they'd probably think all black people over in Jamaica are really dark, if they just watch that programme. I mean telly's a real great influence really isn't it?...about black people.

196

Photo 8: Enoch Powell meets Jon Girling [Birmingham, 21st December 1986]

While not all of those interviewed had developed such an awareness of the subtle inflexions of racism, few had failed to be politicised in some way by their experiences. In order for young whites to maintain their affiliations and relationships, at least some reflection on their "whiteness" was required. The distinctive social identities inhabited by those with strong cross-racial friendships and affiliations generated a particularly acute awareness of the boundaries and dynamics of "race". The extent and intimacy of those interactions produced a range of crosscutting identities, allegiances and social spaces where the salience of divisions premised on racial difference was attenuated. These processes did not banish racist ideologies, particularly in their more diffuse and structural forms, but they could dampen their effects in certain specific local circumstances. At the very least, they acted to demystify and undermine notions of racial difference. For some of these young whites, they were clearly undercutting and problematising their investment in racialised categories of "whiteness" and "Britishness".

This much was reflected in the constant attempts to reduce "race" to an irrelevance of skin colour, by invoking discourses of "unity" and equality. These arguments might have been less convincing were it were not for the fact that black youth appealed to the same discourses in their interactions with their white peers and friends.

Underlying these seemingly clichéd slogans were practical and genuine attempts to negotiate the oppressive categories that were seen to detract from, and dehumanise, social relationships.

Those who had mixed-race children with black partners (three of the men and four of the women) had a considerable personal stake in upholding such beliefs. In this sense, these young white people were laying the foundations for a future mixed-race Britain, carrying through their youthful experiences into their adult lives and passing them on to their own families. Pat, for example, pointed to her own offspring as "living proof" of the triviality of racial difference, arguing that "if black and white people's gonna keep to themselves, there's gonna be nothing".

Sentiments such as these were articulated time and again by those in the study. While expressed in various forms, from humanistic proclamations, to quoted reggae lyrics and Rasta-inspired reasonings, they were motivated by the same basic desire, namely to deprive "race" of its significance as a source of division and difference in everyday life.

Epilogue

What has happened is that a substantial section of the chavs…have become black. A particular sort of violent, destructive, nihilistic gangster culture has become the fashion. And black and white, boy and girl, operate in this language together…this language which is wholly false, which is a Jamaican patois which has been intruded in England. And this is why so many of us have this sense of literally a foreign country (David Starkey, BBC *Newsnight*, Friday 12th August, 2011).

It's like, I love this place. There's no place like home. Balsall Heath is the centre of the melting-pot, man, 'cos all I ever see when I go out is half-Arab, half-Pakistani, half- Jamaican, half-Scottish, half-Irish, I know 'cos I am! Who am I? Tell me? Who do I belong to? They criticise me, the good old England. Alright then, where do I belong? You know, I was brought up with blacks, Pakistanis, Africans, Asians, everything, you name it. Who do I belong to? I'm just a broad person. The earth is mine. You know, we was not born in England, we was not born in Jamaica. We was born here, man! It's our right! That's the way I see it…That's the way I deal with it (Jo-Jo, Balsall Heath, Birmingham, 1983).

In an appearance on BBC2's *Newsnight* in the aftermath of the 2011 riots, television historian David Starkey confessed that he had been re-reading Enoch Powell's "rivers of blood" speech from 1968. Powell, he said, had been "absolutely right" in prophesising such disorder, but was "completely wrong" about the violence being inter-communal. Instead, Starkey suggested, what had happened was that a substantial section of white working-class "chavs" had become "black" and that a particular kind of black youth culture had taken hold amongst young people and lay behind the rioting.

Starkey's outburst reiterated many of the themes in Powell's earlier response to the 1985 riots (see *Introduction*). Starkey played on similar themes of race, crime and urban disorder, the sense of an alien, black presence invading England, turning parts of it into a "foreign country". But what was different about his intervention was that this racialised pathology now included white youth. His comments were a remarkable acknowledgement, albeit in distorted and racialised terms, of some of the profound cultural changes that had indeed taken place in the 26 years since Powell's 1985 speech.

The second quote above, from Jo-Jo, was originally used to conclude the first edition of this book. His personal testimony and his "all nations" concept of community offered a quite different vision of the "new England" that was already emerging in 1983, and had since come to fruition in many parts of urban Britain.

In the passage of time since Jo-Jo's quote, and the first publication of this book, a lot of water has obviously gone under the cultural bridge. The late 1980s marked the prelude to an unprecedented period of cross-fertilisation in British youth culture and popular music. This cross-cultural traffic increased in the 1990s as music became a crossroads for various transnational and diasporic cultural flows, generating a torrent of polyglot musical forms.

Cross-cultural identities and affiliations in youth culture that were relatively marginal in the early 80s, became increasingly commonplace by the 1990s. A series of parallel studies published after this book suggested that similar processes to those observed in Birmingham were occurring in other areas of urban Britain between young people of different ethnic backgrounds (Rampton, 1995; Baumann, 1996; Back, 1996; Nayak, 2003; Harris, 2006). In parts of south east London, Les Back found a syncretic, working-class youth culture that drew on a rich mixture of South London, African-American and Afro-Caribbean cultural symbols. Rampton focussed on the role of south Asian youth in multi-ethnic youth cultures, looking specifically at "language crossings" between young people of south Asian, white English and Afro-Caribbean descent. Rampton found speech patterns which variously exhibited influences of Panjabi, patois, stylised Indian English and white working-class regional dialects (Rampton, 1995). From the mid 90s onwards, these linguistic forms were increasingly combined with idioms and terminology from hip-hop culture to form a generalised, non-ethnically marked, urban vernacular used by young people.

Reggae culture continued to be a central reference-point in post-80s popular music and youth culture. Particularly evident was the adoption of reggae by Asian youth of Indian, Pakistani and Bangladeshi heritage. In Birmingham, this was perhaps best exemplified in the music of Apache Indian, whose *bhangramuffin* style fused elements of traditional Bhangra music and panjabi language, with dancehall reggae and patois lyricism. Reggae sound system culture was also adopted by Bengali youth in London's East End, with groups such as Asian Dub Foundation fusing the rhythms and basslines of hip-hop, bhangra, dancehall reggae and dub.

While the centrality of reggae in black British culture was eclipsed by subsequent music movements, its rich legacy continued to permeate all of the post-1986 genres, from soul and hip-hop, through jungle and dub-step, to speed garage and grime. The influence of reggae DJing was clearly audible in many of these new, black British genres where African-American rap aesthetics were rearticulated and overlaid with Jamaican, black British and working-class regionalisms. The central place of *orality* in these genres has been one of the core threads of continuity running through them. The democratic character of these oral practices is grounded in the human voice as a primary resource of symbolic creativity. Much of their populist power and artistry is drawn from their improvised, spontaneous character in local performance settings. These oral practices offer modes of poetic expression which are infinitely adaptable to local experiences, providing all young people with a platform from which to express their own points of view and write their own history.

Many of the cross-cultural interactions described in the book around *reggae* continued to be played out around rap and hip-hop culture. White youth's mass identification with hip-hop exhibited many of the same processes, dynamics and contradictions. White engagement with hip-hop, for example, entailed similar kinds of negotiated affiliations to blackness and radical "pro-black" discourses. Rap provided similar discursive spaces and didactic resources for disaffected white working-class youth suffering from the effects of the marginalisation and deindustrialisation. Its universalist, double-voiced symbols, and its critiques of state power, found a resonance amongst young white listeners, fans and practitioners. Rap provided them with a language through which to comment on the micro-dynamics of everyday life, and a means to dissect the wider social and political forces that affect their lives (Bennett, 1999).

The legacy of the reggae tradition in British popular culture was also apparent in the profound influence of sound system culture on post-80s popular music. The methodologies and principles of that culture provided a blueprint for countless genres, through its technologies, performance practices, organisational forms, and spatial politics. For third and fourth generation black Britons, sound system culture represented a rich cultural heritage that key practitioners continued to draw upon. Within black British music genres, these connections have been mediated by cross-generational links within black communities and families.

The influence of sound system culture was evident throughout dance music in the configuration of sound technology, and in the use of dub techniques and performance aesthetics drawn from the reggae tradition. Its echoes could be heard in the bass lines and rhythm tracks of Jungle and speed Garage, in their dubplate-inspired recording and distribution practices, and in various forms of creative turntablism and interactional dialogue between DJ and audience. The collaborative ethic of sound system culture was also a major influence on post-80s music, through its principles of self-organisation and collective production. That influence was visible in the collective groupings and support systems which coalesced around disparate musical movements, from hip-hop to rave, in the form of crews, tribes and posses. These connections gave rise to a number of multi-ethnic sound system-based cultures, emerging from provincial towns and cities out of a melting pot of music styles, tastes and identities.

The struggle for autonomous cultural space has been an ongoing and recurring feature of many of these movements. Young people's struggle for their own unregulated leisure spaces, independent of mainstream commercial leisure provision, have been prefigured by the black community's own struggles around cultural space. Here, sound system culture has played a significant role in shaping and inspiring these autonomous leisure institutions through its characteristic fusion of "politics" and "entertainment". Through its ability to combine the pleasures of musicking with elements of protest and education, reggae culture has highlighted young people's resistance to attempts to confine their leisure to particular forms of orderly consumption. From the sound system dances of the 70s, to the warehouse parties and mass open-air raves of the 80s, these spaces have evolved as alternative networks to the regulated and exclusionary forms of mainstream commercial entertainment. Modelled on the blues party and sound system dance, these movements have survived in a network of unauthorized venues. This has often put them at the sharp end of increasingly draconian forms of monitoring, surveillance and disciplinary measures by the authorities. A whole battery of policing tools and legal powers has been deployed to suppress these spaces as part of a wider strategy of controlling urban space which has progressively restricted the freedom of movement and assembly.

Some of the cultural power of these movements lay in their ability to bring fleeting alternative public spheres into being in which participants were connected to each other through collective sensibilities and common affiliations. In doing so, they revealed something of the power of musicking to create spaces where alternative notions of belonging and identity could be articulated. They suggested music's ability to create soundscapes in which the spatial and temporal relations of the dominant culture could be suspended, and to establish collaborative connections that bridged racial and ethnic differences. This was particularly evident in many forms of post-80s dance music culture with their expansive and inclusive multi-ethnic sensibilities.

Through its ability to prefigure different visions of social life, through its modes of production, performance and reception, music continues to have important ethical values and lessons to deliver. Music has the potential to embody alternative ideals in the face of consumerism and the privatisation of culture that have permeated life under neoliberalism. Where musical performance and consumption are turned outwards into expressions of sociability and collective awareness, they go against the grain of dominant modes of consumption in the leisure industry around screen-based models of digital entertainment and mobile privatisation, whose ideal consumer is the atomised, private, individual.

The original conclusion of this book included a fair amount of speculation about the anti-racist potential of the processes that it documented. Racism's hold over significant sections of young white people, and their commitment to nationalist and racist ideas, it concluded, was more precarious than had been assumed hitherto. Not all white working-class youth were monolithically "racist" in the same way, or to the same degree. The cultural formations and identities described in the book suggested that racial fragmentation was not an immutable, incontestable reality. Some of the most powerful rebuttals of racism lay embedded in the situated interactions, social arrangements and solutions evolved by young people themselves. The notion that cultures were homogeneous, impermeable blocks that were the fixed attributes of particular racial or ethnic groups was completely undermined by many of the cross-cultural identifications and affiliations documented in the book.

These findings were echoed by many of the subsequent studies cited above. Back found evidence that young whites were distancing themselves from whiteness and Englishness in favour of identifications with blackness and black people (Back, 1996). There were signs that national racist discourses were being subverted by neighbourhood discourses of inter-racial harmony based on familiarity and established links. For Nayak, the dichotomising of white responses into "anti-racist angels" versus "racist demons" belied various subtle gradations and complexities in white youth's cultural identities (Nayak, 2003). The development of hybrid forms of musical and cultural expression that couldn't be defined as either "black" or "white", but were a synthesis of both, undercut some of the binary dualisms of racial difference. The new ethnicities and hybrid cultures that emerged out of these spaces of cultural inter-meshing made a mockery of absolutist definitions of racial identities as mutually exclusive phenomena. For music continued to be a crucial space in which such identities were not only expressed, but in which the boundaries between them were also tested and realigned from all sides.

These observations, however, always came with a number of qualifications and caveats about their liberatory potential. Cultural hybridity was never a panacea for racism. Non-racist subjectivities could not be simply "read off" from musical affiliations, or from proximity to, or engagement with black cultures. The contradictory aspects of some forms of youthful white identification with black music could reinstate racial differences and racialised discourses (Nayak, 2003). In the case of rap and hip-hop culture, this was partly a consequence of music video's role in mediating these processes, and the heavy promotion of particular genres of rap which skewed the accompanying imagery towards reified images of blackness, masculinity and urban "ghetto culture".

204

Racism, as Paul Gilroy reminds us, can co-exist with cultural patterns that embody its overcoming (Gilroy, 2005). Disabling racist discourses continually threaten to insert themselves into everyday living. While *some* cross-cultural processes might attenuate *some* forms of inter-personal racism at the local level, their capacity to challenge the more diffuse, institutionalised structures of racialised inequality can be limited.

Many of these tensions and contradictions have been glossed over in superficial versions of multicultural hybridity which have been accommodated to serve various ends (Back, 2016). Some of these symbols, for example, have been incorporated into political discourses of nationalism which have been given a youthful multicultural face. The styles and sounds of an exoticised cultural hybridity have been commercially appropriated by the entertainment industry, while bland, corporate forms of multiculturalism have also emerged, premised on shallow notions of "diversity".

While many parts of Britain are more ethnically diverse than ever before, "race" continues to play a volatile role in British political culture, as seen in the ongoing controversies about immigration and "British values" and the continued salience of racialised codes of national belonging. Older forms of racism have been overlaid by newer forms of xenophobia, nationalism, and racisms mobilised against new targets.

These dominant versions of nation, culture and identity, however, are at variance with many aspects of everyday life in urban Britain where the reality on the ground is increasingly one of cultural mixity and syncretism premised on commonality and shared experience. This is a state of affairs that Paul Gilroy has called "conviviality", one founded on everyday patterns of sociability and co-habitation in Britain's urban communities, one in which "race" is ordinary, nothing special (Gilroy 2005). Much of this reality has been built up organically through the entanglements of kinship patterns generated by successive generations of mixed relationships and family households. This is just one facet of a gradual passive revolution of incremental changes that Stuart Hall called "multicultural drift" (Back, 2010). It is a process comprised of multiple, cumulative and mostly irreversible changes towards heterogeneity in British society and culture. The musical traditions, cultural formations and identities that are the subject of this book form a significant part of these changes. At the very least, these provide a base of experience from

205

which to push back against exclusionary forms of national identity and belonging, and to counter the dehumanising effects of racialised hierarchies. At their best, they can point to forms of social living where alternative, non-racialised ethical values and conceptions of humanity might be imagined and realised.

Bibliography

Abrahams, R. (1972) "Joking, The Training of the Man of Words in Talking Broad", in Kochman, T. (ed.) *Rappin' and Stylin' Out.*

Back, L. (1987) "Coughing up Fire: Sound Systems in South-East London", *New Formations* No. 3

Back, L. (1996) *New Ethnicities and Urban Culture: Racisms and Multiculture in Young Lives*, Routledge.

Back, L. (2002) "Out of Sight: Southern Music and the Coloring of Sound", in Ware, V and Back, L, *Out of Whiteness: Color, Politics and Culture*, Verso.

Back, L. (2010) "Stuart Hall in conversation with Les Back", *Dark Matter* 7, 28th November. Available at: http://www.darkmatter101.org/site/2010/11/28/stuart-hall-in-conversation-with-les-back-audio/

Back L. (2016) "Moving Sounds, Controlled Borders: Asylum and the Politics of Culture",
Young: Nordic Journal of Youth Research Vol.24, No.3.

Barker, M. (1981) *The New Racism*, Junction Books.

Barrett, L. (1976) *The Sun and the Drum*, Heinemann.

Baumann, G. (1996) *Contesting Culture: Discourses of Identity in Multi-Ethnic London*, Cambridge University Press.

Bebey, F. (1975) *African Music: A People's Art*, Lawrence Hill.

Beckford, G. and Witter, M. (1980) *Small Garden...Bitter Weed: Struggle and Change in Jamaica*, Zed.

Bennett, A. (1999) "Rappin' on the Tyne: White hip hop culture in Northeast England - an ethnographic study", *The Sociological Review*, Vol.47, No.1.

Bilby, K. (1985) "Caribbean Crucible", in Haydon, G. and Marks, D. (eds) *Repercussions: A Celebration of African-American Music*, Century.

Brathwaite, E. (1981) *Folk Culture of the Slaves in Jamaica*, New Beacon Books.

Cabral, A. (1973) "National Liberation and Culture", in *Return to the Source*, African Information Service.

Caesar, I. (1976a) "Strictly Rockers", *Black Echoes*, 27 March.

Caeser, I. (1976b) "It Dreader", *Black Echoes*, 12 June.

Campbell, H. (1980) "Rastafari: Culture of Resistance", *Race and Class* Vol.22, No.1.

Campbell, H. (1985) *Rasta and Resistance: From Marcus Garvey to Walter Rodney*, Hansib.

Caribbean Times (1981) *Sistrens: The Women Behind the Rasta Movement*, 23 August-3 September.

CBI (1984) *Birmingham Community Action Programme Report*, Birmingham City Council.

Chernoff, J. M. (1979) *African Rhythm and African Sensibility*, University of Chicago Press.

Clarke, S. (1980) *Jah Music: The Evolution of the Popular Jamaican Song*, Heinemann.

Cone, J. H. (1972) *The Spirituals and the Blues: An Interpretation*, Seabury Press.

Crahan, M. E. and Knight, F. W. (eds) (1979) *Africa and the Caribbean-The Legacies of a Link*, John Hopkins University Press.

Craton, M. (1982) *Testing the Chains: Resistance to Slavery in the British West Indies*, Cornell University Press.

Dennison, Sam (1982) *Scandalize my Name: Black Imagery in American Popular Music*, Garland.

Dalby, D. (1971) "Ashanti Survivals in the Language and Traditions of the Windward Maroons of Jamaica", *African Language Studies*, No.12.

Dalby, D. (1972) "The African Element in American English" in Kochman, T. (ed.) *Rappin'and Stylin' Out.*

Dalke, R. (1979) *Ska to Reggae: UK Label Discographies Volume 2*, Top Sounds International.

Dalphinis, M. (1978) "Approaches to the Study of Creole Languages – the Case for West African Language Influences", *The Black Liberator*, No.1.

Dalphinis, M. (1985) *Caribbean and African Languages: Social History, Language, Literature and Education*, Karia Press.

Davis, S. (1983) *Bob Marley: The Biography*, Arthur Baker.

Donald, J. (1982) "Language, Literacy and Schooling" in *The State and Popular Culture,* Open University Press.

Field, S. and Southgate, P. (1982) *Public Disorder: A Review of Research and a Study in One Inner-City Area*, Home Office Research Study No. 72, HMSO.

Frith, S. (1983) *Sound Effects: Youth, Leisure and the Politics of Rock 'n' Roll*, Constable.

Frith, S. (1988) "Playing with Real Feeling-Jazz and Suburbia" in Frith, S. *Music for Pleasure*, Polity.

Furnell, J. (1980) "The Lover's Beat", *Black Echoes*, 13 December.

Garratt, S. (1985) "Lovers' Rock", *The Face* No.59, March.

Gayle, C. (1974) "The Reggae Underground", *Black Music* (July).

Gayle, C. (1975a) "Reggae Explosion", *Black Music* (October).

Gayle, C. (1975b) "Dread in a Babylon", *Black Music* (September).

Gayle, C. (1976a) "The Pressure Drops", *Black Music* (May).

Gayle, C. (1976b) "Oh What a Rat Race!", *Black Music* (June).

Genovese, E. (1976) *Roll, Jordan, Roll: The World the Slaves Made*, Vintage.

Gillett, C. (1983) *The Sound of the City: The Rise of Rock and Roll*, Souvenir Press.

Gilroy, P. (1982) "Steppin' out of Babylon: Race, Class and Autonomy", in CCCS Race and Politics Group, *The Empire Strikes Back: Race and Racism in 70s Britain*, Hutchinson.

Gilroy, P. (1987) *There Ain't No Black in the Union Jack: The Cultural Politics of Race and Nation*, Hutchinson.

Gilroy, P. (1991) "Sounds Authentic: Black music, Ethnicity and the Challenge of a Changing Same," *Black Music Research Journal* Vol, 11 No. 2.

Gilroy, P. (2005) *Postcolonial Melancholia*, Colombia University Press.

Griffith, P. (1977) "The Drum in Reggae", *Black Echoes*, 12 November.

Gutzmore, C. (1978) "Carnival, the State and the Black Masses in the United Kingdom", *The Black Liberator*, No. 1 (December).

Hall, S., Critcher, C.,Jefferson, T. and Roberts, B. (1978) *Policing the Crisis: Mugging, the State and Law and Order*, Macmillan.

Hebdige, D. (1974) *Reggae, Rastas and Rudies: Style and the Subversion of Form*, Stencilled paper 24, Centre for Contemporary Cultural Studies, University of Birmingham.

Hebdige, D. (1979) *Subculture: The Meaning of Style*, Methuen.

Hebdige, D. (1981) "Skinheads and the Search for White Working Class Identity", *New Socialist*, No. 1 (September/October).

Hebdige, D. (1983) "Ska Tissue: the Rise and Fall of 2 Tone", in Davis, S. and Simon, P. (eds) *Reggae International*, Thames and Hudson.

209

Henry, I. et al. (1982) "Power, Culture and Identity: the Case of the Afro-Caribbean People", in *Minority Experience*, Open University Press.

Hewitt, R. (1986) *White Talk Black Talk*, Cambridge University Press.

Hilliard, B. (1981) "Sensitivity Without Paralysis", *Police Review*, 24th July.

Hind, J. and Mosco, S. (1985) *Rebel Radio: The Full Story of British Pirate Radio*, Pluto Press.

Hinds, D. (1980) "The "Island" of Brixton", *Oral History*, Vol. 8, No. 1.

Hiro, D. (1973) *Black British: White British*, Monthly Review Press.

Hoare, I. (1975) "Mighty Mighty, Spade and Whitey: Black Lyrics and Soul's Interaction with White Culture", in Hoare, Ian (ed.) *The Soul Book*, Methuen.

Hobsbawn, E. J. (1959) *The Jazz Scene*, Weidenfeld and Nicolson

Hoetink, H. (1979) "The Cultural Links", in Crahan, M. and Knight, F. (eds) *Africa and the Caribbean - The Legacies of a Link*.

Howe, D. (1973) "Fighting Back: West Indian Youth and the Police in Notting Hill", *Race Today*, Vol.5, No. 11 (December).

Howe, D. (1980) "From Bobby to Babylon: Blacks and the British Police, part 1", *Race Today*, Vol. 12, No. 1 (May/June).

Humphry, D. (1972) *Police Power and Black People*, Panther.

Hylton, P. (1975) "The Politics of Caribbean Music", *The Black Scholar* (September).

Institute of Race Relations (1979) *Police Against Black People*, Race and Class pamphlet No. 6, Institute of Race Relations.

John, A. (1970) *Race in the Inner-City*, Runnymede Trust.

Johnson, L. K. (1975) "The Politics of the Lyrics of Reggae Music", *The Black Liberator*, Vol. 2, No. 4.

Johnson, L. K. (1976) "Jamaican Rebel Music", Race and Class, Vol. 17, No. 4.

Johnson, L. K. (1977) "Bob Marley and the Reggae International", *Race Today*, Vol.9, No. 4 (June/July)

Johnson, L. K. (1983) "From Mento to Lovers Rock: A History of Jamaican Music", BBC Radio One.

Jones, S. (1993) "Crossover Culture: Popular Music and the Politics of 'Race'", *Stanford Humanities Review*, Vol. 3, No. 2.

Kettle, M. and Hodges, L. (1982) *Upising! The Police, the People and the Riots in Britain's Cities*, Pan.

Kochman, T. (ed.) (1972) *Rappin' and Stylin' Out: Communication in Urban Black America*, University of Illinois Press.

Kopytoff, B. (1976) "The Development of Jamaican Maroon Ethnicity", *Caribbean Quarterly*, Vol. 22

Laing, D. (1985) *One Chord Wonders: Power and Meaning in Punk Rock*, Open University Press.

Lawrence, E. (1982a) "Just Plain Common Sense: the 'Roots' of Racism", in CCCS Race and Politics Group, *The Empire Strikes Back: Race and Racism in 70s Britain*, Hutchinson.

Lawrence, E. (1982b) "In the Abundance of Water the Fool is Thirsty: Sociology and Black 'Pathology'", in CCCS Race and Politics Group, *The Empire Strikes Back: Race and Racism in 70s Britain*, Hutchinson.

McGlashen, C. (1973) "The Sound System", *Sunday Times* Magazine, 4 February.

Martins, B. (1983) *The Message of African Drumming,* Kivouvou and Editions Bantoues.

May, C. (1977) "British Reggae: Part 3, Getting out of the Ghetto", *Black Music*, Vol.4, Issue 46.

May, C. (1978) "Sticksmen", Black Music, Vol. 1, Issue 9.

Middleton, R. (1972) *Pop Music and the Blues*, Victor Gollancz

Mulligan, B. (1969) "Kingston's Kong is King of Reggae", *The Record Retailer and Music Industry News*, 20 December.

Mungham, G. (1976) "Youth in Pursuit of Itself" in Mungham G. and Pearson, G. (eds) *Working Class Youth Culture*, Routledge and Kegan Paul.

Murdock, G. and Troyna, B. (1981) "Recruiting Racists", *Youth in Society*, No. 6 (November).

Nayak, A. (2003) *Race, Place and Globalization: Youth Cultures in a Changing World*, Berg.

Nketia, J. H. K. (1975) *The Music of Africa*, Victor Gollancz

Nketia, J. H. K. (1978) "Tradition and Innovation in African Music", *Jamaica Journal*, Vol. 11, No. 3 and 4 (March).

Nketia, J. H. K. (1979) "African Roots of Music in the Americas", *Jamaica Journal*, No. 43

Nketia, J. H. K. (1982) "Interaction Through Music: the Dynamics of Music Making in African Societies", *International Social Science Journal*, Vol. 34, No. 94

Partridge, R. (1973) "Reggae...the Hits you Never Hear", *Melody Maker*, 21 July

211

Patterson, O. (1966) "The Dance Invasion", *New Society*, 15 September.

Patterson, O. (1967) *The Sociology of Slavery*, Associated University Press.

Phillips, M. (1982) "Thirty Years of Black Britain: Language and Originality", *Frontline*, Vol.2, No.2

Pollard, V. (1980) "'Dread Talk": The Speech of The Rastafarians in Jamaica", *Caribbean Quarterly*, Vol.26, No.4

Pollard, V. (1982) "The Social History of Dread Talk", *Caribbean Quarterly*, Vol.28, No.4

Post, K. (1970) "The Bible as Ideology: Ethiopianism in Jamaica, 1930-38", in Allen, C. and Johnson, R. W. (eds) *African Perspectives: Papers in the History, Politics and Economics of Africa*, Cambridge University Press.

Post, K. (1978) *Arise Ye Starvelings: The Jamaican Labour Rebellion of 1938 and its Aftermath*, Martinus Nijhoft.

Powell, E. (1985) "My Challenge to Mrs Thatcher", *The Times*, 21 September

Price, R. (ed.) (1973) *Maroon Societies: Rebels Slave Communities in the Americas*, Anchor Books.

Price, R. and Mintz, S. (1976) *An Anthropological Approach to the Afro-American Past: A Caribbean Perspective,* ISHI Occasional Papers in Social Change, No. 2, Institute for the Study of Human Issues.

Rampton, B. (1995) *Crossing: Language and Ethnicity among Adolescents*, Longman.

Randall, R. (1972) "The Trojan Story", *Melody Maker*, 30 December

Reckford, V. (1982) "Reggae, Rastafarianism and Cultural Identity", *Jamaica Journal,* No.46

Rice, J. and T., Gambaccini, P. and Read, M. (1977) *The Guinness Book of British Hit Singles: 1952-1977,* Guinness Superlatives.

Rimmer, D. (1985) *Like Punk Never Happened: Culture-Club and the New Pop*, Faber and Faber.

Robinson, C. (1983) *Black Marxism: The Making of the Black Radical Tradition*, Zed Books.

Ross, A. (1989) *No Respect: Intellectuals and Popular Culture*, Routledge

Schuler, M. (1979) "Myalism and the African Religious Tradition in Jamaica", in Crahan, M. and Knight, F. (eds) *Africa and the Caribbean - The Legacies of a Link.*

Sims Holt, G. (1972) "Inversion in Black Communication", in Kochman, T. (ed) Rappin' and Stylin' Out.

Sivanandan, A. (1982) "From Resistance to Rebellion: Asian and Afro-Caribbean Struggles in Britain", *Race and Class*, Vol.23, No. 2/3.

Small, S. (1983) *Police and People in London: A Group of Young Black people*, PSI Report No. 619, Policy Studies Institute.

Small, C. (1987) *Music of the Common Tongue: Survival and Celebration in Afro-American Music*, John Calder

Small, C. (1998) *Musicking: The Meanings of Performing and Listening*, Wesleyan University Press.

Smith, D. (1977) *Racial Disadvantage in Britain*, Penguin.

Smitherman, G. (1977) *Talkin' and Testifyin': The Language of Black America*, Houghton Miflin.

Solomos, J. (1986) "Political Language and Violent Protest: Ideological and Policy Responses to the 1981 and 1985 Riots", *Youth and Policy*, No. 18.

Steward, S. and Garratt, S. (1984) *Signed, Sealed and Delivered: True Life Stories of Women in Pop*, Pluto Press.

Storm Roberts, J. (1973) *Black Music of Two Worlds*, Allen Lane

Sutcliffe, D. (1982) *British Black English*, Basil Blackwell.

Toop, D. (1984) *The Rap Attack: African Jive to New York Hip Hop*, Pluto Press.

Wallis, R. and Malm, K. (1984) *Big Sounds from Small Peoples: The Music Industry in Small Counties*, Constable.

Walton, Ortiz (1972) *Music: Black, White and Blue*, William Morrow.

Ward, R. (1979) "Where Race Didn't Divide: Some Reflections on Slum Clearance in Moss Side" in Miles, R. and Phizacklea, A. (eds) *Racism and Political Action in Britain*, Routledge and Kegan Paul.

White, G. (1967) "Rudie, Oh Rudie!", *Caribbean Quarterly*, Vol. 13, No. 3.

White, G. (1983a) "Music in Jamaica", in Davies, S. and Simon, P. (eds) *Reggae International*. Thames and Hudson.

White, G. (1983b) "Mento to Ska: the Sound of the City", in Davies, S. and Simon, P. (eds) *Reggae International*. Thames and Hudson.

Widgery, D. (1986) *Beating Time*, London, Chatto & Windus.

213

Williams R. (1972a) "The Facts About Reggae", *Melody Maker*, 19 February.

Williams, R. (1972b) "Black Gold of Jamaica", *Melody Maker*, 30 September.

Williams, R. (1973a) "The First Genius of Reggae", *Melody Maker*, 24 February.

Williams, R. (1973b) "The Fire This Time", *Melody Maker*, 17 March.

Willis, P. (1977) "Learning to Labour: How Working Class Kids Get Working Class Jobs", Saxon House.

Printed in Great
Britain
by Amazon

31394068R00127